New Essays on Narcissism

ever-present

'Narcissism' has become a suspiciously ubiquitous topic in the psychoanalytic literature and in the wider cultural debate on the spirit – or lack of it – of the times. Most participants in these debates would readily agree that the writings of Béla Grunberger have provided the touchstone for the recent literature. He has thought longer and more deeply about it than anyone since Freud's basic paper 'On narcissism'.

The present volume contains his further reflections, with original ideas on the prenatal and biological dimensions of narcissistic phenomena. He develops a concept of the 'narcissistic drive dialectic' and sees the processes of maturation in these terms. In normal development there is an integration of drives as a result of the resolution of the Oedipus complex. Narcissism is on the other side of the dialectic – the drive to go back to a prenatal state. His analysis extends to cultural and literary phenomena. He also uses his model for the explanation of dissidence in psychoanalysis itself.

Béla Grunberger was born in Hungary and studied medicine in Lyons and economic and social science in Geneva. He is a Training Analyst of the Paris Psychoanalytical Society, the author of *Narcissism: Psychoanalytic Essays* and co-author (with Janine Chasseguet-Smirgel) of *Freud or Reich? Psychoanalysis and Illusion* (Free Association Books, 1986).

David Macey is a freelance translator and writer.

New Essays
on Narcissism

BÉLA GRUNBERGER
Translated and edited by David Macey

'an association in which the free development of each
is the condition of the free development of all'

FA^B

Free Association Books / London / 1989

First published in Great Britain 1989 by
Free Association Books
26 Freegrove Road
London N7 9RQ

British Library Cataloguing in Publication Data
Grunberger, Béla, 1913–
    New essays on narcissism.
    1. Narcissism
    I. Title II. Macey, David
    155.2′32
    ISBN 1-85343-105-2

Typeset by Photosetting, Yeovil

Printed and bound in Great Britain by
Billing & Sons Ltd, Worcester

Contents

Acknowledgements

Certain of the papers included in this volume have been previously published as follows.

'The oedipal conflicts of the analyst', *Psychoanalytic Quarterly* XLIX, 1980; translated by Marion M. Oliner. 'The anti-Semite and the oedipal conflict', read at the 23rd International Psycho-Analytical Congress, Stockholm, July–August 1963, published, *International Journal of Psycho-Analysis* 45, 1964; translated by Sidney Stewart. 'Narcissus and Oedipus: a controversy', presented at the Klinik für Kinder- und Jugendpsychologie, Munich, on 17 September 1985. 'On narcissism, aggressivity and anti-Semitism', published as 'Brève communication sur le narcissisme, l'aggressivité et l'antisémitisme', *Revue française de psychanalyse* 4, 1984. 'The oedipal crossroads or psychoanalysis at the parting of the ways', read to the Swiss Psychoanalytic Society, 20 September 1983. 'The struggles and the failure of Don Quixote-Narcissus', read to the Psychoanalytic Association of Madrid on 23 February 1985. 'On fetishism', read to the Société Psychanalytique de Paris on 18 November 1975, published as 'Essai sur le fétichisme', *Revue française de psychanalyse* 2, 1976. 'On purity', read to the Société Psychanalytique de Paris on 17 January 1984, published as 'De la pureté', *Revue française de psychanalyse* 3, 1984. 'Narcissism: genesis and pathology', lecture presented at the Institute of Psychology, University of Bologna on 13 April 1985. 'The monad', read to the Paris Psychoanalytical Society, 1985, and published as 'Über die Monade', in *Narziss und Anubis*, vol. 2 (Munich/Vienna: Verlag Internationale Psychoanalyse, 1988). 'From monad to perversion: avoidance of the Oedipus', read in 1986 at a symposium organized by Professor Jochen

Stork, and published as 'Von der Monade zur Perversion. Ein Modus der Vermeidung des Ödipuskomplexes', in *Narziss und Anubis*, vol. 2 (Munich/Vienna: Verlag Internationale Psychoanalyse, 1988). With the exception of Chapters 3 and 6, all translations are by David Macey.

Preface

The present work is a collection of studies consisting of clinical and literary *applications* of my hypotheses about narcissism. This is in fact the second series of articles I have devoted to the subject. The first was published in Paris by Payot in 1971 (Grunberger, 1971), and was then translated into English and published by International Universities Press in 1979 (Grunberger, 1979a). My first essay on the role of narcissism in psychoanalytic treatment dates from 1956.

I have, then, been studying narcissism and its manifestations for over thirty years. The various contributions I have made over this long period of time testify to my involvement in a process of research which involves the use of impressionist brushstrokes but which constantly moves in the same direction. That process inevitably influences the way in which I attempt to present material which is always new but always related to the same theme. This necessarily results in a certain amount of repetition. That may be regrettable, but it is also unavoidable.

I would add that my early work, in which I stressed the 'positive' aspects of narcissism in psychoanalytic treatment and in culture in particular, and in which I saw narcissism as a key to our understanding of the human condition, was initially rejected, sometimes violently so, in France. My conceptions did, however, gradually find an audience, so much so that most of them have fallen into the public domain (by which I mean that no one even thinks of mentioning me by name in discussions of, say, the opposition between narcissism and the drives). Despite their familiarity, I am still in the habit of reiterating certain elements of my conception in every paper I write, in accordance with both a certain pedagogic method and ancient traditions whose effectiveness has been demonstrated by the resounding success of advertising. I might add that I never repeat myself without introducing some new element which modifies the perspective I have adopted.

I also make use of the formula 'as I have said elsewhere' without giving any specific reference. This is simply a way of alluding to my earlier essays, which can now be found in the two published collections. To give detailed references would overload the text, simply because there are so many of them.

In the introduction to my first collection of essays, I quote Lou Andreas-Salomé (1958, p. 164 emphasis added): 'Narcissism accompanies all the strata of our experience, independently of them. In other words, it is not only an immature stage of life needing to be superseded, but also the *ever-renewing* companion of all life.' I would add that the same could be said of the theory of narcissism itself. I would like to take this opportunity to point out that the first analyst to elaborate a theory of narcissism thus identifies a basic element of the Freudian theory of narcissism (Freud writes 1914, pp. 75-6: 'an original libidinal cathexis of the ego ... fundamentally persists'), extends its field of application and is fully aware that the new concept of narcissism opens up a new continent to the 'science of the soul.'

In that same introduction, I also cite Baudelaire's: 'Even when quite a child, I felt two conflicting sensations in my heart: the horror of life and the ecstasy of life' (Baudelaire, 1887, p. 73) in order to allude to the conflict the child experiences between the elational modalities of narcissism and the drives. Twelve years later, I described an apparently identical conflict in an article entitled 'Narcisse et Anubis' (Grunberger, 1983), but situated it in a totally different perspective. Anubis does not represent the aggressivity of the drives (which turn against the child or attack its introjected objects), but the dark, negative aspect of primary narcissism itself.[1]

---

1 It has frequently been objected that there may be such a thing as the pathology of the foetus, and I have often thought about this problem. If it were correct, this objection would destroy my concept of absolute prenatal bliss, even though the traces found in myths, culture, religions and the very organization of the human mind all testify to its existence. We are in fact talking about a coenesthesis which cannot be perceived by the ego because, in the prenatal state, there is no perception in the psychological sense of the term and, what is more important, no ego. In my view, the foetus records impressions, which are independent of one another and which are the sources of the future ego nuclei.

I subsequently completed my initial hypothesis by taking into account those factors that might invalidate it and by incorporating them into my schema. I adopted the notion of positive and negative imprints (the future nuclei of the ego), and even took the view that negative imprinting might result from a failure to achieve positive imprinting, arguing that a combination of the two results in the formation of the double narcissistic nucleus. That concept is central to my work of this period. The title 'Anubis and Narcissism' is also an allusion to Jean Cocteau's play *La Machine infernale* (1934), which deals with the tragedy of King Oedipus. Sophocles describes the

The history of anti-Semitism provides another example of how my work has evolved through a number of different stages, though it should be the topic of a separate discussion. I have always been interested in the subject, and presented a psychoanalytic study of it in 1963 ('The anti-Semite and the oedipal conflict'). Although that study contained elements of the theory of narcissism, it was dominated by the oedipal problematic and proved not to be fully satisfactory, especially after the historic event known as the 'Six-Days War'. Far from making the oedipal theory obsolete, the new wave of anti-Semitism stirred up by the Israeli–Arab war – and its effects are still being felt – revealed the importance of the narcissistic factor. My response to this displacement of the problem took the form of the short essay entitled 'On narcissism, aggressivity and anti-Semitism', which first appeared in 1984 (both essays are included in the present volume). I do not take the view that my research is now complete, and I am currently writing a book (*Anti-Semitism and Christianity*, Free Association Books, forthcoming) which is intended to identify a supplementary reason – to which I attribute a definite heuristic value – for the existence of anti-Semitism.

On the one hand, I am convinced that every stage in my research project has born fruit; on the other, no science is ever complete, and no one can lay claim from the outset to having produced a body of work which is both totally valid and definitive.

When my first collection of essays on narcissism was published, I found myself faced with a number of difficulties which could, I thought, be alleviated by writing a short introduction which at least admitted to their existence. I attempted to situate my theory within the general theory of psychoanalysis. Whereas classical theory is part of a theory of the drives (*Triebtheorie*), my theory is concerned with a specific psychic dimension. Whilst narcissism (as I understand it) can indeed develop parallel to the drives, and whilst the two can be synthesized (and this is indeed the aim), it can also become antagonistic to the drives, as the aim of pure narcissism is to find (or find anew) bliss and narcissistic perfection in a non-instinctual, or even anti-instinctual, mode. This is a perfectly logical demand, but it can be fulfilled only in fantasy. The interplay between narcissism and instinctual development (both pre-oedipal and oedipal) takes the form of a series of

---

conflict between Oedipus and the Sphinx, who is a *divinity* (a narcissistic ideal) but who has a *dual* nature: she is at once a radiantly beautiful young woman and Anubis, the jackal-headed god of Egypt. Like the palaeo-narcissistic primal nucleus and the archaic aggressivity which I describe as 'Anubian', her dual nature corresponds to a primal and bipolar coenesthesis. This bipolar ego may retain a certain autonomy within the complete ego; it remains, however, outside the structure of the ego proper, and is not bound up with the ego drives characteristic of the central oedipal agency.

dialectical situations involving two contrasting positions, which may be harmonized to a certain extent, but which are also quite contradictory. The problem of the dual orientation of narcissism is raised by Lou Andreas-Salomé (1921, p. 11), who attempts to explain the paradox of 'the dual disposition of narcissism, turned on the one hand toward self-assertion and on the other toward abandonment in the primal boundless state.'

My theory of narcissism centres upon the paradox that stems from its unconscious physiological origins. It originates in a prenatal coenesthesis which man has to disavow for narcissistic reasons. Indeed, all the psychic pecularities we habitually ascribe to man and which he cathects in a supremely narcissistic mode – completeness, omnipotence, an awareness of his own special worth, the exultant tendency to expansion, serenity, the feeling of freedom and autonomy, absolute independence, invulnerability, infinity and purity – derive directly from the prenatal coenesthesis experienced by the foetus. At the same time, and in the conscious mode, all these characteristics are – and must be – experienced as being essentially non-instinctual. Man wishes to deny the physiological origins of his aspirations towards the absolute. He wants to be a pure spirit, to rid himself of his body and, in the best of cases, he projects his aspirations on to God. This gives rise to a fundamental ambiguity, which is the source of a major existential conflict: the newborn child is forced to repress its prenatal regime in its entirety or, rather, to deny it access to conscious perception (I am thinking here of a specific aspect of infantile amnesia), and to disavow its materiality. It has had to give up this regime in exchange for the support which subtends its new 'instinctual solution', namely its own body. It will, however, continue to cathect the psychic derivatives of its initial existential system in a specific way, and will thus cling to a regime whose psychic derivatives have become abstract, disembodied, immaterial, non-instinctual and conflict-free. They know nothing of their corporeal support and regard it as an antagonist.

It is said that God created man in his image, but man created God in the image of himself as a foetus, and does not want to stop identifying with it.

Two of the essays in this volume deal with the perversions and point out that perverts do not merely regard themselves as 'normal'; they consider themselves to be superior, and claim to be indulging in an ideal, pure sexuality, unlike those who 'make love like Dad' and therefore wallow in a banal, down to earth and degrading sexuality. I also recall Freud's remark (1905b, pp. 161–2): 'The highest and the lowest are always closest to each other in the sphere of sexuality; *vom Himmel durch die Welt zur Hölle.*' It might be said that Freud's words in a sense endorse the claims made by perverts, and he does in fact suggest that perverse behaviour opens on to a vision of purity and spirituality based upon a sort of *a posteriori* dematerialization of the regressive, perverse act which thus allows the subject to regress to the prenatal state. My paper on fetishism describes this 'renarcissization' of anality at some length and in somewhat repetitive terms, and mentions Hitler's perversion in order to show how it relates to the idea of purity. I also take the opportunity to describe a whole category of perversions which have until now, in my view, been poorly classified in nosographical terms. They are based upon contact with the mucous membranes, sexual and otherwise. Contact with them reawakens memories of contact with the mucous membranes of the uterus, and recollections of an exultant elational sensation. I failed, however, to point out that the intestinal content which penetrates the mouth of the coprophile pervert and which, significantly enough, comes from the body of the woman he worships (the real object of his adoration is in fact the intra-uterine environment) can easily change register. It is an odorous, warm surface which recalls the mucous membranes of the uterus but which is transfigured as it suddenly takes on the characteristics of an object which is narcissistically cathected in a regressive process of purification and exaltation. After all, 'innocent' children play with their excrement, and it would be a brave man who attempted to establish a dividing line between the innocent, pure pleasure of the narcissist and the perverse anal-sadistic games of the pervert.

Parmain, April 1989

A note on terminology

Béla Grunberger occasionally refers to narcissism as an 'asexual self-love' [*aimance de soi*]. Elsewhere (Grunberger, 1983, p. 929) he explains that the term is adopted because it introduces an 'objectless' nuance and can therefore be applied to an affective state which may have no real object. The term *aimance* itself was once proposed as a translation of 'libido'. 'Captation' is to be understood in the sense of identification with (or being trapped by) an image; it also relates to the notion of *captativité*, which is sometimes used for the young child's tendency to appropriate the outside world. In order to avoid a degree of repetition and to ensure conciseness, the expression 'the Oedipus' has sometimes been used in preference to 'the Oedipus complex'. This usage has no specific semantic or theoretical connotations.

David Macey

Chapter One

The monad

At the dawn of time, there was an age of gold when man
was at one with nature, when the eternal harmonies and
laws of nature were more clearly expressed in man
himself than they have ever been expressed since. Even
today, we regard those moments in which our being is at
one with the whole of nature as instants of perfect bliss.
(von Schubert, 1808)

say again

I MUST ASK the reader's forgiveness for reiterating my theory of narcissism
but, given that it does differ greatly from other theories, I feel that I am
under an obligation to stress just how different it is. There are theories of
narcissism which follow the *Trieblehre* of the founder of psychoanalysis, but I
am proposing a theory which postulates the existence of a psychic dimension
that escapes the purely instinctual dimension. This is, to use Ferenczi's
phrase, a 'bioanalytic' theory. We can therefore posit the coexistence of two
dimensions, one governing the drives, and one deriving from what I term pure
narcissism. (There are, of course, parallelisms between the two; they intersect
and can be synthesized and give rise to a dialectic which generates a wealth of
mixed formations and nuances and is governed by the laws that govern the
instinctual and narcissistic dimensions respectively, and must be studied
from different perspectives.)

Narcissism, in the sense in which I understand that term, extends beyond
the limits that are normally assigned to it. Narcissism is often described as a
form of self-love [*aimance de soi*] (positive or negative), as self-valorization
(micro- and megalomania), or in terms of specific problems at the level of
object-cathexis. These descriptions remain within a classically Freudian
metapsychological framework. By adopting a bioanalytic theory, I have been
able to trace narcissistic phenomena back to a hypothetical *prenatal
coenesthesis*, to a factor which is primarily biological, to an unconscious and
archaic lived experience. Only certain of its derivatives become conscious,
belonging to an earlier time

This paper was presented at the Paris Psychoanalytical Society, 1985.

and in its pure state it tends to deny its origins at any cost, to reject any reference to biology. One of narcissism's essential characteristics is a disavowal of its biological origins.

I would now like to take the opportunity to add that the domain of the narcissistic factor, in the sense in which I understand that term, extends to the social, the intellectual, the cultural and the mystical. In advancing this theory, I am of course going against the psychoanalytic *Zeitgeist*, which tends to argue against *Kulturanalyse* by promulgating the doctrine that psycho-analysis is restricted to the narrow framework of couch and consulting room. I in fact think that prenatal coenesthesis is the matrix for a whole number of derivative psychic formations, such as serenity, the feeling of happiness, the feeling of sovereignty (all these formations may of course be distorted and can take either a positive or a negative form), completeness, omnipotence, a sense of one's own worth, an exultant expansionism, feelings of absolute freedom, independence and autonomy, feelings of invulnerability, eternity and immortality. Man is a mammal who thinks he is God – and, given that he is a fallen angel, there is a logical and a quasi-juridical basis to his demand to return to this ideal state.

The prenatal lived experience seems at first to be unorganized and to have no specific content, but it will later be integrated into the ego by deferred action [*nachträglich*] and will, so to speak, be *interpreted* and will thus give rise to highly cathected primal fantasies which serve to express its original potential. Man comes into the world with this as his baggage, but he is immediately confronted with the implications of the fact of having been born: namely, the loss of the prenatal state.

A text by another German romantic (Lichtenberg, 1844, p. 32) contains not only a description of the prenatal paradise both in its primal state and in a projected form – and that description is itself banal for anyone who explores the depths of the psyche – but also an allusion to the obligation to give it up. That obligation is incumbent upon the newborn child, and the prenatal condition must in fact gradually give way to the new *instinctual solution*, as opposed to the earlier *narcissistic solution*. Lichtenberg writes:

> I cannot get this idea out of my mind: before I was born, I was dead, and when I die, I will go back to that state. We refer to dying and being reborn with a sense of having had a previous existence as 'fainting'; we refer to waking up with new organs that have to be educated as 'being born'.

I would add that there is a dynamic difference between the prenatal and postnatal realms because, as I have often stressed, *a child is neotenic when it is born, but not before it is born*. In its prenatal existence, it has at its disposal an energy reserve that is quantitatively and qualitatively different to – and probably greater than – that available to postnatal energetics in the true sense.

This prenatal energetics corresponds to an untouched biological heritage. For some time after birth the newborn baby is still living through an embryological phase in which its vital coefficient is increased to the power of X. Experiments have, for instance, shown that a fifteen-day-old baby which is submerged in water has a spontaneous ability to swim. This is a natural phylogenetic ability which subsequently disappears. (A newborn baby has more nerve cells or synapses than it will have at any other time in its life. Its nervous system may develop in any direction, but as it becomes more specialized it also becomes more limited.)

The mother, or care-taker, attempts to reproduce the infant's prenatal conditions of existence (Ferenczi, 1913a), not only to foster its illusion of enjoying, without any solution of continuity, the narcissistic elational regime of which it has been deprived, but also to facilitate the transition from one existential system to the other, from past to present, from narcissism to the drives.

To a certain extent, a newborn baby still enjoys its prenatal autonomy, and its beatific smile expresses a triumphant bliss which is 'not of this world'. It uses this vicarious technique to avoid giving up its prenatal condition: *it has not yet been born*. An appropriate education thus allows the transition to be made in a rational manner, and – provided that the timing is right – allows the child to sustain the prenatal elational state. Such techniques are supposed to attenuate and, to a certain extent, to annul the sudden shock of birth. The care-taker (or mother) builds an 'incubator' for the newborn baby. This implies that the child is in physical proximity to the mother or to something representing her (I am thinking of the custom of swaddling babies). This incubator or brooder is, so to speak, an extrojected uterus. The newborn infant thus finds itself in a sort of virtual space which protects it from both the outside world and its deep and overwhelming instinctuality. I refer to this structure as *the monad*. The monad is a nonmaterial womb which functions as though it were material; on the one hand, it encloses the child in its narcissistic universe; on the other, it prepares it for the partial dissolution of that universe – or, in other words, for the dissolution of its own essence.[1]

The function of the monad's existence is to *reassure* the newborn child. (Kafka, 1919, p. 138: 'A fine wound is all I brought into the world; that was

---

1 The Hebrew word *rak'hmime* is one of the attributes of the Divinity; it in fact means 'uterus' (*rek'hem* is the singular of *rak'hmime*). According to the Jews, God possesses, along with other qualities, the quality of being *el maale rak'hmim*, meaning 'full of compassion', but literally 'full of womb' (in his omnipotence, the father also possesses maternal attributes). There is therefore a direct link between the divine (which I regard as a projected derivative of the narcissistic coenesthesis of omnipotence) and the organ which provides it with its biological substratum or envelope. The divine realm is the natural environment for cosmic narcissism. The foetus, like God, is both the centre and the circumference of this universe.

my sole endowment.') Experiments have shown that if a recording of its mother's heartbeat is played to a two-day-old infant when it cries, it will immediately stop crying because it is under the illusion that it is still inside her body. Except in moments of deep regression (such as sleep) the infant needs to be near its mother, or to certain rhythmic patterns which imitate the rhythms of the body of the pregnant mother. When modulated in a certain way, the voice and gaze of the mother can also function as a monad. We have, then, a binary unit [*Zweieinheit*] in which the infant merges with the internal surface of its foetal envelope. Together, the two form the monad. The mother is not yet an object for the child in any metapsychological sense, because there is no ego to perceive her as an object. That is why we cannot speak of relations or fusion at this stage. Mother and child form a double unit which exists inside the monad. Literary images of this double unit can be found in stories of doubles or *doppelgängers* and, though differently, in those about mirrors and shadows.

My own view is that the monad can be identified with a transitional object, and that a connection can thus be established between narcissistic projection and object relations; I also find the same connection in the 'imaginary playmate' fantasy and, as I will describe later, in the *analytic situation* itself. The role of the monad can also be fulfilled – for the child – by an animal, a set of toys, or other objects from his 'treasure horde' (Grunberger, 1967). For the adult, its role can be played by a sublimated object or by a set of ideas or beliefs (which may or may not be represented by a charismatic figure – by, that is, a figure who is narcissistically cathected or 'narcissophoric'). Individuals who feel a great need for the companionship provided by a pet have probably experienced very early frustrations at the level of the monad.

The monad is part of the psychic structure, and it is obviously bound up with the psychosexual component. It may come to the fore during certain phases of maturation, such as passionate love (in which the monad obviously lives on) or, at the other extreme, in the Darby and Joan existence of some old couples. In the monadic relationship, the one thing that the child asks of its mother is that she 'be with' [*mitsein*] it in a certain way, though even a tentative explanation of that mode of being is beyond the scope of the present essay. The *pure narcissistic demand* the monad is called upon to satisfy is not to be confused with the child's instinctual demands, which are situated at a different level. The latter demands can and must manifest themselves in a parallel or complementary mode, but in the initial stages of the child's evolution they are antagonistic to its *pure* narcissistic demands. If we do confuse the two, the child will point out what we are doing and hold it against us, and – at a later stage – the adult will address the same criticisms to his or her analyst, just as he or she once criticized his parents by saying 'Is that all you can give me?'

The narcissism–drive dialectic is reproduced in the dialectic that occurs at an emblematic level between the penis as part-object and the phallus or phallic image (in my view, the former has a strictly sexual meaning, whilst the latter has a narcissistic significance). It may be useful to make the same distinction in other domains too. It may, for instance, be of some help to a young analyst who, at an early stage in his career, encounters a predominantly narcissistic (platonic) male homosexual who loves his own image by loving the other. If the analyst alludes to the sexual nature of the bond between them, or raises questions about it, he may find that his visitor makes a hasty exit. If he does so, it indicates that he has chosen the narcissistic solution (a mirror relationship) precisely because it allows him escape the entire instinctual dimension.

I once had a hysterical analysand whom I will call Bettina. Her case history illustrates the narcissism–drive and penis–phallus dialectic, and sheds some light on both her 'identification' with the penis (this might be said to be a characteristic of narcissism) and the phallic nature of the monad itself. The phallic image is in fact the unconscious emblem of narcissistic completeness and, as we have seen, the function of the monad is to preserve that narcissistic completeness. This is true for both children and adults – or at least some adults.

Bettina was a young woman of Italian origin who lived with her father in modest circumstances which allowed them little privacy. She told me about a memory from her adolescence. In the middle of the night, she felt an overwhelming urge to get up and leave the room she shared with her father and go out into the courtyard to admire 'the thing that stands up' (meaning the moon). She also recounted a dream in which her father was a theatre director; the theatre in question was known as 'The Comet'. Analysis revealed that this young woman was running away from oedipal sexual excitement, taking refuge in narcissistic regression, and looking at the mirror image of the phallus with which she identified in a narcissistic and desexualized mode. She and the image formed a monad which protected her; a heavenly monad, so to speak (the moon and the comet). If we now turn to 'cosmic narcissism' (in which the foetus merges with its universe, which is synonymous with the universe as a whole), this typically narcissistic formation sheds some light on the enigma posed by certain religious mysteries. I pointed out to the subject that on the tympani on some Romanesque churches Christ is depicted by an image emerging from an *ovoid* shape known as a mandorla (the term derives from a Greek word meaning 'almond'). The mandorla represents 'Christ in glory' and has eminently narcissistic connotations, particularly in that the egg, the organ for the reproduction and preservation of the species, is identical to the monad's precursor and model: the uterus.

It will be apparent that the conception of the monad that I am outlining

5

lends itself to multiple applications which cannot be dealt with here. The monad has its own history (in so far as it is a process), its own pathology and its own vicissitudes. Narcissism induces a specifically monadic feeling of guilt, and every aspect of psychic life can be viewed in this perspective. The monad has a role to play in religions, ideologies and perversions, and its role in sublimation opens a whole cultural dimension up to analysis. I have even been able to make use of it in studies of anti-Semitism and racism. The theory of the monad will, I believe, add to our understanding of phenomena of contemporary relevance, such as aggressivity and violence. Here, however, given my topic, I shall restrict the discussion to the study of the monad in the analytic situation.

For a long time I have been studying the analytic situation (I make a distinction between the analytic situation and the historical transference) as an instance of narcissistic regression. For the moment, however, I would like to narrow the focus by applying the monadic schema to the same analytic situation. I will illustrate my point by describing a case described to me by a colleague: an exceptional and highly schematic case history but also, in my view, rich in meaning.

A young man went into analysis because he was having difficulties in establishing contacts and relationships, and was experiencing sexual problems; he also displayed some somatic symptoms. Having listened to the therapist explaining the fundamental rule, he lay down on the couch and remained silent until the end of the session. He returned for further sessions, and behaved in the same way for several months. Then, during one particular session, he made his verbal presence felt by saying: 'We're not there yet, but things are definitely getting better.' He then lapsed back into silence and after again saying absolutely nothing for several months, he got up at the end of the hour, declared that he now felt fine and thought he had been cured, thanked his therapist, and off he went.

Let me make my intentions quite clear: this is, as I said, an exceptional case. I am in fact well aware of the importance of interpretations and therefore of the analytic material, and I am convinced of the dangers inherent in certain analytic attitudes, such as maintaining a systematic silence. I am referring to the silence of the analyst. As for the analysand, some forms of silence may result from specific blocks which may give rise to anxiety, and it may be necessary for the analyst to intervene, whilst others introduce the prenatal process itself into the framework of the analytic situation, which then functions as a monad. The monad itself is silent but it is the site of an intense, accelerated metabolism, just as analytic treatment is a second and accelerated form of education. Analysis has sometimes been seen as a new beginning, a *Neubeginn* (Ferenczi; Balint, 1932), and whilst the monad does preserve the narcissistic factor, it also paves the way for its own destruction by going through a series of stages which – in a well-conducted analysis – must follow on from one another in the appropriate order. Just as the monad is made up of a container and a content, the analytic situation consists of a fixed material perimeter which contains the fantasy and recollected material and is supported by a preordained narcissistic programme designed to realize the narcissistic ideal. This is the driving force behind analysis. And just as the monad paves the way for a gradual synthesis of narcissism and the drives, so each phase in the process, interpreted or not, implies a repeated rejection of phantasmic narcissistic solutions and reorientates the pure narcissistic factor in such a way that it can be introduced and integrated into the ego in a manner which is both effective and economically valid.

The 'basic trust' the child places in the monad is reproduced in the analytic situation when a narcissistic idealization is projected on to the analyst inside the monad. I am referring to the 'positive transference', which Freud (1916–17, p. 440) compares to a period of fine weather. As for the 'negative transference', we will discuss that in connection with the 'history' of the monad (in analysis).

The case I described above demonstrates that there is a process centred on the monad, and that the monad is a framework whose nature explains the richness of certain silences and elucidates the link between the analytic perimeter and the material, which combine to form a monad represented by analyst and analysand alike.[2]

We often hear talk of a 'therapeutic alliance' based upon the symmetry between transference and countertransference. The notion of analytic neutrality is being undermined and there is a tendency to place an unwarranted emphasis on the proposal Ferenczi put forward towards the end of his life, when he began to recommend that analyst and analysand should, so to speak, take turns in analysing one another (Ferenczi, 1985; Grunberger, 1979b). All this presupposes that there is a *relationship* between analyst and analysand. In my view, the analyst is involved in a relationship with the analysand only to the extent that he is the focus for a specific historical transference – in other words, for the conflict-ridden pre-oedipal or oedipal phase of the analysis.

In a purely narcissistic analytic situation, the analysand forms a monad by narcissistically cathecting the analyst (and the analytic situation), but the analyst does not reciprocate, as to do so would mean promoting the subsequent transferential relationship, whereas it is supposed to be dissolved. It is rather a bad sign if an identification (positive or negative) outlasts the analysis, as is so-called hysterical 'identification', which is in fact a form of

2 We know that if analyst and analysand meet outside the 'monad', their clinical relationship within the monadic framework will be damaged. We also know that the analysand may know nothing at all about the layout of the consulting room if he has not cathected it in a specifically monadic manner.

imitation or *mimesis* (and as we know, it is sometimes impossible to tell the difference between the analyst and a candidate who imitates not only his gestures or style, but even his way of dressing; we also know that there are 'clubs' made up of the disciples of certain 'masters', to say nothing of their aesthetico-philosophical or political loyalty to the master, which merely testifies to the fact that the transference has been badly 'dissolved' – to use a superficial expression when we should really be undertaking a study of the pathology of the monad).

There is, however, a lasting bond between analyst and analysand, but I prefer to use an ethological term and speak of *imprinting*. The notion of the monad may help us to come to terms with this enigmatic variation on identification if we adopt a psychobiological perspective. I refer to certain fixed behavioural constants which remain unconscious for both analysand and analyst. They are 'transmitted' from analyst to analysand, and only a third party who happens to know both well will see them. These characteristic forms of behaviour are of secondary, or even minor, importance, and a biologist would find them reminiscent of the disproportion between the great size of certain portions of the brain – such as the rhinencephalon – and the minimal significance, for our purposes, of their actual role. But the perspective changes if we recall that we are dealing with relics of certain functions which fulfilled a much more important role in the phylogenetic past or during prenatal life. We have here an index of the continuity between prenatal life and the analytic situation, in so far as it is a postnatal monad. In this context, the terms 'identification' or 'transference' are not appropriate. In both its intrauterine form and its extrauterine form, the monad serves to reproduce certain forms of behaviour.

In one sense, the family cell functions as a monad, not only because it is, in its early form, centred on the mother, but because it is also the locus for sexual and aggressive conflicts which are antithetical to the monadic universe, which therefore facilitate its partial fragmentation at the appropriate time and in the appropriate mode, and which therefore, in theory, promote the synthesis of narcissism and the drives. There are family environments in which the mother is unable to play her role as a monadic centre. If, for example, the phratry is too large, she may choose a 'favourite', thus disadvantaging her other children, who often have to form a monad of their own – sometimes the family splits up into 'pairs', at least one of which (irrespective of the sex of its members) becomes the true monad. Everyone refers to the pair as inseparable, and they often regard themselves as aristocratically superior to the rest of the family, but their unconscious life shows that they are interchangeable as well as inseparable (as becomes obvious if one of the couple is in analysis). It is commonplace to find the same phenomena in the dreams of mothers who form a monad with their children, and vice versa, as they adopt the rule of 'container equals content'. If sexual elements are then grafted on to the monad – and this is quite in keeping with the evolution of a monadic organization, as narcissistic purity itself opens the door to sexuality by providing it with an alibi – we will find that narcissism becomes synthesized with the instinctual dimension and that the monad gradually (but never completely) breaks up to make way for the dimension of drives and objects.

The narcissistic regression which characterizes the beginning of the analysis finds its expression at the end of the session in certain motor disturbances such as minor forms of vertigo. Elsewhere, I have adopted Ferenczi's description of this phenomenon (Ferenczi, 1929), with reference to the narcissistic regression induced by the analysis. It represents the coming together of two dimensions: that of narcissistic regression on the one hand, and that of reality on the other; at the same time, motor-function acquisition mobilizes the anal component. The combination of the two results in vertigo. I once had a woman patient whose analysis appeared to be stagnating somewhat, despite my analysis of her instinctual conflicts. One day, she said to me: 'You know, for some time now I've been feeling a little dizzy when I get up from the couch. It reminds me of what you describe as the "end of the session syndrome" in your book.' At that point it suddenly occurred to me that she really was about to enter the instinctual dimension, and she promptly confirmed my *Einfall* ('insight', but literally a 'falling into', an appropriate term to describe how thought suddenly falls into the unconscious or, rather, how the unconscious slips into thought). She did in fact produce the association 'I would like to go to bed with you', and for the first time, and much to her own surprise, she used a vulgar expression that was quite out of keeping with her usual style. The monad she had been living so fully had provided an opening on to the oedipal conflict, with all the pregenital anal components which make it truly authentic. The monad had begun to self-destruct, and narcissism was now bound up with instinctuality.[3]

The analytic monad is, like any monad, a sort of virtual membrane which shelters a matrix of completeness, and that structure is present from the outset. This is why, without being at all psychotic, the analysand begins analysis by believing that the therapist is a 'subject supposed to know' (Lacan,

---

3 During our next session, she described a dream which confirmed that an oedipal transference had occurred. I figured in the dream, together with an uncle. The analytic couch had become a sofa, and a parrot perched on a horizontal bar above it. My patient was German and knew a lot about psychoanalysis, and she spontaneously noted that the parrot was a *Papagei*, a bird (*Vogel*). [*Vögeln* is 'the vulgar term for sexual intercourse' referred to by Freud (1900, p. 583) while 'Papa' in French means Daddy; trans.]. She had already used the word the day before. As for the uncle, he had once had incestuous relations with her. The choice of the bird suggests a slightly ironic gesture towards the analyst, and thus signals the appearance of the negative transference.

1973, p. 230), someone who understands all languages, who is familiar with all the sciences. This notion is reminiscent of that of divine omniscience, which is a narcissistic projection on the part of the subject. The monad is at this point supported by a pre-object (the analyst), but that support is itself experienced as having an immediately obvious and absolute source in the analysand's narcissistic self. (Analysand and analyst or pre-object are in intimate contact, but there is at the same time a distance between them; the two protagonists meet only on the narcissistic level and in a narcissistic mode.) The support gives the subject a profound feeling of security. It appears to be so solid as to be proof against everything that the subject will attribute to his parental imagos, once the monad has gradually been destroyed. The monad's place will be taken by a series of maternal imagos and – more important – paternal imagos corresponding to the different stages of the maturation process: the gradual 'narcissization' of the drives, the smothering of the narcissistic factor by the drives, and the almost total destruction of the monad.

If the monad is well constructed (and in real life this depends upon its being constructed by the subject's care-takers), it may facilitate this development. But the premature introduction of conflict constitutes a trauma which may upset the analytic situation, lead to the failure of the analysis, or even, in certain cases, result in delusions. In one case which has come to my notice, the fact that a young analyst became pregnant just as she was beginning to analyse a woman patient had a traumatic effect lasting for more than a year because it mobilized the patient's psychotic defences; both the analytic situation and the psyche of the patient reacted as though they had been hit by a seismic shock. It was only thanks to her tact that the therapist was gradually able to undo the damage she had unwittingly caused to a patient who had been prematurely driven out of the monad to make way for the analyst's real child.

But analytic technique itself can lead to the break-up of the monad, or make its establishment impossible. At one extreme we have Lacan, for whom the analyst is a sovereign ruler who exploits the analytic Law to his own advantage – notably by deciding the length of the session on a whim and by keeping absolutely silent. At the other we have Ferenczi, who late in life recommended the reciprocal analysis of analyst and analysand. Between these two extremes we have the Freudian rule of 'benevolent neutrality', which makes it possible to respect both the monadic nature of the analytic situation and the possibility that the monad will gradually break up. Being a constituent element in the monad, the analyst must remain neutral. Most analysands – those for whom analysis is clearly indicated and who have established a therapeutic alliance with the analyst – confirm his neutral position because they spontaneously understand the analytic attitude, an attitude which would be experienced outside the analytic situation as unbearably frustrating, offensive or even insulting. The analyst does not, for instance, answer the analysand's questions. The analysand tolerates that fairly well (whereas he would rebel if his parents behaved in similar fashion, thus proving that there has been no transference in any real sense) and remains convinced that whatever the analyst does (or does not do) is in his interests. The analyst is in a sense the patient's guardian angel (guardian angel and patient form a variant on the monad).

The guardian-angel analyst is, however, only one aspect of the analytic situation, and we know that the mother herself must behave in such a way as to allow the monad to dissolve in an adequate manner[4] after a long dialectical interplay between narcissism and instinctual development. Within this process of development, we find that pregenital and genital conflicts have a permanent role to play (as does the so-called negative transference). One has the impression that as the subject progresses towards maturity and object relations, the monad, which is an abstract but biologically based formation, gradually gives way to the phallic image. The latter is also an emblem of completeness, but this completeness has been enriched by and integrated into the real. Whereas the monad allows the newborn child to go on living its prenatal existence as though it were still inside its mother's womb, the phallus is a support for the wish to return to the womb, which explains why it is so important, and why we constantly encounter it as a symbol (Ferenczi, 1924).

Because man is born neotenic and to some extent remains neotenic, his neoteny gives him a capacity for constant self-renewal [Neubeginn]. As we know, the best analyses are those which continue in the form of a self-analysis, which is a maturational process triggered by analysis proper. We terminate analyses when we have reconstructed the monad under the right conditions. I am thinking of a young woman, a drug addict, who went into analysis. She would lie on the couch, surrounding herself with a variety of objects, such as cigarettes, sweets, a handkerchief, lipstick, gloves, and so on. She had been brought up by a mother who, acting on the advice of a paediatrician, avoided all contact with her child, coming into close contact with her only to perform a minimal number of mechanical acts as neutrally and impersonally as possible. It can safely be assumed that the circle of objects with which the patient surrounded the couch represented the 'extrojected' uterus of her mother, and its substitutes (her mother's arms and cuddles), which she had also been denied. Her drug addiction obviously plunged her back into a prenatal paradise from which she had been torn prematurely and without compensation. For such a patient the analytic situation is probably too frustrating because of its implied absence of tactile or visual contact. (She was not my

4 It is well known that a mother who resists this development instead of encouraging it can do her child a great deal of harm, and can practically smother it in a permanent monad.

patient, and I am not sure that I would have asked her to lie on the couch.) Even so, it seems that she did arrive at a sort of compromise on the couch; having abandoned the monad she and her drugs formed, and being unable to tolerate the lack of physical contact characteristic of the analytic situation, she used her objects to cobble together a sort of monad which was supported by the presence of the analyst. The objects – some of them recognizable as transitional objects – definitely seem to me to have the characteristics of a substitute uterine envelope.

Once the monad has been reconstituted, the analysand can relive his conflicts and retrace his evolution in more adequate economic conditions. We have already seen the importance of the monad within the analytic situation. Certain analytic techniques remind me of the case of the mothers Jochen Stork described in a talk organized by Serge Lebovici in Paris on 5 December 1983. They had suddenly lost their infants, but it had not been possible to determine the cause of their deaths. The mothers were interviewed using psychoanalytically inspired techniques, and it transpired that one of the children had died – and here I am thinking of a specific case – at the age of three months in a room next door to its mother's bedroom. The mother in question lived alone, and woke up one day to find that her child had died during the night. She was therefore psychically separated from her child. I do not think it takes an in-depth analysis to realize that this mother had probably been unable to construct a monad with her child.

Similar sudden and unexplained deaths have been observed amongst the Boat People who reached the United States after so many terrible experiences. These people die for all sorts of reasons: some real, obvious or manifest, some mysterious or simply strange. Their deaths remain unexplained, or seem to. I think it would be useful to try to establish a link between these sudden deaths, for which there is no apparent explanation, and a monadic deficit, a lack which, at some point in the victims' lives, must have been reactivated.

As we have seen, the monad has its history, but it also has its pathology, and both are determined by the way it comes to terms with the demands of instinctual life. It both fights those demands and transforms them. For a while, the newborn child which enters the postnatal dimension stands at a crossroads between two worlds: the world of the drives that urge it to master the real, and the world of prenatal elation, the 'other world', for which it will always feel nostalgic. It will also experience feelings of rebellion and indignation at having been driven out of paradise, and will look back with nostalgia on the perfection, bliss and purity it once knew. It will miss that marvellous world, whose one defect is that it exists only in terms of an *a posteriori* interpretation of prenatal coenesthesis. Given that it is part of his subjective reality, man will go on demanding to return to the ideal state he experienced in the womb and which, for a while and in a sense, he continued to experience in the monad. The same demand will be put forward with particular force by the frustrated, the weak and the immature on the one hand, and by mystics, lovers, believers in utopia, artists and narcissists on the other. (It goes without saying that love and art are satisfactory answers to this demand – and they are not the only ones – while some other solutions are more debatable.)

Analysis contains this dimension of the psyche. Indeed, that is its very essence. The analytic situation in its specificity functions as a new monad, guaranteeing and establishing in the outside world something the foetus once enjoyed in an inner world.

An examination of all the potential the monad offers in life and in psychoanalysis is obviously out of the question here. The aim I set myself in this essay was to introduce the concept of the monad, which is the site and container of prenatal narcissism. Having attempted to study narcissism as a derivative of the physiological entity known as the foetus, I wanted to extend the discussion to include the derivatives of the container which envelops it and is in a sense both its counterpart, the surface on which it is reflected, and its complement.

Chapter Two

Narcissus and Oedipus:
a controversy

A s WE KNOW, the Oedipus complex plays a fundamental role in structuring the personality. At the same time, it transcends individual lived
experience and lies at the origin of culture, sublimations, morality and
social institutions, etc. As we shall see, it also plays a central role in the
maturational process which takes the individual from birth to adulthood.

As for narcissism, Freud first uses the term in a note added to the *Three Essays
on the Theory of Sexuality* in 1910 (Freud, 1905b, p. 145n), and then 'introduces'
it as a concept in 1914 (Freud, 1914) when he describes narcissistic forms of
behaviour, notes the 'persistence' of narcissism ('an original libidinal cathexis
of the ego ... fundamentally persists': p. 75) and makes a distinction between
narcissistic libido (ego-libido) and object-libido. It will also be recalled that he
draws a comparison between object-cathexis and the pseudopodia put out by an
amoeba, and states that secondary narcissism derives from the libido that is
taken back from objects (1916–17, p. 416). According to Freud's second
conceptualization, the prototype for primary narcissism is to be found in
intrauterine life (Freud, 1921, pp. 130–1).

In showing that the narcissist takes himself as a love object, Freud
introduced narcissism into the theory of the drives, and it does not seem to me
that his second conceptualization, according to which the origins of narcissism
lie in intrauterine life, can be regarded as invalidating that view. Yet as
Laplanche and Pontalis (1967, p. 338) note, Melanie Klein (1952, p. 51) takes

This paper was presented at the Klinik für Kinder- und Jugendpsychologie in Munich, 17
September 1985.

the view that 'a relation to objects is present' from birth onwards, and that it is therefore not possible to speak of a 'narcissistic stage', but only of 'states'. This modifies the status of the concept in relation to Freud's *Trieblehre* (the theory of drives).

My own reflections on the subject long ago led me to the conclusion – and I must apologize for repeating myself yet again – that narcissism must be conceptualized in such a way as to make it autonomous – that is, in such a way as to situate it *outside* the corpus of the theory of drives. Narcissism enters into a dialectical relationship with the drives, and whilst the two may develop in parallel, narcissism can become anatagonistic to the drives, and this *basic ambiguity* constantly creates problems that may prove difficult to resolve.

In my view – and my clinical experience confirms my view – the prenatal origin of narcissism is a fact of enormous importance whose effects tend to be ignored, even though they are constantly at work in the depths of the unconscious. The foetus experiences no conflict and no desires; its host takes care of its metabolism, and it exists in a state of perfect completeness. This coenesthesis leaves sufficient traces for it to be fantasized as a state of *perfect bliss, absolute sovereignty* or *omnipotence.* Folklore, religions and literature all confirm the existence of this fantasy, which corresponds to an ideal which man has lost and continues to seek. Indeed, he seeks it all the more eagerly in that although it is a fantasy, *the demand for that ideal state is based on the reality of a lived experience with an undeniably biological substratum.*[1] As I demonstrate in my article on the phallic image (Grunberger, 1964), the phallus is emblematic of all the attributes of prenatal coenesthesis, and its image – a primal fantasy – is present within the psyche from, and probably before, birth. The future ego retains a memory of the spontaneous satisfactions of the foetal age, and therefore feels justified in attributing its elational narcissistic happiness to the complete absence of conflict and to the absence of activity on the part of the drives, and can think of this state as one of absolute purity – purity being confused with an existential regime in which it is protected from the drives. That state is then transformed into an ideal. As a result of this fantasy, the ego – or a certain sector of the ego – opposes the instinctual solution, even though that solution will inevitably be forced upon it.

We can further deduce from this that the subject will have great difficulty in accepting reality and integrating it into his ego, particularly in that an absolute and totally independent narcissistic omnipotence (absolute in subjective terms, at least) will be the source of an overevaluation of the self

---

1 This intrauterine bliss may, of course, be disturbed, but even if the foetus does register the fact, it does so independently of the traces left behind by the positive experience, and here we might adopt Glover's nuclear theory of the (future) ego (Glover, 1930). Indeed, the contrast between the two lived experiences may be an essential element in the structuring of the content of the bipolar ego.

that will further justify the omnipotence (Lacan's 'The analyst's only authorization comes from himself': 1967, p. 14). The subject will live all the affects that derive from his narcissism in an exalted mode as a result of the specific coefficient which heightens the intensity of the lived experience by introducing a narcissistic hypercathexis. It might be objected at this point that I am describing a psychotic state, and we do indeed find all this in an overt form in the psychoses. In 'normal' cases, these manifestations are of course tempered by other sectors of the ego which are less involved in the process, but they still betray their presence. Narcissism is never in fact devoid of a certain pathologization, if only because of the inevitable frustrations which force the ego to negotiate over this state of affairs.

Having said that, I shall give a summary description of psychosexual development from the viewpoint I have just outlined, but before doing so I should point out that this study takes as its object a *certain variety* of narcissistic subject whose structure is characterized by a conflict between narcissism and the Oedipus, and that such subjects react to that conflict in a particular way.

I will take the adolescent as a model. Conflict between narcissism and the Oedipus is normal in adolescents, given the instinctual and narcissistic changes they have to come to terms with, but if that conflict *persists* and becomes the kernel of a psychosexual organization, it poses a certain number of problems which we will now try to examine.

A child brings into the world with it its prenatal elation, because during the first postnatal phase the regime under which it lives is still narcissistic (we know that its environment does all it can to perpetuate, as far as possible, the conditions in which it lived before it was born). As we know, when a child is born it experiences a huge trauma, to which it responds with an aggressivity of cataclysmic intensity. That aggressivity is the object of immediate repression (primal repression).[2] Seen in this light, then, birth is a castration of the narcissism represented by the phallic image. It is a castration because of the loss of prenatal coenesthesis, and because birth represents the moment of transition from that loss to the other primal fantasy, which consists of attributing narcissism, and therefore the phallus, to the adult (the father). It stimulates the birth of a specific urge to recover the phallus. If, like Freud (1929, pp. 124–5), we accept that the sense of guilt derives from the renunciation of aggression (see the account of the Wednesday meeting devoted to this topic given by Sterba, 1982), it seems only logical to assume that this prototypical castration provokes an enormously aggressive response,

---

2 Cf. Freud (1926, p. 94): 'It is highly probable that the immediate precipitating forces of primal repression are quantitative factors such as an excessive degree of excitation and the breaking through of the protective shield against stimuli.'

and that this aggression might be the *primal source of a future and equally powerful sense of guilt*. If we consider the absolute helplessness of the newborn infant, which is *overwhelmed by the devastating effects of the trauma*, and the ill-defined but profound feeling of guilt that results from it, and then compare them, we find the image of crisis provided by the legend of the Flood that was sent to punish mankind for its sins.

Here, I am summarizing my earlier remarks (Grunberger, 1983) on the double primal imago, on the positive and negative nucleus of narcissism. The negative nucleus is a surface for the projection of an aggression which is not expressed, is therefore transformed into guilt, is inevitably persecutory and terrifying (all terrifying imagos are maternal). I am of course describing a matrix structure whose existence is purely hypothetical, but there can be no denying that it has a biological support. The spontaneous succession of these two primal nuclei (the presence of the bad mother is an omen of the appearance of the good mother who was there at the beginning, and who will therefore *return* bearing the narcissistic ideal: stories about the wicked witch and the good fairy) is another of mankind's basic fantasies: the fantasy that the *total destruction of reality* (the apocalypse) *will spontaneously give rise to a new world corresponding to the narcissistic ideal*, to the New Jerusalem. (If birth and access to reality destroyed narcissistic coenesthesis, we can return to our primal state simply by suppressing reality.) This schema is implanted in the psyche at the very dawn of life; the analysand relives it as he or she analyses his or her conflicts of the moment; the recurrent themes of analysis are castration (both auto- and hetero-) and guilt.

Shaken by the trauma, the narcissistic self will henceforth be organized with the help of the mother. Even before any object relations have been established, mother and baby form a binary unit (which is not yet a dyad) and the neonate is thus able to go on living its narcissism because it is enclosed within a monad,[3] and because its own narcissism *reflects* that of the mother. We know the importance, for children of this age, of the *gaze* and of *reflection*. This reflection has no formal or chromatic content, but it does contain the narcissistic 'point of similarity' to which the monad is attached (narcissistic mirroring is also found in theophanies, transfigurations and in certain perversions such as fetishism).

---

3 See chapter 1 above. By 'monad', I mean a narcissistic existential form which exists prior to the existence of objects and drives. Its derivatives are to be found in certain adolescent relationships, as well as in love and, of course, marriage: the 'ideal marriage' has a great deal to do with the monad, as do sublimation and 'imaginary playmates', a topic on which there is a considerable literature (like 'transitional objects', they are imaginary and do not really exist). Cf. Winnicott's description of primary narcissism: the subject is supported by the environment, merges with the environment, but remains oblivious of its existence. André Green (1976) says of Winnicott's 'subjective object': 'From the point of view of the *infans*, the object is part of its own narcissistic organization.'

The monad is therefore a predominantly narcissistic phase, but the predominance of narcissism is gradually undermined by inevitable and repeated frustrations which gradually mobilize the instinctual apparatus – again with the help of the mother, who eventually comes to be cathected in an instinctual, as opposed to a narcissistic, mode. As for the father, the phallic image is present within the psyche from the outset, the corresponding sign being the emblem of both narcissistic completeness and phallic energy (the penis). The child can use it to 'triangulate' in a sense, but it cannot be integrated by a child in Abraham's second oral (oral-sadistic) stage (Abraham, 1924), and certainly not by a child in the anal-sadistic stage. It is impossible to speak of the Oedipus in this connection, as it is only the integration of the latter component that allows the child to engage in oedipal *conflict*. Involvement in oedipal conflict is useful in two senses: it restores the child's illusion of a completeness (because its intrinsic immaturity is transformed into a prohibition from the outside), whilst a sense of guilt bound up with a specific conflict provides it with an anchoring point.

The anal stage also provides a framework for the struggle for the phallus. The effects of the narcissistic coefficient of this search are reflected in such legendary images as the quest for the Holy Grail or the Golden Fleece. Now, because of its regressive component, this search is a matter for the bipolar ego (Grunberger, 1983) which combines the 'pure' elational level with a very archaic aggressive component, and thus provokes a feeling of guilt that can be overcome only with great difficulty. It would seem that oedipal involvement makes it possible to avoid this pitfall by genitalizing the deep aggressivity. When, in his discussion of the dissolution of the Oedipus complex in boys, Freud (1925c, p. 256) states: '*Whereas in boys the Oedipus complex is destroyed by the castration complex, in girls it is made possible and led up to by the castration complex*', he can be understood as meaning that the boy attempts to rid the archaic aggressive component of guilt by giving up the father's phallus (at the end of the Oedipus complex the boy will be granted his own phallus), whereas the girl does so by acquiring receptivity, which annuls the 'savage' character of her *captation* of the father's penis (a combination of fear of castrating and a wish to castrate) and genitalizes the deep component. [7]

As it happens, the neonate does not come into the world empty-handed, and its baggage does contain something that can inspire 'fear and trembling' (here one thinks of dreams about black suitcases which are both persecutory and precious, and which the dreamer dare not open because they contain his aggressivity). I have on several occasions spoken of analysands who, in the course of treatment, come up against difficulties which prove insurmountable because of the need to integrate the anal component. Narcissists find it immensely difficult to give up the narcissistic regime which ensures them the protection of the Primal Mother and their identification with her, and they refuse to take the plunge.[4] Oedipal conflict does open up the oedipal world to them, but it is also a world of *sin*. Until now, the child has been *guilty*, but as he enters the anal phase (which is also the phase of knowledge) he becomes a *sinner* (the state of sin is washed away by the Christian ritual of baptism, in which the child is reimmersed in water – amniotic fluid – or, in other words, in the pre-instinctual mother).

The anal period is therefore predominantly instinctual and marked by an oedipal attempt to release the subject from his deep feeling of guilt.

The Oedipus is a duel with the father, who both comes into conflict with the child and supports him. René Girard (1978, p. 135) speaks of the 'fierce' father; the phallus is indeed a permanent challenge to the nebulous blur of narcissism, but at the same time the father has his place in both the ancestral line and the line of descent which support his child's existential project. The male child identifies with his father (just as the girl identifies with her mother, though cross-identifications are also necessary) and grows stronger in the course of the conflict. He thus succeeds in synthesizing his narcissism and his drives. As I have said elsewhere, anyone who really does kill his father has, like Oedipus himself, failed to come to terms with the Oepidus.

We now come to the latency period which, whilst it does have a certain obsessional tonality, is primarily narcissistic. During this stage, the ideal of purity is often signalled by what has been described as the *mystical crisis of adolescence*, or rather of pre-adolescence. The mystical crisis of adolescence and pre-adolescence, which will subsequently reappear in later mystical tendencies, also has its counterpart in the analytic situation itself; I refer to certain aspects of the positive transference. This is not a purely theoretical issue, as I have on occasion heard analysands say that coming to the session was like going to church, whilst others, who are afraid of going into analysis, express their fears in terms of a *non dignus sum intrare*, rather as though the analyst were God. And we all know that analysis is surrounded by a somewhat mystical halo because it does touch upon a deep narcissistic kernel and awakens corresponding reactions in the unconscious.

The resurgence of the Oedipus occurs during puberty and is short-lived (though true maturity comes much later – at the age of twenty-five, according to Freud – and we can therefore also speak of a second latency period). And Freud (1924b, p. 177; emphasis added) does indeed state that this may cause problems: 'If the ego has not in fact achieved much more than a "*repression*" of the complex the latter persists in an unconscious state in the id and will later manifest its pathogenic effect.' The resurgence of the Oedipus might, then, be

4 Cf. Freud's circular letter of 15 February 1924 to Committee members: 'The obstacles that evoke anxiety, the barriers against incest are in contrast to the intrauterine fantasy. Where do they come from? They seem to be represented by the father, reality, authority which does not permit incest.'

more accurately described as a remanence which has not really been dissolved – as, that is, an Oedipus which never really began, and on which the subject remains fixated, unable to resolve the problem or to let go. It is not the complex that produces the pathogenic effect, but the internal conflict provoked by the need to engage with it. This is not an oedipal conflict but an anti-oedipal conflict between narcissism and the Oedipus. As we shall see, this particular position might be termed a 'pseudo-Oedipus' or 'inverted Oedipus'.

I once treated a young scientist whose problem included a *'fate neurosis'*. Within his own specialist area he was highly qualified, very gifted and well respected, and he was on the threshold of a brilliant career. But he was unable to cross that threshold. He was a 'good analysand' who had cathected his treatment well, attended regularly and was making considerable progress in the kind of improvements that I attribute to the narcissistic component in the analytic situation. His main problem, however, remained intact and it seemed to me that it was high time for him to emerge from his narcissistic cocoon and to begin to analyse his conflicts (I had also learnt from other sources that in his private life he was sometimes given to violent outbursts of brutal aggression, but that he was careful to restrict them to his immediate family. These outbursts were not a form of 'acting out' but undirected explosive reactions; the aggressivity was expressed in superficial terms, but its origins lay deep within him and he seemed to be terribly afraid of it).

One day he told me that he had applied for an extremely important and interesting position and had received a reply in the form of an invitation to meet the relevant authorities. This was to be the final interview, and would no doubt be a pure formality. He did not attend the interview, with predictable results. I should add that this was not masochism (that much had been clear to his previous analysts; this was his third analysis); nor was it a phobic inhibition along the lines of: 'It was too much for me, I couldn't bring myself to go'. What struck me about his case (and it must have struck him too, otherwise he would not have told me about it) was that at the end of the story he said: *'I was very pleased with myself; I showed them all right'* (!).

Fortunately for the analysis, he followed up these strange remarks by telling me about an *explicitly transferential* dream which I was able to interpret by telling him that he was sabotaging his analysis in order to prevent me from carrying it out, throwing down a challenge to Freud and psychoanalysis in an attempt to prove that it was worthless, and that he needed to prove its worthlessness just as he needed to prove to the relevant professional authorities that he rejected the entire system over which they presided. I added that all this masked a fantasy that one day he would suddenly achieve immediate and spontaneous success without making an effort; that he would not owe his success to the official institution and the whole system it represented but would succeed *despite it*. As to the astonishing remarks with which he concluded his story, they fulfilled his fantasy in advance; it was rather as though it had already become a reality.

He seemed to be moved by my interpretation, and I immediately noted a significant change in his behaviour. The patient tended to speak very softly, had a slight hiss to his voice and articulated his words badly, as though his phonatory muscles were impaired in some way; his previous analysts had in fact complained about this. He spoke as though he were sure that his incoherent mumblings would be heard, as though he knew that he would somehow make himself understood. After the session I have just described, his speech became much clearer, more audible and comprehensible. He suddenly began to speak as though he were *addressing an interlocutor*.

This difficult and complicated patient, whom I categorize as a borderline case, had settled down into a narcissistic regression, and whenever reality intruded he reacted by regressing still further (and had a great capacity for doing so). He had resolved to negate his narcissistic trauma in this way rather than allowing himself to be shaken by traumas which would help him to make progress with his conflicts. When I offered him an interpretation he could not in a sense reject, he would rush off to 'get plastered'; as a result everything was wiped out, and we had to start all over again. By behaving in this way he was attacking me, but it was impossible to see his attitude as anything other than an attempt to *avoid* any conflict with me or with the oedipal existential situation, from which he wanted to distance himself at all costs. I have had other analysands who, in the same situation and with the same aim in mind, have reacted by adopting a violently projective and provocative attitude and by erecting a similar wall between them and myself as representative of the oedipal world.

For the patient I am describing I represented the Oedipus he rejected, but it was for that very same reason that he was bound to me and analysis. By constantly rejecting me, he was protecting his regressive haven: the narcissistic ideal defended by the omnipotent Mother. He displaced the conflict downwards, turning it into a conflict between the Good Mother and the Bad Mother, and then projected it on to me *without* abandoning his secret quest for the *paternal* phallus that lay behind the image of the Mother, or in her belly. *This is why marginality is bound up with constant provocation and with constant attacks upon the paternal principle and the world it governs.* These constant attacks show that the father is always there. The narcissist fights the Oedipus, but his entire organization is based on a negative form of the Oedipus. As I said earlier, I refer to this mechanism as a 'pseudo-Oedipus' or an 'inverted Oedipus'.

The marginal subject may well elaborate an anti-oedipal ideology designed to negate and narcissistically decathect the Oedipus (the precise role of that ideology within his psychic economy remains to be determined), but its entire content is bound up with the Oedipus in a variety of ways which can readily be identified and classified. The presence of the Oedipus in the discourse of the narcissist may be betrayed by:

1 *Opposition*: 'You say this, I say that.' That suffices because the narcissist refuses to argue (the idea of causality originates with the Oedipus, with the father; *'Cause toujours'*, as Lacan (1953, p. 40) used to say, playing on the double meaning of *causer*: 'to cause' and 'to chat'.

2 *Raising the odds*: 'You are not Oedipal enough.' And so we see a group of German-speaking analysts campaigning to attack their 'father analysts' who – in their view – did not do enough to resist Nazification. Certain of their criticisms are no doubt justifiable; others fail to take account of the concrete situation in which those analysts found themselves. Indeed, the behaviour of the 'righter of wrongs' masks a sadistic attack on the part of the id disguised as a superego.[5]

3 *Inversion* or 'return to sender'. 'You forbid; I forbid you to forbid' – not that that prevents the narcissist from behaving as an intellectual terrorist or from projecting 'terrorism' on to the Law. And in one sense he is right to do so; because he rejects the very existence of the Oepidus (and the Law), he experiences the very existence of the oedipal order as a form of castration.

The narcissist maintains a balance between the narcissistic solution and the repression of the oedipal perspective by adopting a Manichaean position: all that is good is on his side (the narcissistic ideal); all that is evil is on the side of the other.[6] But Manichaeism has been known to fail, and we often find that the peculiar violence the narcissist projects on to his adversary is an expression of his serious but secret doubts as to the validity of his own system (as is the contempt he displays and the alienation he uses to maintain his contemptuous attitude).

The conflict experienced by the narcissistic analyst compels him to avoid the oedipal situation with which he is constantly confronted in the course of his work, and that in turn explains his paradoxical sensitivity to the oedipal

5 The narcissist's 'superego' is a hardliner [*pur et dur*]. I place 'superego' in inverted commas because in the absence of the Oedipus there is only the early maternal superego. The superego brandished by the narcissist is merely an intellectual copy which is used as a superego-stick to beat the father with. The narcissist makes much of this moral agency, but at the same time we find in the content of his ideology the very opposite of the oedipal superego: namely, a systematic and programmed transgression of the laws of that agency.

6 Because of this Manichaeism, the narcissist's every act and every idea is governed by the same subjective criteria which electively decide the validity (or nonvalidity) of the real.

position. He is therefore faced with two temptations. He may openly regress to the narcissistic regime of the Mother and orientate everything towards language, speech, abstraction and a circular narcissistic theorization, deriving his criteria from his speculations and becoming lost in arcane aesthetic-philosophical arguments. Alternatively, he may project the abyssal problematic outwards on to reality. The reality in question (the environment, social and economic factors, society, education, capitalism . . .) will, however, have been tailored to meet his needs on an *ad hoc* basis. His 'commitment' will *appease his guilt* by locating it outside the internal dimension, which he holds in contempt (just as one German analyst expresses his contempt for the *Innenschau*). He will reject epistemophilic pleasure and replace it with the narcissistic quest for a pure illusion devoid of any materiality.

We now have to look at the position the narcissist adopts in relation to the *other* – or, rather, others. This is an important question for us, as the narcissist's tendency towards expansionism, and his ability to seduce and captivate those he wants to drag along in his wake, pose a threat to the survival of psychoanalysis. We must therefore examine the deep origins of this particular subversion of our discipline.

The manner in which the narcissist discovers himself for what he is is part of normal adolescent development. At a given moment, the adolescent suddenly becomes aware of a change in his opinion of himself. He experiences a revelation based upon a coenesthesis which he interprets: he suddenly has the impression of being different and superior to others. Initially he feels superior to members of his family, but his feeling of superiority does not end there, as we shall see later. For the moment, I leave aside the possible *pathologization* of the psychic effects of this coenesthesis, as that would involve us in a lengthy discussion. The effects of its pathologization tend, however, to conceal or mask the basic process, in the same way that a tree with lush foliage may have completely invisible roots.

The important point is that this feeling places the adolescent *outside* the family, and divorces him from his social milieu; he will of course use the mechanism of projection to attribute to his background the origins of his feelings of having been abandoned, of being misunderstood, of being unfairly or cruelly treated. His insertion into the world will be painful. In self-defence, he will build a wall behind which he can organize his loneliness. Not only does he cut himself off from others; he violently rebels against them in a particular way, and his extreme reactions reveal the fragility of his protective wall.

It need scarcely be pointed out that this systematic rebellion does not have the *positive* import of the 'no' uttered by a child in the anal stage: on the contrary. Yet in a way the narcissist is right to complain that he is misunderstood by the oedipal world, because although he is starving for affection (and would like to be supported in his deep distress) he will deny this and vehemently reject anyone who tries to approach him. His narcissism is such that this is a major point of honour (compare 'the abject desire to be loved' described by Deleuze and Guattari, 1972). The observer is thus placed in a contradictory position.

This raises the question of narcissistic identification and identity. As we have seen, the narcissist is fundamentally opposed to the oedipal process. It is a matter of definition to say that the narcissist identifies with *his own image*, but as that identification is based on the exclusion of all instinctual elements, it remains superficial, rigid and isolated from any maturational urge. The narcissist lives within the infinite and boundless dimension he has inherited from prenatal life, and therefore has a tendency towards expansionism; he will project the corresponding feeling (one of the components of his specific coenesthesis: when he was at his mother's breast he was alone and he merged with his own universe) on to his *fellows* – or, in other words, on to those with whom he is bound by an 'elective affinity'.[7] The resultant narcissistic group is composed – for all its members – of multiple self-images, rather as though it were a hall of mirrors.[8]

The narcissistic group is constituted *in opposition* to the paternal principle (the reality principle) and places itself under the aegis of the omnipotent Mother in a narcissistic regression which provides it with a feeling of completeness and bliss. Didier Anzieu argues (1971, p. 73) that 'every group situation is lived as an imaginary wish-fulfilment' and that the group is 'that fabulous place where all wishes are gratified', and therefore compares the group to a *dream*. He adds (p. 75) that 'birds which think they are of a feather flock together', and is even inspired to allude to the essentially narcissistic factor of belief, as we do not in fact have any objective criteria to judge 'elective affinities' [*Wahlverwandtschaften*], to borrow the title of Goethe's novel (Goethe, 1809).

The narcissist may recognize himself in his fellows (but if he does, we might well ask if we are dealing with a true narcissist). In fact, and as we have seen, he is by definition violently hostile to others (one thinks of the Dreyfus Affair and of Forain's famous picture of a totally devastated family dining-room; it bears the legend: 'They talked about it'). It might also be noted in passing that

7 In fantasy, the point of similarity will be projected on to the analyst, thanks to narcissistic regression, in complete disregard for his reality (hence the importance of his neutrality), and the specific way in which the process is cathected. If the analyst's lack of neutrality – or, worse still, a seductive captation or a sadistic attitude – interferes with the subject's ability to settle into the analytic situation, the result will be either a pathological fixation or a real possession (in the quasi-demonological sense of the term).

8 Cf. Erikson (1956, p. 125): 'When there is no strong sense of identity, even friendship and love affairs become desperate attempts to outline the blurred edges of identity through a mutual mirror game.'

the content of the ideologies which support the narcissist's self-satisfaction is relative, and possibly self-contradictory. It is curious to note in this context that those who violently berate others for not having resisted the Nazis are often the very same people who adopt the slogan *'besser rot als tot'* ('Better red than dead'), a slogan which expresses submission rather than resistance. It has also been noted that certain of the themes currently used as propaganda by narcissistic groups were once part of the arsenal of the right (regionalism, ecology, the consumer society, etc.). Narcissists are found amongst *all* extremist groups. What I have tried to stress is the relativity of the content of the ideologies upon which they rely.

The point of similarity is often openly paradoxical and contrary to any known logic. Its origins are mysterious and its nature has yet to be defined. It may be contained in a minor detail which we discover after the event and via a process of logical deduction, or in bizarre details which are at first sight totally insignificant. In that sense, it is reminiscent of love (and love is blind, as the saying has it) and of dreams; Freud notes how the affective charge of a dream may lie in a tiny detail which is easily overlooked. One also thinks of a phenomenon that can be noted in some analyses, where certain minor behavioural patterns may be *transmitted* from analyst to analysand, from unconscious to unconscious, without either party being aware of it; this may be noted by an observer, such as a case supervisor who happens to notice what is happening. It may well be accurate to make systematic reference to latent homosexuality in this connection, but the homosexual element is usually problematic and will certainly not help to resolve the enigma. It is, however, quite certain that a content which is narcissistically cathected by a group may provide it with a 'point of similarity', with the cathexis moving from group to content, and then back again: in other words, it is reflected back on to its bearers.[9] We can safely assume that the idea of narcissistic similarity contributed to Freud's initial concept of transference. He does in fact use the word transference [*Übertragung*] in his introduction to the dream of Irma's injection (Freud, 1900, pp. 105–6):

> And now I must ask the reader to take my interests for his own for quite a while, and to plunge, along with me, into the minutest details of my life; for a transference of this kind is peremptorily demanded by our interest in the hidden meaning of dreams.

9 Proust (1919, p. 385) gives a good description of this ineffable element, which is so difficult to grasp, when he writes: 'That invisible but harmonious link, like a warm shadow, an atmosphere which made their cortège a whole which was as homogeneous throughout all its parts as it was different from the crowd through which it was slowly making its way.' Note the difference between the crowd and the group.

The rules that govern the way in which 'similar' people come together to form a group are not those that govern the formation of a crowd, and we must not view the leader of the crowd in the same perspective as the central charismatic figure who often presides over the destiny of the narcissistic group. We know that when 300,000 young people gathered together at the Woodstock festival for several days (with music acting as a narcissophoric factor) none of the expected characteristic crowd phenomena occurred. A group may also be cemented together by an idea, but woe betide anyone who ignores the possibility of narcissistic disappointment or, on the other hand, of the irruption of the instinctual factor, which may well prove fatal to the group's cohesion if *expansion* turns into *fragmentation*. The narcissistic (unorganized) group is fragile, as it has no pregenital component; that makes it *sacred* in its members' eyes because the absence of the pregenital component unleashes an outburst of pure narcissism. The content may also be completely replaced (exchanged for another content which is equally sacred but still homogeneous), in which case we can speak of a 'transference of sacramentality', of 'the Internationale, a new communion of saints', of 'faith in the coming', of the 'Fourth Estate', of 'waiting for the great day', or the hope for 'a new era' or 'a fraternal world'. New saints (Varlin, Louise Michel, Sébastien Faure) replace the old, and new rituals are devised (see Pierrard, 1984).

The labour movement has its martyrs, and it commemorates its saints. It has its liturgies, feasts, pilgrimages, hagiographies, etc. (I will not go into the question of the analogous sacralization of Hitlerism, or of what goes on in Communist countries.) But the details cannot be changed; the narcissistic world will not tolerate sacrilege, and demands absolute loyalty. It is also characteristic that sacralization has more to do with the expression of narcissism than with its content, as only the Word is narcissistically pure, and its content cannot but be soiled by causal oedipal thought. The narcissist lives in language ('Analytic discourse is accredited by its style alone': Lacan).

For the narcissist, all that exists is himself and language, in so far as he cathects it. Anything that is not him does not exist, and if it persists despite him it must be repressed into nonexistence by all possible means. Come what may, he will act as if it did not exist. As Pierre Vidal-Naquet notes (1980, p. 8) in a discussion of Faurisson's claim (Faurisson, 1978) that the gas chambers never existed and even that the Holocaust never took place: 'One of the features of contemporary "culture" does seem to be the tendency to deny the existence of what seemed to be well established social, ideal, cultural or biological realities.' The same Professor Faurisson once published a small volume (Faurisson, 1961) which proved that 'Le Bateau ivre' (Rimbaud, 1883) was no more than a jumble of reminiscences and plagiarisms – or, in a word, that the poet Rimbaud never existed. But, to adopt Charcot's famous dictum, 'ça n'empêche pas d'exister'.

This essay represents an attempt to put down a few markers that might help us to arrive at an adequate identification and understanding of the conflict between the Oedipus and narcissism in the light of tensions within psycho-analysis which seem to be expressions of that conflict. The implications of that conflict reach far beyond our professional community, and should be examined in much greater depth. Having mentioned Rimbaud, let me express the hope that 'other horrible workers' will appear to go on with the task.

Chapter Three

The oedipal conflicts
of the analyst

I

MY EXPERIENCE has convinced me that there are special oedipal difficulties for those who prepare themselves for the psychoanalytic
profession, and that these oedipal problems are more important in
training analyses than in therapeutic analyses. The so-called training or
didactic analyses develop in a different way; they *are* different from others.
They require a supplementary effort (often in vain) tied to the working
through of a specific oedipal dimension which I will describe in this essay. To
choose a banal example, some physicians in analysis were helped in the
affective, social, and even professional spheres of their lives. Although they
essentially possessed the necessary attributes to become psychoanalysts, they
nevertheless continued to encounter difficulties in conducting their own
psychoanalytic work. This difficulty is well known, yet the problem continues
to present itself acutely and has an impact on the selection and training of
analysts. Some young analysts conclude a therapeutic analysis with
particularly favourable signs for their future psychoanalytic careers, but after
the analysis is terminated and they start to practise psychoanalysis they face
unexpected complications and require 'some more analytic work'. I have been
able to establish further that certain analysts have great difficulty in
recognizing and identifying oedipal situations in their clinical work. This is
probably due to specific deep-seated structural conflicts which must be
detected.

This paper was first published in *Psychoanalytic Quarterly* XLIX, 1980, translated by Marion M.
Oliner.

There is a resistance to this 'nuclear complex of neurosis' which exists in every one of us; and if it manifests itself with an almost indomitable force in some, it survives even in those who may seem to have worked it through and analysed it exhaustively. In fact, it seems that the ubiquitous resistance to psychoanalysis crystallizes around the negation of the 'dirty little family secret', as the authors of *Anti-Oedipus* (Deleuze and Guattari, 1972) call the 'father complex' of Freud (see also Chasseguet-Smirgel, 1974).

My reflections have led me to consider the central importance of the Oedipus complex to psychoanalytic activity. This was Freud's principal discovery, and it issued directly from his working through the mourning he experienced after the death of his father. The analyst must have acquired a solid oedipal dimension in order to develop a specific receptivity based on oedipal maturation that is as complete as possible. But the Oedipus, the centre of the complex constellation aimed at assuring the subject's psychosexual equilibrium, is of necessity confronted by the narcissism of the individual. The Oedipus is confronted especially by the 'solutions' (other than psychoanalytic treatment) in which narcissism predominates, such as love, religions, or ideologies (attempted sublimations straddling narcissism and the Oedipus complex). The avoidance of the Oedipus complex may be related to the narcissism of some analysts.

Indeed, if psychoanalysis had to fight at the beginning in order to establish itself, and if the small group of pioneers had to suffer the attacks of its scorners, the battle now continues on the *inside* of the movement, which seems to have secreted its own opposition ever since the beginning. In this essay I will identify certain roots of this opposition.

If the Oedipus complex is universal, its open discovery and recognition are contrary to the pleasure principle and necessitate a particular structural receptivity and psychosexual maturity. For the 'oedipal discoverer', to be in the world is to be engaged in a dynamic process, a task involving an effort which must be renewed continuously (the 'combat with the angel' will be taken up later). This task and orientation are essentially antithetical to the pleasure principle.[1] In summary fashion, I shall call 'narcissists' those whose

---

[1] In 'The symbolic representation of the pleasure and reality principles in the Oedipus myth', Ferenczi (1912c) treated Oedipus as the representative of the reality principle. The woman (mother) of the hero tries to divert him from his search for the truth and promises him peace and happiness if he can be satisfied with make-believe. Oedipus represents the reality principle, and Jocasta signifies mysticism and illusion, the negation of reality. In *The Ego and the Id*, Freud (1923a, pp. 31- 2) stated that the birth of the Oedipus complex arises in the child's discovery that the father constitutes an obstacle to the fulfilment of his wishes.

The myth, as it is narrated by Sophocles through the staging of his own fantasy, is above all an oedipal drama in the proper sense of the word, but it also contains references to narcissistic omnipotence on the subject of the origin of the hero, of the intervention of divine powers, and

conduct seems to be largely governed by the pleasure principle, corresponding to a definition which I have often tried to eludicate.[2]

What I have just alluded to concerning the history of psychoanalysis in the vertical direction, in terms of permanence and succession of 'deviations', can also be discerned in the horizontal direction, probably for the same reasons. The disposition of the Oedipus takes place differently according to a certain cultural context, but always within the framework of the dialectic between reality principle and pleasure principle, Oedipus and Narcissus. Originating in Central Europe, psychoanalysis has spread throughout the world, but it has taken on different aspects in the Germanic and Anglo-Saxon countries on the one hand, and Latin countries on the other; in the Judaeo-Protestant milieus and those dominated by Catholicism, and especially beyond the cultural area having a European origin: thus, after a brief classical beginning, the Japanese and Indian psychoanalyses have been entirely transformed and are – in relation to the original model – basically unrecognizable, as far as we know. If the Oedipus complex, as Freud has shown us, is at the origin of our moral and sociocultural life, the manner in which the individual tries to arrange his oedipal conflict, to 'negotiate' it, is in itself a function of certain cultural factors which, having their own historic evolution, are liable to impose the

---

finally, of the apotheosis of Oedipus (*Oedipus at Colonus*); it is always a matter of two levels in which the two elements become mixed – of the earthly level and the heavenly level, of the narcissistic domain and that of the drives. When Freud described the transference phenomenon, he used the adjective 'grotesque' (1916–17, p. 442) and one can understand perfectly if one thinks that transference is induced by narcissistic regression which, as a dimension, is absolutely independent of contingencies of reality and materiality.

2 I have considered narcissism as derived from an absolutely specific elational prenatal coenesthesis, and I have shown the derivatives of this state in the narcissism of the individual. Narcissus did not love his body ego, since he rejected sexuality (and, of course, autoerotism): that is to say, the postnatal solution, the drive dimension. He could admire himself only narcissistically in an elational way, plunged into this state of felicity but lacking adequate psychosexual support. 'To be absolute' he went astray in the universe of materiality, therefore of finiteness, contrary to his principle, and he could not (nor did he want to) effect the necessary synthesis between the two dimensions which are, in principle, antagonists – narcissism and drives. He could therefore only disappear into absolute regression, which (in his postnatal state) could only be death. It was Resnick who drew my attention to the passage in Ovid (p. 83) which retells the birth of Narcissus: 'Liriope . . . was the nymph whom Cephissus once embraced with his curving stream, imprisoned in his waves, and forcefully ravished. When her time was come, that nymph most fair brought forth a child with whom one could have fallen in love even in his cradle, and she called him Narcissus.' The myth enlightens us both on the fate of Narcissus – whose return to the maternal bosom (water) coincides in fact with his birth, his two parents being rivers – and with regard to his profound structure being made of vagueness and imprecision, the span of time confusing the present moment with eternity.

effects of this evolution and its oscillations on the Oedipus itself and, through it, on psychoanalysis in general.

Before undertaking my demonstration, I shall again take up the study of the concepts in question, from the point of view of a dialectic between narcissism and the Oedipus.[3]

Since discretion precludes my use of clinical illustrations, I will instead consider Oedipus himself. I shall take as the starting point the opposition between Oedipus and Jocasta, as Ferenczi has interpreted it. I shall adopt this interpretation by considering this conflict as fundamental, a conflict which becomes confused with the one in which Oedipus confronts the Sphinx. Moreover, I shall propose as a working hypothesis a certain analogy between the plague which struck the population of Thebes through the monster and the crisis which prevails in our civilization, and particularly in our small psychoanalytic world – a crisis which seems to have adhered to the steps of our young discipline from its birth onwards.

In addition, it would be logical to apply this viewpoint – i.e. the opposition between Oedipus and Narcissus – to the individual professional fate (theoretical and practical) of each analyst. Indeed, all of us are subject to cultural influences outside our psychosexual development and to permanent oscillations with regard to our positions. Freud himself was no exception. It would be easy to demonstrate, I believe, the effects on him of a pendular movement between the strict enterprise of the researcher (Oedipus) – he was ridiculed because of his 'scientism' – and the yielding to a narcissistic seduction of philosophic speculation, against which he defended himself desperately, only to succumb to its charms eventually. Research feeds upon imagination and rigour, but if the Freudian undertaking corresponds to this synthetic orientation, then the work of the analyst is made up simultaneously of a succession of sectors stemming from one or other of these two factors. I regret that I cannot elaborate this point of view.

II

I have said that analysis is a global process with a beginning, an unfolding, and an end, having a goal which could be formulated as 'the narcissistic fulfilment of the individual'. Psychosexual development in its entirety cannot have any other finality, and the individual ultimately achieves this fulfilment through a

---

3 In my first study devoted to this subject (Grunberger, 1956) I considered only the narcissistic factor and how it characterizes especially the initial period of the treatment. Furthermore, the theme of my essay was the analytic process in general and not, as in this present work, the analysis of the future analyst, particularly his oedipal phase. Nevertheless, I implied that narcissism was, in my conception, an essential and quasi-unique factor – the motor of treatment – and I take advantage of the present occasion to complete my position, which exceeded the scope of my earlier discussion.

process of drive maturation which will be narcissistically cathected, and vice versa. Treatment consists of a taking up again, a resumption of the maturation process on a new basis. During this *new birth* (compare Balint's [1932] *Neubeginn*) the analyst helps the analysand to push away from his path, one by one, the obstacles stemming from complexes (coming out of the experience of the repetition compulsion reactivated through analysis). He functions as a support for the analysand in his *existential project*. It seems that if the destiny of the subject is not *programmed*, as a computer is, the particular facts which govern his fate (his personal equation) can determine its trajectory to a certain extent, and in any case it corresponds to his wish: he wishes to complete himself, to be himself. This wish stems from and is directed by his narcissism projected on to the analyst, cathected in an omnipotent manner. The individual restructures himself in this way, and his problem is first of all narcissistic, since it is a problem of identity itself: Who am I? – with the equally narcissistic answer: 'I am who I am' (I want to be really who I am virtually). He becomes God in this way, but in order to *realize himself* he must change his perspective to become a man – that is, to use his bodiliness, the fate of his drives embodying in this way his narcissistic project. This is the whole problem, to which maturation through the Oedipus is the key. Oedipus, adoptive son of Polybus and Merope, reigning couple of Corinth, has doubts about his identity and wants to know who he is. This is how the drama begins.

This conception takes into account certain aspects of the quasi-mute role of the analyst, whose presence counts above all else. That presence is necessary to complete, by valuing it, the phase of the process that, at a given moment, touches maturity, which it attains through the analyst's often mute confirmation. Without this concomitant narcissistic cathexis, every interpretation stays intellectual and can be considered as wild analysis. Moreover, the interpretation must follow exactly the maturational process, whose unfolding the analyst must, of course, respect. The analysand, like the child, has the right to his own research, which is an important element of well-tempered timing. Oedipus had left to search for his identity and was on the point of discovering it through a series of conflicts when the oracular agency of Delphi, through its precipitation as a wild interpreter, cut the ground from under his feet.

I have insisted upon stressing the importance of the original narcissistic factor and its ties with the Oedipus, the psychosexual development, and the analytic transference.

I would like to recall here once more that the child, in being born and projected into the world of drives, must of necessity refind his lost narcissistic equilibrium through his new psychophysiological equipment. I have stressed the role of the mother, on whom falls the task of reproducing, around the child, an approximation of his original milieu and of permitting him to try to complete himself with the help of his *external* milieu (merging narcissism). Here the child profits as if externality did not exist, since the mother is not yet an object. But together with these early narcissistic 'developments' (in the sense of a passage or transfer from one state to another) the child brings with him at birth the *Anlage* for an image of the father who procreated his developmental trajectory. This is the father who presided over the programming of his becoming and maturing in the sense of a *fundamental reorganization* of his libidinal economy (and his concomitant narcissistic equilibrium).

Since the child is condemned to leave his cocoon and to *integrate himself into the world*, he must acquire a new existential dimension based on drives, on castration, and on the defences against them. Henceforth frustration and narcissistic mutilation will be his daily bread. This whole maturational process is orientated towards the Oedipus, for reasons which we will examine below. This evolution centred on the paternal imago takes a certain time, if only because the neonate insists on holding on to his primitive existence (often his mother also has the tendency to maintain him there) and because the passage to the other shore required a particular effort of him. (This is where the paternal model can support his progress in an adequate manner.) It is in this profound Oedipus that we find foreshadowed the historic Oedipus induced by the mother as the support of the first pregenital feelings.

At the end of a certain developmental period, the child usually accepts his new drive orientation and opts definitely for this new maturational direction, although he still runs the danger of keeping a certain fear – that is, a dread of the drives: we know the importance of this problem in psychosexual pathology. Schematically, we can say that it is a *nodal point* which rotates the child in his new universe. His subsequent evolution will, from then on, take place under the sign of the Oedipus, and we could paraphrase Freud in this way: where Narcissus was, there Oedipus will be.

But what happens when things take a different course? Then the child may remain blocked at a precocious phase of his development and fixated on the mother in a particular way. On the one hand, he will continue to obtain from her satisfactions derived from narcissistic fusion with her, needing the narcissistic supplies from outside because of his blocking, and he will identify himself with her at the same time in order to benefit from her narcissistic omnipotence. On the other hand, he will begin to fear her precisely because of this evil power – evil, because he will end up projecting on to her a reactive primitive aggression, especially since he will be incapable of integrating his aggression due to the lack of an adequate pre-oedipal development. The anal-sadistic component which is not integrated results in a fragile ego, since it lacks the synthesis between the primitive sadism and the elational narcissism, a circumstance whose effects will be discussed below. It can touch upon certain psychoaffective sectors of the ego without involving others – particularly, I think, of the intellectual sector itself.

As we know, developmental disturbance of the anal-sadistic component complicates oedipal evolution. Full 'genitality' designates a state of integration of paternal power. (One is father on one's own; one is a father among fathers.) The subject is disengaged from the anal-sadistic phase of the conflict, on which certain people remain fixated as a result of the internalized conflict with the introjection of the paternal phallus (the 'combat with the angel'). We view this in a certain light as the 'reconciliation with the father'. Here I suggest that just such intrusions of disturbance in oedipal development may echo in the tendency of the future analyst to approach psychoanalysis from a strictly intellectual angle. Indeed, psychoanalysis – like any other discipline considered from the strictly intellectual angle – can be 'learnt' as a sort of pidgin-analysis (I borrow this term from J. F. Revel [1978], who writes about pidgin-Marxism). Everything will depend on the integration of this knowledge into the global personality and on the degree of its evolution. One can become an analyst in order to enrich one's *having* (increasing one's acquaintances, acquiring a social position, etc.) or one's *being* (modifying oneself in the sense of an oedipal project).

In general it is the Oedipus which opens the analytic treatment in emerging constantly during the session in all modes of psychosexual relations; it functions like a structuring element of the ego and as a source of energy nourishing the process of individuation; as the oedipal strivings must be taken up repetitively during the evolution of the subject in order to flesh itself out, it must be worked through continuously during the treatment. In the absence of this repeated analysis and appropriate timing, the subject may not be able to maintain his oedipal position to the point at which it could really be considered definitely acquired. He will be particularly exposed to a regression to the level of identification with the Primal Mother. This is particularly valid for the so-called training analysis, a deep didactic treatment, the only guarantee actually at our disposal while we suffer the pressure of the reigning narcissistic, anti-oedipal – and therefore anti-analytic – collective superego and collective ego-ideal.

I hear at this point the argument which recalls that the first analysts were often poorly analysed or not analysed at all, but were nevertheless good analysts. This is a perfectly valid argument which is at the same time questionable, and we shall discuss it in particular with regard to the difference in the conditions of recruitment then and now. But in fact, what are we concerned about? The therapeutic analysis can correspond to a whole gamut of treatments which range from the amelioration of symptoms to real structural modifications. It can fail to accomplish the 'revolution' and remain truncated with regard to a theoretical ideal. It has, by the way, a tendency to complete itself by a decathexis after the acquisition of the global therapeutic result, according to the principle: 'The Moor has done his duty, the Moor can go.'

Now, this is never the case for the didactic analysis, for the simple reason that the analyst remains in permanent contact with the unconscious of his analysands and therefore with his own, with its conflicts which have either been resolved or at least sufficiently mobilized to make their presence known. That is why a didactic analysis cannot remain satisfied with a partial result and must be terminated only after running a complete trajectory. It will have had to attain and to consolidate a post-oedipal position endowed with this particular density which was mentioned above. To remain fixated at a pseudo-Oedipus (avoidance) – that is, the anal-sadistic phase expressing itself through sadistic tormenting of the father – would be a sign of regression which precisely constitutes the defence against the Oedipus.[4]

The study of a certain aspect of narcissism seems to me to be particularly enlightening about the importance of a solid didactic training; it also introduces us to a whole dimension of psychoanalysis which tends to metamorphose these days into a cult of language.

Oedipus was expelled from the maternal womb at birth, which constitutes a narcissistic injury, even though it is the lot of all humans. We have seen, however, that it is incumbent upon the mother to supply the adequate gratification and environment in order to help the neonate accept gradually what I have called the drive solution. Coming into the world is therefore relatively reparable – relatively, since the wound will always be open to a certain extent. Oedipus's mother not only failed in her duty of reparation, but inflicted on him a threefold narcissistic injury by radically abandoning her child (expelling him, in a way, a second time); the third affliction is a true castration (swollen foot), a somatic expression of the phallic narcissistic loss. The future king of Thebes was able to undertake the reparation of his initial injury in a narcissistically satisfying way, which is reserved for heroes, but he

---

4 As for the first analysts, the founders of our discipline, whatever their inevitable therapeutic errors, many of these pioneers possessed a special endowment. They had, from the start, a certain spontaneous oedipal maturity, as is proved by the circumstances of the choice of their vocation, which constitutes, in my opinion, a genuine natural selection of absolute value. Without this oedipal maturity, at least in a certain sector, they would never have recognized the value and the scope of the Freudian discovery, against that which was fashionable and against the 'beautiful people' of their time who heaped insults on them. And they would never have been capable of the deprivation and the courage that defending their discipline against a hostile environment demanded of them. Like Oedipus, they were in search of the truth with an absolute determination. They pursued their research undaunted by the narcissistic injuries they suffered. This search was anti-narcissistic in the sense of regression (all deviations restructure themselves at a particular narcissistic position by denying the Oedipus complex). As to their motivation, it had a profound authenticity – different, in any case, from that of some young analysts who say: 'Everyone in my department is in analysis. If I don't do it, what will I look like?'

also had to pass through the crisis of identification with the Primal Mother in order to complete himself in this sense.

Some years ago there was an account in Canadian and other newspapers of how a drunkard behaved badly in a pub, and the owner asked him to leave; in other words, he was 'treated like dirt'. Afterwards, he came back armed with a Molotov cocktail and 'blew up the joint'. There were no survivors. This can be explained as his desire to make his narcissistic injury null and void by causing all those who were witnesses to disappear.

This mechanism seems to have been perfectly grasped by the dramatist Peter Shaffer, the author of *Equus*. This is the story of a young man who pierces the eyes of all the horses in a stable (although he adores horses) because they witnessed his sexual fiasco with a girl. Of course, a psychoanalyst will immediately think that this is a superficial motive and that behind it is an oedipal story (complete with primal scene and regression to anal-sadistic coitus). But precisely who, if not the parent, is the most direct witness of the original narcissistic injury, especially of the oedipal narcissistic injury linked to the physiological inadequacy of the little boy confronted with his precocious desire? In addition, I have insisted many times on the role of the oedipal interdiction as a defence against the narcissistic injury expressed in the thought: 'I am not impotent; it is the other person who is blocking the road (but when I am like him, I shall be able to marry Mother without exposing myself to the repetition of the same narcissistic injury, since I shall be an adult myself).'

I have mentioned witnesses, but the most troublesome witness is, without doubt, the parent who is at the same time the rival, which adds the narcissistic injury of defeat to that of inadequacy. We know, however, how to distinguish between what relates to the rivalry doomed to fail and what is imputable to the narcissistic injury proper (inadequacy). Guilt diminishes with expiation, punishment and repentance, whereas shame does not cease until the witnesses have disappeared. Moreover, things introduce themselves differently to the girl and to the boy, if only because the narcissistic injury of the girl is less dramatic and more profound: on the one hand, she can hide her inadequacy from herself or transform it into a fear of penetration; on the other hand, her injury in the form of penis envy may stretch across her psychosexual life in general. Apart from the further complexities of how matters differ for the boy and the girl, I am here stressing that although the Oedipus as rivalry with the parent of the same sex (historical Oedipus) may be visibly evident throughout analysis, the profound Oedipus linked directly to the narcissistic injury proper is infinitely more difficult to grasp and has a tendency to resist analysis until the end. We could even say that the former functions as a defence against the latter. The two can easily become intermingled, because the Oedipus *in general* is repressed. The analyst who has this problem will regularly encounter oedipal situations without being aware of them; or, on the contrary, his historical Oedipus will be used, exhibited and relived (acted out) in order to camouflage the primitive Oedipus. The inverse does not exist. In order to grasp the nature of the primitive Oedipus we have to reconsider its origin: i.e. the narcissistic injury.

We have seen that the fact that the narcissistic injury has a witness is very important. The testimony of the witness can be external or internalized into the ego. In the most severe cases of narcissistic injury, which end in suicide (see Grunberger, 1966), it is the evidence of the projected ego-structure which pushes the narcissist to eliminate himself. But this testimony can be fought, and injury annulled, in various ways. One can either suppress the witness or at least wish for his disappearance; but one can also *project* on to him the injury in question – that is, the failure or the insufficiency of which one accuses oneself on the narcissistic level. The latter method is extremely widespread and almost 'physiological'. Narcissism being a question of value, the narcissist can also *devalue* the witness by covering him with insults, by diminishing him narcissistically, which prevents the injury from being reflected: by clouding the mirror. We know that this reflection can go a very long way and that the whole world can suddenly take on the aspect of an immense mirror, causing the injury which has been suffered to stand out. This can result in end-of-the-world fantasies (apocalypse complex), as if only the total disappearance of all humanity could put an end to the shame which has been suffered. In more modest cases, it is only a matter of causing the psychoanalytic society to which one belongs to disappear.

The father of the fundamentally narcissistic Oedipus is not a person, since we are far from the literal Oedipus rivalry. This does not involve the historical Oedipus but the Oedipus principle structuring the world in conformity to its derivatives; it is the paternal function in the wide sense of the term. In the conflict we have, on the one side, the subject in his wounded narcissistic omnipotence and, on the other, the paternal function, the ambient material world, reality, since all this is considered by the narcissist as his antagonist, which must disappear. Their existence reminds him of his failure, of the shame of not having been able to master the complex and not having been able to evolve to the level of post-oedipal drive organization.

In order to apply this view to our speciality we establish, for instance, that the narcissistic analyst cannot endure the notion of training, since being trained means organization, hierarchy, 'establishment', and the notion of difference and maturation without mentioning manipulation by instructors. He is the anointed, whose perfection is already there from the beginning, since he is the heir of the absolute charismatic narcissism. If he becomes involved with the 'system' anyway, it is only with his lips and with a mental reservation by inverting the situation, by making a 'gift of his person' to the institution. But heaven help the one who puts in doubt his immediate and total adequacy (that is, his uniqueness), who would give him a narcissistic injury by way of a criticism or a refusal. This is a genuine test which is applicable only when it is already too late. The witness to his shame must disappear; the institution which served as a framework for his humiliation must be broken into pieces; the very theory which served as a basis for the recognition that turned against him must be devalued, all of which results in the annulling of his injury. In fact, if the doctrine whose representative gave him the injury is no longer valid and is replaced by another – if possible, by one which is diametrically opposed to it – the criterion by which he was judged is invalidated, and the injury annulled.

The oedipal person reacts to failure as a stimulus to attempt the fulfilment of his oedipal wishes with renewed determination, but for the narcissist there is no next time, since he prefers the disappearance of the system in which the injury took place. He will 'get out of line' with regard to the system and, in this way, will annul the injury by eradicating the possible bases for the repetition of his shame. He will not try to triumph over the father (to identify with him in order to surpass him later) but will try to abolish the principle of paternity itself and the whole frame of reference of which it was the organizer.

However, this does not mean that in this way he will be assured of total independence with regard to his constellation of complexes. Indeed, he will actually surrender to other instances more absolute and more compelling than the ones of which he thought he was ridding himself. It is this problem that we are now going to examine.

We follow Oedipus on the road to finding his identity, which is a double problem since it is independent of his identity of origin. His sexual identity also constitutes a problem: Laius, his father, is in one sense homosexual, while he, Oedipus, has pierced feet and is therefore from the start the carrier of a certain representation of femininity. On his way, Oedipus meets the Sphinx (I think that in the light of the primary process we can afford to overlook the chronological succession of the episodes), a monster which is half animal and half woman, carrier of masculine and feminine attributes corresponding to what we usually call the Phallic Mother. We know that she threatens with disaster those victims, mostly young people, who cannot answer her riddles concerning sex. It is the Primal Mother, who is castrating and seductive at the same time, whom Sophocles calls the 'cruel singer' (whereas in another passage in *Oedipus Rex* the monster is referred to as 'poet': 'How is it that when the bitch recited her verses for you, you didn't issue a word of delivery for these Thebans?') alluding, no doubt, to the maternal function linked to the learning of language.

This apprenticeship of the infant is preceded by a glossolabial play which uses not only the tongue and the lips but the mucous membranes of the oral cavity with its content (air, saliva); thus the infant produces noise and sound. At the beginning this is an oral autoerotic play activity, but the quasi-concrete productions of the child, as well as the rumbling of the bowels transposed to the mouth, evoke the highly cathected activity of the later narcissized and eroticized anal phase (upward displacement). Here the libidinal erotic element involving the child and the mother dominates, to the detriment of the following phase: that of the learning of speech as a vehicle with precise content. The precocious sexualization of this game in which the mother and child participate can furnish the basis of a perverse duo, the third member being excluded and useless, leading to a general tendency to avoid the Oedipus. At the same time the game paves the way for a clear disequlibrium of the affective charge, especially belonging to the glossolabial[5] function itself (it will have the lion's share), which will be withheld from the mental functions involved in the oedipal struggle, such as reality testing.

The father is the reality which troubles the couple. The father also represents causality in the sense of one fact necessarily begetting another, and the negation of this causality is the destruction of the paternal function. Here I suggest the parricidal implications of confusing such cardinal considerations of causality as the distinction between the essential and the contingent, the true and the false, the primary and the secondary, the perception of the limit of things and their respective position in time and space, etc. Much could be said about the cathexis of lallation becoming, through a kind of pseudo-sublimation, a 'superior twittering', but if I continue in this direction I shall go beyond the scope of this essay.

The child, seduced and fascinated by the phonic play, could stay fixated at this stage or fall back upon it (it seems that this has been foreseen by Sophocles as a dangerous abuse, a plague, and a genuine castration, since it cuts the road to maturation).[6] Oedipus triumphs, however, over the 'maid with the pointed claws', resolves the enigma and, by discovering its content,

5 This whole activity, considering its location, often produces the diphthong 'bl', from which is derived the designation of a confused and empty discourse as 'bla-bla-bla'. The Bible story of the Tower of Babel is undoubtedly linked to the cathexis of this phase of phonation. The construction of the Tower of Babel itself is an anal function, and its aim is eminently narcissistic: to reach the heavens and to be like the Divinity. Besides 'bl' (and 'vl', which is similar) there are suggested etymologic linkages with the French words *volubile, babiller* [to babble], *bléser* [to lisp], *balbutier* [to stammer], and with the English word babble. In his Italian etymological dictionary D. Olivieri (1965) states: '"Babel" is onomatopoeic in origin and refer to the bla-bla of children.' He also cites Greek and Sanskrit words having the same significance.

For pejorative implications we may allude to the 'bl' in *hâbleur* [boaster]; in the Hebrew *hevel* [*hevel havalim*, or *vanitas vanitatum*]; the name Hübelé Balazs designates in Hungarian someone who talks without rhyme or reason. (In Hungarian there is generally a vowel between the two consonants.)

6 Another hero of Greek mythology, Ulysses, defends himself against the siren song. By asking to

revealing its precise theme (which is begetting and the line of descendants), puts the monster out of existence. The enigma is in fact presented in the overloaded esoteric style proper to the oracular language of the period (sufficiently known by Sophocles' public, so that he took it for granted), and it is the demystification of this language that results in the Sphinx's being precipitated into Nothingness (which can also represent the interior emptiness of the monster suddenly brought to light by the hero).

The episode of the Sphinx lends itself to an interpretation which makes of this combat a confrontation between the oedipal ideal and the fixation to the Primal Mother, which seems to have been the problem of the great century during which Sophocles lived. As a culturally sensitive, politically experienced public man, Sophocles grasped the impact of the impingement of two civilizations expressed by the superstitious, idolatrous language of the Sibyl in contrast to the voice of Oedipus and the language of clarity and reason. It was, after all, an era of Greek philosophic ascendance. In his fundamental work on matriarchy, Bachofen (1861) stresses the importance of Sophocles' era for the birth of our civilization. Harold Stewart states (1961, p. 428): 'It has been suggested that the Oedipus story represents the changeover from the matrilineal society... to the patrilineal, where the line of descent and influence runs through the males.'

The pendular movement of history actually seems to favour the matrilineal tendency with the narcissistic regression which is supported by the Primal Mother imago. What concerns us is the reorientation, in this respect, of our own discipline, with the inversion of the oedipal tendency and of the principles derived from it and the negation of clinical reality as such. Instead, the cathexis of the analyst's narcissistic intellectual activity displaces the focus to the regressive and at the same time superficial expression of the psyche in a position which is defensive against the principle of oedipal maturation.

In fact, we know that Oedipus's combat with the primal maternal imago does not end in this way. If we follow the account we establish that Oedipus, like the Sphinx, will be the cause of a scourge (the pestilence with which the gods will afflict Thebes for leaving a regicide unpunished). And, again like the Sphinx, he will cause the misfortune of his environment by tormenting it with his disquiet and his insidious questioning as well as by the implacable pursuit of his goal, which is a problem finally linked to his own downfall, analogous in a sense to that of the Sphinx. By means of a wise poetic condensation, Sophocles opens a perspective on the telescoping of the levels and on a simultaneous perception of the different degrees of the hero's evolution. It is

---

be tied to the mast of the ship (to the paternal phallic emblem which protects him), Ulysses resists the fatal regressive temptation.

the negative aspect of his story which appears this way, bearing witness to – or, rather, representing – the survival of his fixation. In fact, by apparently triumphing over the monster, Oedipus has *introjected* it, thereby becoming like it. The monster disappears from the tale without a trace, as if swallowed by Oedipus: it can be found from then on inside, as if Oedipus himself will disappear (miraculously) into the entrails of the Earth Mother, swallowed by divinity. The hero will remain from then on in conflict with his introject and will be torn between his two contradictory tendencies, the paternal and the primal maternal identifications.[7]

At the end Oedipus will succumb, a victim of the introject that persecutes him and of his cruel, sadistic superego, but we can interpret the murder of Laius, whose identity he does not know, as his identification with the introjected sadistic mother.[8] As to the scene in which Oedipus penetrates into the palace looking for Jocasta, it has been interpreted by van der Sterren (1948) as a sadistic version of incestuous coitus. (Oedipus, at the peak of anger, demands a sword, forces the double doors, tears down the curtain, etc.)

In fact, the conclusion we can draw on the subject of the story of our hero is that – if one can say this – he could not resolve his Oedipus. (Of course, I consider Sophocles' play a fantasy creation.) He never completely left his fixation on the early mother. He was king indeed, and he engendered and procreated, but he was in reality neither king nor father. He abandoned the reins of his government to his brother-in-law Creon (his uncle as well) and never had the relationship of a father with his children. He brought his sons to the point of killing each other and his relationship with his daughter Antigone (undoubtedly his preferred one, compared to her sister Ismene) vacillated between a pseudo-incestuous and a homosexual tie. (Pasolini had the role of Antigone played by a young boy, thus yielding to an inspiration which could be justified, in my opinion, as a replica of the homosexual grandfather.) After his fight with the Primal Mother and the oedipal killing, Oedipus *regresses* by returning to his birthplace (Thebes) rather than joining his family in Corinth. The story is also a regressive movement when considered in a sociohistorical light:

7 'The Sphinx is the enigma which Oedipus will have to resolve, and the enigma has two possible solutions: either the mother Sphinx or Oedipus the human child' (Roheim, 1934).

8 According to one version, Oedipus was supposed to recover certain horses belonging to his adoptive father, which had been stolen. This makes the incident banal, while lending it a trivial aspect in the style of a Western. The attack on the occupant of the chariot, who asks permission to pass, is tinged with provocation and projection ('You are the bad one'). The incessant harassing of the father is not the expression of oedipal aggression but a defence against it through identification with the sadistic mother.

The Oedipus cycle has a definite matriarchal orientation. As in the Jason saga, it describes a world seen through matriarchal eyes. Neither gods nor goddesses populate this world. But its matriarchal sprites and bogies are very much present and figure in events... the Sphinx, the Erinyes, and Fate. (Balter, 1969, p. 265)

As I have stated, the psychosexual evolution, as it traverses the oedipal phase, is determined by the pre-oedipal imago of the parental couple. The project of narcissistic completion becomes transferred to the acquisition of impulse mastery, a long and complicated process stretching over the whole duration of psychosexual development. There is no space here to examine these under such headings as 'maturation', 'guilt', 'aggression', 'castration', 'neutrality' (of the analyst). What we must remember is that as the process unfolds the positions become constantly fraught with guilt, not only because of the ambivalence stemming from the nature of object relations (in the strictly oedipal framework) but also because of the antagonism between narcissism and the life of the drives, since the oedipal rival, the father, is at the same time the carrier of the narcissistic projection. Also, we must understand why a perfect mastery of the analytic situation demands from the analyst an equally perfect mastery of the oedipal problem, *the permanent penetration into the unconscious taking on for him (and not for the analysand) a clearly incestuous aspect.*

Moreover, the analysand – i.e. the analytic candidate – faces the 'didactic' analyst who is his father in the transference relation, but who is at the same time his real rival – not to mention the specific analytic phallus of which he is the carrier.

The failure to recognize the unique character of this position ('there is no difference between the therapeutic and the didactic analysis; there is no didactic analysis') can only be intentional; otherwise, those very persons who would like to confer upon *every* analyst the right to conduct didactic analyses would not be as demanding as they are today about granting these same analysts access to the status of senior analyst, conferred in principle on those who can express themselves by producing texts. They therefore subordinate the analyst's essential activity to an activity which can be undertaken by anyone. Yet the narcissistic aura surrounding them is used to cathect a fringe activity which is an *expression* of the essential task. But in this case, we are facing exactly the antagonism which strangely resembles what we have just described in referring to the difference which separated Oedipus from the Sphinx.

There is an antagonism between two fundamental and, in fact, contradictory positions: that of the analyst whom I shall call oedipal (since the adjective

'Freudian' has been usurped), and the analyst for whom treatment, even as an object to be cathected, is negligible. What he retains of analysis is *his* intellectual construction, and he shortens the analytic session to be sure that no specific atmosphere could take shape which would favour the vital emotional engagement of the unconscious of both patient and analyst. Having pushed aside the experience that should be lived through, one could, at a pinch, do without the patient, and analysis could become a philosophy, or even a metaphilosophy, to the extent to which it applies its reflection to a philosophico-grammatico-linguistic construction which is called psychoanalysis.

Oedipal psychoanalysis pursues a scientific method by exploring clinical reality, little by little, by verifying the results in a sufficiently reiterated way. It seeks to understand the clinical situation with the help of the discovery of unconscious motivation and also with the help of working hypotheses. Anti-oedipal analysis, however, proceeds in the opposite way: it is a kind of global and immediate *gnosis*, proceeding from an immovable dogmatic whole, unalterable and definite because it is sacred, that which one imposes on every reality (clinical or not), a scheme to which clinical practice must conform.

Psychoanalysis *applies* its knowledge to all psychic manifestations, where-as the anti-oedipal doctrine *protests* against this way of doing things and, on the contrary, proceeds in the reverse direction. It is not experience or practice that counts, but the mystical initiation. This results in a situation in which a candidate can be 'consecrated' an analyst at the end of three to six months, whereas *practically* his analysis can last up to ten or fifteen years or more. Thus the Sphinx expresses herself through enigmas, and thus language becomes the essential element which replaces all the rest for the anti-oedipal analyst, and receives the whole narcissistic cathexis.

Chapter Four

The oedipal crossroads or psychoanalysis at the parting of the ways

I

A S THE TITLE INDICATES, this essay will centre on the study of the oedipal crossroads, of a crossroads within the process of *maturation*. It will examine the crossroads in the light of the dialectic between narcissism and the Oedipus as, in my view, the crisis within psychoanalysis reflects that primary dialectic. Given that the aim of analysis is to allow the analysand to achieve a satisfactory degree of maturity, posing the problem in this way allows us to begin by pinpointing a fundamental divergence of opinion between the supporters of two different theories. The notion of maturation is in fact essentially anti-narcissistic – and this explains why even the use of the term is proscribed in certain quarters – in that the narcissistic dimension presupposes a state of absolute, definitive and immutable perfection, a phantasmic position which can, thanks to a splitting mechanism, quite easily coexist in the unconscious alongside an accurate perception of the real.

In order to dispel any possible misunderstandings, I should make it clear that I am in no sense referring to the way a certain form of American psychoanalysis has developed this concept. Thanks to a deliberately maintained confusion between work carried out on the other side of the Atlantic and the term 'maturation', the idea that man has to mature, that he does not spring fully armed from the head of Zeus, is tending to disappear. Because the notion of maturation is, as I will have occasion to point out below, antinarcissistic, it is oedipal, and the narcissistic factor works against the Oedipus

This paper was read to the Swiss Psychoanalytic Society, 20 September 1983.

until such time as the two are synthesized. If they are not synthesized, we have not only an absence of reciprocal integration, but a situation of conflict.

In analysis, the narcissism of the subject is reflected, as it were, by the analyst in accordance with the model of narcissistic confirmation, but in theory the analytic situation also immediately introduces the frustration it inevitably implies. The analytic process puts the subject on the road to oedipal conflict and thus induces a synthesis. Narcissism is therefore gradually metabolized, and the ego takes the path of oedipal maturation. 'Where Narcissus was, Oedipus shall be.' (I am not thinking here of the problematic specific to narcissism, or of any specific form of guilt.)

The course of the maturation process (a process identical to that of individuation) must not be confused with a phenomenon that is to be observed in certain analyses, namely a hysterical, and often caricatural, identification with the analyst on the part of the analysand; in terms of the Oedipus and individuation, I consider that *mimesis* to be a bad prognosis. It is in fact a mirror identification, and we know that the bearers of a certain structure have great difficulty in giving it up, if indeed they can do so at all. Indeed, why should anyone wish to achieve the goal of the Oedipus? Why should we wish to become our own fathers (ourselves)? In our day, the Primal Mother known as the state takes care of the individual's every need, so why should anyone make the effort necessary to reach adulthood? The image of the power of the father has now been devalued for reasons which cannot be discussed here – not least because the problem has already produced an immense body of literature, from Federn (1919) to Mitscherlich (1967), Gérard Mendel (1986) and others.

For a long time, the future individual oscillates between sustaining an oral-narcissistic fusion with the mother and engaging with the oedipal project; this results in the phenomenon of *a prolonged and conflict-ridden adolescence*. This question has, it seems to me, inspired no in-depth psychoanalytic studies, but it has attracted the attention of non-analytic sociologists. Once again, we have to ask *why*?

In an issue of *Le Débat* devoted to adolescence (*Le Débat* 25, 1983), Hervé Lebras – who, like the other contributors, is a sociologist – devotes an article to 'interminable adolescence', and André Bégin introduces the term 'post-adolescence'. He notes that this 'age can last for many years' (he mentions thirty, but I know of cases in which it has lasted much longer) and adds that it may even '*represent the high point of existence*' (emphasis added). He also makes the point that I have just made: that 'physiological puberty' and 'social puberty' are 'two very different things, and it is very rare for the two to coincide' (here he cites van Gennep's book on *Les Rites de passage*, which dates from 1909). In Paul Yonnel's view, adolescence is becoming a new 'social continent', an 'international ethnic community' or 'a cosmopolitan nation with great horizontal generational gatherings', though all these ideas had already been outlined by André Stéphane (1969).

This oscillation is observable both in analysis and in life as a whole: the subject may display conflict-ridden oedipal attitudes and *pseudo-oedipal* attitudes which are in fact merely a defence against the Oedipus. The subject seems to want to attack the father in an authentic oedipal conflict, but this is in fact a way of warding off or *avoiding* conflict; it is a defence against any real structuring and maturational conflict with the father. There is indeed a conflict, but it is a conflict between the subject, on the one hand, and the world and the oedipal dimension on the other. This position manifests itself in a constant 'harassment' of the paternal figure; the subject preserves the paternal figure rather than attacking it. The aggressivity that is unleashed does not represent an attempt to make contact with the object; on the contrary, it is a means of avoiding the very possibility of true object relations. It is an 'alienating'[1] movement in which the other is not opposed, but denied the right to exist. The object of this alienating tends, rather, to be preserved or kept in reserve for a future oedipal conflict.

A nonintegrated primary narcissistic kernel which lives on in this manner functions like a real agency; whilst an oedipal structure is beginning to develop, the subject can simultaneously adopt a pseudo-oedipal mode of behaviour, and does so for narcissistic reasons (ego-ideal). One of my patients, who came originally from Vienna, used to say '*Alles was gut und teuer*' ('anything of value belongs to me'), and another used to 'go to the demo' in his Porsche (the demo was in support of the workers). These contradictory attitudes appear to coexist without causing any serious problems, as narcissism ignores the principle of noncontradiction.

The combination can, however, result in real conflict, and I have seen that conflict *in statu nascendi*. I am thinking of a young analyst who described how he had given his patient an interpretation in the course of a session; it was an adequate interpretation of a typically oedipal situation. But he immediately took fright and at the first opportunity he began to criticize his own actions, desperately attacking the theoretical basis of his interpretation. He had gone too far in identifying with the father and wanted to redeem himself (in the eyes of his regressive maternal superego) by demonstrating that he had *restricted the power of the father*. The interest of this stance will emerge later, as will that of the rather analogous significance of a certain '*purity*' and '*rigour*'.

Narcissism is not simply an elational self-love [*aimance de soi*], or a love of the bearers of the narcissistic cathexis which the subject projects into the

1 Hitler uses similar mechanisms in his definition of Aryan and Jew. If one is a man, the other must belong to a different species, an alien being which does not belong to the natural order. Compare the conversations recorded by Rauschning (1939).

mirror; it is also an omnipotent feeling of absolute autonomy, of faultless perfection, an overevaluation of the self and a spontaneous tendency towards expansion, a feeling of infinity, of boundlessness, of eternity. All these components are destined to be worked through in and by the Oedipus. If, however, the narcissism of the subject resists that working through, it will defend itself against it by mobilizing a specific aggressivity, by narcissistically decathecting the obstacle, and by faecalizing it (as one of Sadger's patients said, 'Anything that is not me is shit').

II

In analysis, we often find ourselves faced with patients who suddenly undergo a serious anxiety crisis which prevents them, so to speak, from going on with the analysis. We speak of guilt, the Oedipus, castration fears, and so on, but we analyse in vain, and the therapist has to rely on his *savoir faire* rather than his ability to impart knowledge [*faire savoir*]. (This is not a 'negative therapeutic reaction'; the crisis does not occur *after* a major improvement, and the analysand seems to be afraid of a development which he sees as *threatening* in itself.) The storm may blow over, and the analytic boat may be able to go back to cruising speed, but that does not always happen. In fact these crises do not arise at just any point, and in a sense it is possible to predict when they will blow up: they occur when we come too close to particular material – namely, the *introjection of the paternal phallus* in a specifically anal mode. I refer to the appropriation of the part-object *at a deep, archaic mode, an animal and almost organic level which escapes the conscious mind but still weighs heavily on the fragile ego of the analysand.*

I have pointed out elsewhere that whilst man is born neotenic (and this provides the basis for his humanization), he was not neotenic before he was born, and it would seem that the problem we are discussing involves regression to that level. Diderot (1762, p. 122) seems to have gained a partial insight into this. He gives the underlying fantasy of aggression a terrifyingly animal power:

> If the little savage was left to his own devices, remained totally imbecilic and combined something of the reason of a child in the cradle with the violent passions of a man of thirty, he would wring his father's neck and sleep with his mother.

I should point out in passing that everyone must of necessity go through this phase of anal introjection at some point in the anal stage, but that it remains unconscious; the child integrates it in a highly cathected ludic mode by playing,[2] by listening to fairy stories and, in the present climate, by watching

2 The liturgy for *Passover* (the Jewish Easter) includes the very old custom of *Seder*. Its object is

certain cartoons, etc. The process is, however, often interrupted, either by the narcissistic position itself – should the subject experience the need to resort to this appropriation as a narcissistic wound – or by *an untimely eroticization*, in which case the situation will be relived in analysis (and may have specific pathological effects in the life of the subject). In the meantime the analysis goes on, but the tension increases and at some point the storm breaks. This is the critical turning point in the analysis, the parting of the ways, the alternatives being *an integrated Oedipus or a non-integrable Oedipus*, an analysis that is truly lived or a disembodied, intellectual analysis, '*visceral internalization*' or a failure to achieve internalization. The failure to achieve internalization often results in flight or in an oral-narcissistic regression which is bound up with a fusion-identification with some representation of the Primal Mother, such as a more acceptable or 'bowdlerized' analysis or some other, but equally narcissistic, substitute.[3]

The importance of this crucial stage in the analysis is in fact twofold. If, on the one hand, the subject does acquire the paternal phallus, the fact that he possesses it means that he must abandon for ever the regressive universe of narcissistic omnipotence, the regressive universe of the Primal Mother – or, in other words, his prenatal paradise.

In a paper entitled 'Au dela de L'Oedipe ou "le combat avec l'ange"' [Beyond the Oedipus, or 'the struggle with the angel'], which I read to the Séminaire de Perfectionnement in 1979, I cited and discussed the corresponding passage from the Bible. I now feel that my comments need to be qualified to some extent. The text in question (Genesis 32: 24–32) reads as follows:

And Jacob was left alone; and there wrestled a man with him until the breaking of the day.
And when he saw that he prevailed not against him, he touched the hollow of his thigh; and the hollow of Jacob's thigh was out of joint, as he wrestled with him.

a loaf of unleavened bread which is baked specially by the head of the household, and is known as an *Afrikoman*. The etymology of this word is uncertain, but it may derive from the Greek, and it simply means 'dessert'. When the father breaks the unleavened bread, he hides half of it in his flowing white robes. The youngest son has to find it by outwitting his father's vigilance. Naturally enough, he succeeds. At another specific point in the ceremony, the father has to recover the bread in order to serve it. He cannot find it, and his son is allowed to set his conditions for its return by making demands of his father. He thus integrates his father's phallus in an anal mode (bodily constraints).

3 I recall an old case in which I had to deal with a similar crisis, and failed to do so. I now realize that when my analysand boasted to me about the size of his penis, I wrongly understood him to be attempting a homo- or heterosexual seduction. I initially saw this as a form of resistance. He was in fact attempting to retreat into a narcissistic regression by saying: 'Look at my big penis. It's like yours, so I don't need to introject yours.'

> And he said, Let me go, for the day breaketh. And he said, I will not let thee go, except thou bless me.
>
> And he said unto him, What is thy name? And he said, Jacob.
>
> And he said, Thy name shall be called no more Jacob, but Israel: for as a prince hast thou power with God and with men, and hast prevailed.
>
> And Jacob asked him, and said, Wherefore is it that thou dost ask after my name? And he blessed him there.
>
> And Jacob called the name of the place Penuel: for I have seen God face to face, and my life is preserved.
>
> And as he passed over Penuel the sun rose upon him, and he halted upon his thigh.
>
> Therefore the children of Israel eat not of the sinew which shrank, which is upon the hollow of the thigh, to this day; because he touched the hollow of Jacob's thigh in the sinew that shrank.

This passage describes a decisive incident in Jacob's life: his initiation, or his access to maturity. The new name given to him by the angel, Israel, means both 'victor over God' and 'warrior of [for] God', and there is therefore a close correspondence between it and the unfolding of the oedipal process: only after he has liquidated his conflict with the father does man identify with him and they are reconciled. (It should be noted that this happens every night when the unconscious opens up the Royal Road to fantasies and dreams. All this is clearly indicated by the words: 'Let me go, for the day breaketh'. The light of day chases away the phantoms of the night.)

Jacob appears to have been castrated during the struggle (Delacroix coyly portrays him with a wounded knee). In order to introject the paternal phallus, he must agree to become as a woman – in other words, to submit by going through an inverted Oedipus. This is clearly indicated by the prohibition on eating the sinew of the thigh, which controls movement in the lumbar region. To make matters clearer still, the text specifically states that the angel touches Jacob 'in the hollow of the thigh'.[4]

Man therefore accedes to the Oedipus by identifying with both father and mother, with real historical figures; this allows him to overcome the powers of heaven (the primal archaic kernel of all omnipotence) and to escape the regressive world of the Primal Mother.

III

Freud explains the devaluing and (partial) rejection of the sense of smell and of anal erotism in terms of the adoption of an upright posture. He mentions this in his letter of 14 November 1897 to Fliess (Freud, 1985, p. 279), returns

4 Francis Bacon claimed that man could control nature by submitting to it: *'Naturae enim non imperatur, nisi parendo'* (*Novum Organum*, cxxiv).

to the same theme in *Three Essays on the Theory of Sexuality* (1905b), and then discusses it at some length in *Civilization and its Discontents* (1929). Whatever one may think of Freud's explanation, it seems to me that the very essence of anality in itself provides an *intrinsic* explanation, as it were, as to why it is rejected. At one level, man refuses to accept the definitive nature of the instinctual solution, which involves maturation and, therefore, the anal phase. He wishes to preserve the illusion of prenatal narcissistic bliss, and the Oedipus is the moment of transition between that bliss and the instinctual solution he tends to reject. He seeks equivalents to that bliss by plunging into regressive states which, in terms of both level and quality, are pre-oedipal, and uses them to organize his flight from the oedipal crossroads. He therefore also has to disavow and hold in contempt reality, corporeality and materiality in general – which all find expression in the drives. Should disavowal prove impossible, he falls back upon the mechanism of projection, and at the point when he is obliged to abandon his narcissism – when, that is, oedipal wishes are first activated (together with the narcissistic wound caused by their frustration) – likes become dislikes (so long as the child remains in a merger relationship with the mother, he quite happily (paradoxically enough) accepts himself and his pregenitality, which he sacrifices to the mother because she demands that he should let go of that anal-narcissistic pleasure).

It is because the Oedipus forces the subject to respect reality (or the 'law of the Father', if we prefer to put it that way) that corporeality suddenly begins to *smell bad*, that Jung speaks of the 'rubbish about infantile sexuality', that Deleuze and Guattari (1972) denounce 'the dirty little family secret', and that so many people speak scornfully of 'mamma, dadda, wee wee, caca, titty', all of which are avatars of the Oedipus. This last comment is particularly telling in that it brings together the anal and the oedipal dimensions.[5]

In his discussion of the case of Little Hans, Freud (1909a, p. 112) tells us that 'The fear which sprang from his death-wish against his father, and which may thus be said to have had a normal motive, formed the chief obstacle to the analysis until it was removed during the conversation in my consulting room.' The boy, who wants to take his father's place – a wish that most boys of his age can express without a trace of embarrassment – displaces his feeling of guilt on to the horse he saw fall and injure itself because his oedipal wishes have awakened the guilt bound up with the *anal component* in that wish. That component is present in every oedipal situation, and is the direct source of the guilt feeling. (As we know, the young man in question made a satisfactory recovery and was able to repress the kernel of the complex, but matters are

5 Jones (1954, vol. 2, p. 157) recounts how Jung confided in him that he found the verbal working through of 'unsavoury topics' pointless: 'It was disagreeable when one met them at dinner socially later on.' We are thus in a position to understand the abstract, mystical character of Jungian theory.

rather different for the analyst, who remains permanently in contact with his unconscious.)

In any event, the injured horse which bears with it the young phobic's feeling of guilt (animal phobias are common at this age, and the subject often recovers from them spontaneously) is clearly a projected representation of the animal in man (compare totemism). Chasseguet-Smirgel (1985, pp. 35–43) has shown that Little Hans's fear of castration masks his wish to castrate his father, to take away his large penis; the fallen horses are the opposite of 'erected', and therefore of anality (pure instinctuality). In this connection, it might be recalled that *animal sacrifices* (both as substitutes for human sacrifice and in their own right) have always had a role to play in man's attempts to come to terms with his animal guilt – or, in other words, his *anal component*. This brings us to the notion of *purity* as ideal, and a real discussion of that topic would be a book in itself. This too is a defence against the anal component. According to the morality of the Gospels (the vows of poverty, chastity and obedience – the rejection of the anal component in all its forms, not to mention humility and happiness through suffering, or the annulment of the anal component as such), *purity means the absence of corporeality* and when it attempts to explain the feeling of guilt, it expresses the conflict between corporeality and the narcissistic solution: 'And if thine eye offend thee, pluck it out, and cast it from thee' (Matthew 19: 9). It is because the purity of the Kingdom is incompatible with the anality of the world that 'My kingdom is not of this world'.

The Resurrection itself is a disavowal of reality (of the reality of the Oedipus), and the importance of the anal component emerges quite clearly from the story of Lazarus. His sister Mary says (John 11: 39): 'Lord, by this time he stinketh: for he hath been dead four days.' Yet the miracle does take place: narcissism triumphs over the real.[6]

Purity inspires narcissistic confidence. It allows the subject to project his impurity on to others, but it also frees him from his own aggressivity. The wrath of the pure hardliner is a holy wrath. *The pure purifies and purges* (fascism began with a demand for purity when the impure were forced to swallow castor oil; Hitler's demand that the German race should be pure lies at the origin of the greatest tragedy of our time. Not that there is anything new about it; four hundred years earlier, the Spanish Inquisition was erecting

6 In Dostoevsky's novel *The Brothers Karamazov* (1880, pp. 383–6), the Christlike figure of Ayesha lives, to all intents and purposes, 'within the Kingdom': he is pure. But when his beloved master Zossima dies, it is not the death of the man he loved so much that upsets him as the fact that his body begins to *smell*. This provokes a veritable rebellion, with one monk effectively accusing Zossima of having had commerce with the Devil. The body of a saint, in contrast, was believed to give off an odour of sanctity (idealized anality).

scaffolds in the name of *limpieza de sangre*, or 'purity of blood').[7]

The crisis within our discipline is, in my view, clearly bound up with a growing distaste for corporeality, even though a whole trend within our civilization appears to be moving in the opposite direction. The very wealth of material goods that the triumph of technology places at man's disposal seems to increase his feeling of guilt; it is as though the manna that has fallen from heaven has taken him by surprise; as though he found it particularly difficult to *integrate*. The capacity for integration is in fact conditional on a long process of maturation. It involves a whole exercise in oedipal gymnastics; integration is achieved through repeated conflicts and is taken, so to speak, in small doses. If the process is to be successful, the anal component must in a sense be available from the outset; and that factor depends, in part, upon the structure of the subject himself, but also upon social structuring and 'the mood of the times'.

As I have mentioned elsewhere [see chapter 3], supporting Freud and Freudianism once implied a certain oedipal maturity on the part of the analyst, but the 'savage horde' of the heroic period has gradually given way to a largely narcissistic psychoanalytic community. As a result, the community has experienced such a population explosion that narcissism and psycho-analysis are now almost synonymous. This is not simply a matter of decentring (from the Oedipus to narcissism); it is a matter of a very different motivation and, of course, of a very different form of professional practice, as the criteria for admission are very different from what they once were. The new generation has come under the influence of tendencies which are hostile to the Oedipus (overt or covert versions of the anti-Oedipus theme). Ferenczi foresaw this quite clearly when, in proposing the foundation of an International Association of Psycho-Analysts at the Nuremberg Conference in 1910, he remarked (Ferenczi, 1911b, p. 305; emphasis added): 'We are threatened with the danger of *becoming fashionable*, so to speak, which would result in a notable increase in the number of those who call themselves analysts without being analysts.'

IV

If we look at what happens during an analysis, we find one of two things. We may find that for very good reasons nothing happens; or we may find that the subject undergoes far-reaching modifications: that the analysand visibly changes. The fact that a change has occurred, or is about to occur, is often

7 Some people project their demands for purity on to the Third World, even though events there certainly do not justify their idealistic projections. But the ideal of purity does seem to be essential if they are to preserve an equilibrium between their agencies. *Reality has to be disavowed, despite all the evidence, in order to maintain that equilibrium.*

confirmed by those who are close to the analysand, even before the analyst notices it. Or such changes cannot be ascribed solely to the analysis of specific conflicts (because conflicts are closely bound up with a symptomatology which is modified during treatment) and have to be attributed to a *parallel process* which a well-conducted analytic situation induces and brings to a successful conclusion. This change is particularly obvious to the case supervisor who is able to see the candidate analyst at regular intervals. Those intervals are so spaced that it is possible to observe the progress he has made in the meantime. This is in fact the only criterion which allows us to evaluate the import of the work that has been done.

Now this modification affects a subject who is in analysis in global terms (I am of course simplifying things here; overall change may be the rule, but there are exceptions) and its effects are visible in all his activities, be they physical, superficial or deep, psychic or biological, conscious or unconscious (immunological defences, constants, etc.). This is a real process of maturation, not a theoretical construct, which is why the corporeal aspect of the process awakens a negative attitude on the part of certain analysts who prefer to ignore it and to be protected from the lived experience of the Oedipus (the very word stirs them to anger; it is a real shibboleth which allows us to distinguish between those who are Freudian analysts and those who are not, to paraphrase Ferenczi).[8]

Psychoanalysis is not simply a form of knowledge, nor is it a way of transmitting knowledge: it really does 'engender' a new ego. The whole habitus of the analysand changes and reflects the modifications that have come about to such an extent that, quite apart from these modifications, a certain 'family likeness' appears, and allows one analysand to recognize another.

In 'The dissolution of the Oedipus complex', Freud (1924b, pp. 173–4) asks himself what it is that brings about its destruction. He begins by reviewing various hypotheses as to the fate of the complex, and refers to the 'effects of its internal impossibility' [*seiner eigenen Unmöglichkeit*]. His second hypothesis is clearly biologically inspired, although it is based on a comparison:

> The Oedipus complex must collapse because the time has come for its disintegration, just as the milk-teeth must fall out when the permanent ones begin to grow. Although the majority of human beings [*Menschenkinder*] go through the Oedipus complex as an individual experience, it is never-

---

8 Because of its corporeality, the word 'maturation' has been declared anathema by a whole category of analysts, for whom it brings with it a whiff of brimstone. Lacan used to mock Freudian analysts by calling them 'swimming instructors' (a great compliment in my view) and described Melanie Klein as a 'brilliant tripe-dealer'. The allusion to corporeality has highly pejorative connotations.

theless a phenomenon which is determined and laid down by heredity and which is bound to pass away [*vergehen*] according to programme when the next preordained phase of development sets in [*einsetzt*].

Freud accepts, then, both the ontological and the phylogenetic hypothesis, but he still does not know how the preordained programme is actually carried out within the framework of oedipal development (the threat of castration, the prohibition on incest, the superego). I will not be so bold as to propose the theory that the latency period is a reaction to the *narcissistic wound* that is inflicted when the sexual current is cut off because the subject realizes that his sexual inadequacy means he cannot fulfil his oedipal wishes. I will, however, mention a case in which a similar narcissistic wound had physiological effects which can be understood in those terms. The case involved a young woman whose entire genital development had been blocked at the pubertal stage because of the attitude of her father, who used to display the penises of the patient's two brothers to guests, boasting of their size. Her arrested development resulted not only in amenorrhoea (in itself a banal phenomenon) but also in an involution of the entire genital apparatus. X-rays confirmed that this was indeed the case and the condition proved resistant to all types of treatment, including hormone treatment. But the anomaly gradually disappeared during the analysis, which led to a morphological change, not to mention the birth of three children.

Having outlined these themes, we can now continue by basing our argument on the views expressed by Ferenczi in his paper 'On obscene words' (1911a). In this paper, my illustrious compatriot asks why it is that certain patients find it so difficult to say obscene words, and speaks of the peculiar *power* of such words to make anyone who hears them imagine the organ or sexual activity concerned in its *material reality* [*dingliche Wirklichkeit*]. Freud himself (1905a, p. 98) describes smut as an assault: 'By the utterance of the obscene words it compels the person who is assailed to imagine the part of the body or the procedure in question . . .' Both Freud and Ferenczi allude, then, not to sexuality itself but to a characteristically *anal* mode of sexuality.[9]

Ferenczi (1911a, p. 137) explains the 'peculiar power' of obscene words in terms of their capacity to compel the hearer 'to revive memory pictures in a regressive and hallucinatory manner', and then adds that all words must have possessed these attributes 'in some early stage of psychic development'. Word-presentations are, then, equivalent to reality, and Ferenczi relates them

9 Freud also notes (1905a, p. 98): 'Smut is like an exposure [*Entblössung*] of the sexually different person to whom it is directed.' The Old Testament (Leviticus 18:7) refers to *incest* in similar terms: 'The nakedness of thy father, or the nakedness of thy mother, thou shalt not uncover.'

to Freud's 'perceptual identity' (Freud, 1900, pp. 566-7, 602).

Now, the Oedipus is obscene. When a child going through the latency period says 'It's possible, but my parents don't do filthy things like that', he is expressing the same fear of obscenity. Strangely enough, graffiti seen in May '68 make the same point: 'Responsibility is obscene'.[10] In terms of both psychosexual development and analytic treatment, the Oedipus is a gradual metabolization of narcissism and of the drives (sexuality and aggressivity). The process is based on the narcissism-drive dialectic, but also upon the castration-self-castration pair. *It is essential for the analyst to have gone through the same process of metabolization; if he has not, he may prove unable to induce the process and to follow it throughout its evolution.* At the end of the process, the ego 'possesses itself' in an oedipal mode: it is its own father and it is itself. The protagonists wrestle with one another, just as Jacob wrestled with the angel. The wrestling match is quite unconscious, but as we can see from our day-to-day experience, it involves a great expenditure of energy on both their parts. The Oedipus really is a *Vaterkomplex*, as it gives birth to a new man.

It is, however, possible to refuse to introject the paternal phallus (as a result of an inability to integrate the anal component) and to devalue it (in order to avoid the narcissistic wound inflicted by both the inability to integrate and acceptance of integration). A candidate analyst who refuses to introject takes refuge in a regressive identification with the omnipotent Primal Mother who, like the Sphinx, is endowed with a wealth of highly aestheticized phallic emblems which express the presence of both narcissism and anality. This identification, based as it is on a narcissistic relationship in which he can merge with the Primal Mother, allows him to fight the oedipal dimension and to defend himself against it.

The exciting thing about the profession of psychoanalysis is the passion for *discovery* (tracing the authentic nature of phenomena, the unconscious motivates behind human behaviour), for discovering first causes and origins – in other words, paternity. Oedipus wanted to know his origins, and refused to follow Jocasta's example by concealing the truth. The riddle Oedipus had to answer concerned the three ages of man, three generations, or a line of descent. It is in that sense that our profession can be said to be essentially oedipal or genetic. But it is also possible to avoid this search for the truth by *devaluing* both the Oedipus and the search of Oedipus. Lacan (1953, p. 40)

---

10 Responsibility in fact simply means respect for the real and identification with reality. It is bound up with the Oedipus – or, in other words, governed by the superego, because the superego (the father) and reality merge into one. When Abraham (Genesis 24:1-9) sends out 'the eldest servant of his house, that ruled over all he had' to take a wife unto his son Isaac, the servant has to swear that he will carry out his mission responsibly. He does so by touching his master's genitals: 'And the servant put his hand under the thigh of Abraham his master, and swore to him concerning that matter.'

says *Cause toujours* ['Keep talking/Keep on causing'] and reduces analysis to an *ad hoc* intellectual creation, a narcissistic creation which supplies its own system of reference.

The search for the psychic reality of the Oedipus can, then, be replaced by an oral-narcissistic construct which takes on the features of a religion. The narcissist would conceal the Oedipus — that is to say, incest and the anal component. And as anality eventually results in faecalization,[11] the final phase of annihilation, and as its unconscious assumption or integration proves an almost insurmountable obstacle, incest, which is a return to the mother and therefore a reversal of the ocdipal project ('Onward, ever onward'), is a return to our deepest origins. The narcissistic mother–child pair which emerges from the oedipal dimension is dissolved, or reaches the point at which it dissolves into total nondifferentiation. The oedipal crossroads disappears, and with it the order of the real.

11 Swearing and blasphemy are expressions of both anality and the Oedipus (the law of Moses illustrates the link by forbidding both blasphemy and incest). The Oedipus and blasphemy are not, however, merely linked to one another: swearing *is* the Oedipus (just as the Oedipus implies transgression and the primal scene). In Hungary and the Slavic countries (and no doubt elsewhere), the most common form of oath is 'Fuck your mother', 'Your father's prick', or 'A horse's prick up your arse'. All these expressions are projected oedipal fantasies. This particular kind of insult does not appear to figure in Pichette's (1980) well-documented study of swearing, perhaps because it deals with a Catholic country. I did, however, find 'A consecrated host up a man's arse'. Religion does provide Canadians with the raw material for their swear words (God, the Virgin, Christ, baptism, the host, the ciborium, the chalice, the tabernacle, etc.). The anal component is always present, no doubt because anal regression can conceal the Oedipus (thus, according to Pichette, suppository is used to mean ciborium, and massacre for Holy Mass [*messe sacrée*].

Chapter Five

From monad to perversion: avoidance of the Oedipus

I N THIS ESSAY I propose to show that there is a continuity between what I call the *monad*, meaning a reproduction in postnatal life of certain intrauterine conditions of existence based on a certain mode of relations between mother and infant, and *perversion*. In my view, perversion replaces the monad, but it is filled with the hatred and destructiveness that accompany the break-up of the monad and, presumably, the establishment of an inadequate or precarious monad. Both worlds – that of the monad and that of perversion – are dominated by the mother. In the latter case the subject identifies with the bad mother, who is both dangerous and terrifying.

I will take Hitler, a well-known pervert, as an example. Although his destructiveness does of course go far beyond sexual perversion in the strict sense of the term, it so happens that in his case the two are indisputably bound up together. In the monad, as in perversion, the father is excluded. The transition from monad to perversion allows the subject to avoid the Oedipus complex which, although all subjects attain it at a certain level, may vanish from the scene as a result of regression to perversion. This allows me, in passing, to draw the reader's attention to the fact that those who attack the father in the name of the struggle against Nazism totally fail to understand the nature of Nazism and its leaders, and that such criticisms may be an indication of the return of the repressed. The Hitlerite universe has nothing to do with the father. On the contrary, it is a universe which erases the paternal dimension and puts the Terrifying Mother in its place.

This paper was read at a symposium in Munich in 1986, organized by Professor Jochen Stork.

I have discussed narcissism in a series of articles and papers (Grunberger, 1979) and now feel that I no longer need to repeat myself yet again. I will, however, take the opportunity to stress the importance I ascribe to the *bioanalytic* origins of narcissism (to borrow a phrase from Ferenczi). I would also like to stress that narcissism originates from corporeality, as do all the psychic peculiarities we normally ascribe to narcissism. Completeness, omnipotence, a sense of one's own worth, the feeling of being special, the exultant tendency towards expansiveness, the feeling of freedom and autonomy, absolute independence, invulnerability, immortality, purity, etc. – all derive directly, in my view, from the prenatal coenesthesis of the foetus.

I would add, however, that the origins of narcissism are stubbornly disavowed, as is the existence of its corporeal support. This inevitably gives rise to a basic ambiguity which is the source of a major existential conflict: the newborn child has to repress the materiality of its prenatal regime in its entirety (that regime cannot be an object of perception; I am thinking here of one aspect of infantile amnesia). It has to exchange that regime for the support which subtends its new 'instinctual solution': namely, its own body. It will, however, continue in a way to cathect the psychic derivatives of its first existential system (as listed above) and will thus cling to a regime whose psychic derivatives are now abstract, disembodied, immaterial, divorced from the drives and conflict-free. They know nothing of their corporeal material support and regard it as an antagonist. The child is forced to repress the shock that came with the change of regime; it was an existential trauma because the child was overwhelmed by the multitude of new excitations it had to master (I have, or believe I have, been able to detect traces of the myth of the Flood in this trauma).

Before going on to look at the development of the newborn child, I would like to dwell for a moment on one important point: the *narcissism–drives dialectic*, and the corporeal origins of the drives. This dialectic is an expression of the conflict whose nature I have just described. The resolution of this conflict is all the more urgent in that normally the two protagonists – narcissism and corporeality – are destined to be synthesized. This does not, however, always happen, as the process of maturation that leads to synthesis may be disturbed by the essential difference between the conflict-ridden instinctual processes and narcissism. Narcissism tends not to discharge tension (which is the aim of the drives) but to maintain a conflict-free elational state in which the drives play no part.

The narcissist strives to preserve his spontaneous homeostasis, like the foetus whose entire metabolism is taken care of by its host, the mother (even though the foetus does not know that she exists in any real sense). The narcissist reminds one of the symbolist poet Villiers de l'Isle-Adam (1890) who, in his desire to be free from all instinctual contingencies, said: 'Live? Our servants can take care of that for us.' This state of mind, which strives to free itself from the materiality of existence, later finds its expression in a 'deferred' interpretation which is bound up with feelings based on the notion of *purity* [see Chapter 8 below].

Pure narcissism remains an abstraction, as the narcissist inevitably has to rely on the collaboration of his sensorium or his organs to meet his slightest physical needs (a convincing argument against the ideal of the 'body without organs' described by Deleuze and Guattari, 1972). Essentially, narcissism, which can in theoretical terms be regarded as 'pure', has at its disposal an energetic potential of a different nature and its dynamic power is bound up with its phylogenetic origins, which provide its multiplier-coefficient.

In my studies of this conception of narcissism, I have tried to insist on its specificity so as to isolate a concept which stands, essentially, in a dialectical relationship with the real. That does not, however, mean that I neglect situations in which narcissistic elation comes up against obstacles; in practice, it does so in almost all cases, delusional states being the exception to the rule.

My critics often refer to the possible pathology of the foetus, but far from ignoring that dimension I do take it into account, as will become obvious later. In my view, however, we are dealing here with a coenesthesis which cannot be perceived by the ego, because in the prenatal state there is no such thing as perception in the psychological sense and because – and this is more important – there is no ego. The foetus, in my opinion, experiences registrations of phenomena which remain independent of one another, and they form the future '*nuclei of the ego*'.

In my subsequent work, I extended my early hypothesis (Grunberger, 1983) by not only taking into account those factors which might invalidate it, but also introducing them into my schema. I introduced the notions of positive imprinting (the future nucleus of the ego) and negative imprinting, on the grounds that the latter may result from a failure to achieve positive imprinting. Together, the two make up the *double* narcissistic nucleus, a notion which supplies the central theme of this essay. The title of my essay 'Narcisse et Anubis' (Grunberger, 1983) contains an allusion to Jean Cocteau's play *La Machine infernale* (1934), which deals with the tragedy of King Oedipus. In Sophocles, Oedipus is confronted with the Sphinx, who is a divinity (a narcissistic ideal). The Sphinx's origins are, however, twofold: she is both a young woman of radiant beauty and Anubis, the jackal-headed god of Egypt. Her twofold nature corresponds, that is, to a primal and bipolar coenesthesis, as do the 'palaeo-narcissistic' primitive nucleus and what I term archaic or 'Anubian' aggressivity.

Given that the earliest divinities were various representations of the

Mother Goddess, I associate the bipolarity of the Great Mother (*Magna Mater*) of primitive religions (positive narcissism) with the Terrifying Mother (and the clinical-history imagos of the good and bad mother are, so to speak, their descendants). Images of the 'bad' mother are, it would seem, more common than images of the 'good' mother. The Terrifying Mother lies at the origin of stereotypical representations which are the same for all of us, given that they originate from deep within the psyche ('the object is born in hatred'). These are terrifying representations, and the primitive ego is forced to rid itself of them by projecting them in the form of imagos. All these imagos (the Sphinx, the Witch, Medusa, the Gorgon, the Succubus and the Nightmare) are maternal (the father is unknown in the neonatal dimension).

The *bipolar ego* which appears inside the 'central agency' emanates from these primal narcissistic nuclei, which have, for various reasons, escaped integration by that agency, and can play a variety of roles in this process. We will now look at the possible modalities of the *transition* from the 'narcissistic solution' to the 'instinctual solution'.

I The monad

Ferenczi describes (1913a) how the child's care-takers try to minimize the effects of the break caused by its transition from one existential regime to the other. Freud (1926, pp. 154–5) stresses that the intrauterine existence of the young of the human species 'seems to be short in comparison with that of most animals' and that

> As a result the influence of the real external world upon it is intensified . . . the dangers of the external world have a greater importance for it, so that the value of the object which can alone protect it against them and take the place of its former intrauterine life is enormously enhanced.

I believe it is possible to detect a certain continuity between this aspect of neonatal existence and a psychic derivative of the foetus's prenatal conditions of existence and, therefore, between the foetus and the newborn child [see chapter 1]. I refer to a psychic matrix formation which lives on in what I term the monad, a composite which combines prenatal potentialities and Winnicott's (1956) 'primary maternal preoccupation'. It represents a psychobiological collaboration between mother and foetus, a theme which now occurs with increasing frequency in the specialist literature. The mother does not simply continue to be present; she and the infant form a single unit. We are talking about a sort of personalized 'incubator', or an *extrojected uterus*. The mother does not, of course, exist as an object during this phase in the baby's development, but her *scent* does exist, as do her voice, her smile, etc.

The monad, then, allows the newborn child to go on living in its narcissistic world, but at the same time prepares it for the gradual dissolution of that world by 'narcissizing' elements of the instinctual stage, which has to be integrated into the ego (and timing is an important aspect of this process). The monad is not expressive of either a fusion of a relationship; it is a 'double unit'. Its formation is a matter of instinct or grace on the part of both mother and child – and in this context I have no hesitation about borrowing a religious term, as we know that narcissism rejects rationality, and may often even challenge it.

The monad is made up of a container and a content; in that sense it might be compared with the analytic situation, which consists of a container or a fixed material framework (perimeter) and a content supported by a narcissistic project which remains largely unconscious. The aim of the analysis is to facilitate the accomplishment of that project. In the analytic situation, the monad merges with what is known as the positive transference, especially in the early stages. It gradually makes way for various forms of historical transference corresponding to the successive stages of the maturational process.[1]

The monad may take on a collective form, with the narcissophoric mother at its centre and the children sharing in her charisma, and bathing in its reflection. The children, that is, enjoy unconditional support and can put their faith in the promise of the complete accomplishment of their narcissistic project. The extrojected uterus is concentrically organized around its narcissistic nucleus, and its existence is of course restricted to the initial phase of the monad. Its existence may, however, be unduly prolonged if its initiator, who bears the narcissistic ideal, abuses his or her charm. I have already alluded to this possibility in the context of the analytic situation, and history reveals a wealth of monadic formation corresponding to this schema.

In her *Terre sans mal*, the anthropologist Hélène Castres (1976), for example, describes the Long March to the land without evil undertaken by 12,000 Tupi Indians in Brazil in 1539. She also studies similar migrations undertaken by the Indians at the urging of prophets 'who were born of neither father nor mother as other men are born, but who sprang from the mouth of God the Father' (Castres is quoting extant accounts from participants), a reference to supernatural birth and the concomitant rejection of reality. The

---

1 Given the equation between analysis and monad, we can now begin to understand the importance of how the analyst manipulates the monad by watching over its establishment, its activity and, most important of all, the spontaneity of the process, which must be protected from arbitrary extra-monadic factors. In certain circumstances, the analysand may experience the establishment of time limits for the analysis as a sudden break-up of the monad. The inner structuring of the monad may escape the notice of both analyst and analysand, and rejection can be transformed into an extremely serious narcissistic wound. Seduction may either shatter the monad (narcissistic fixation) or transform it into sadomasochistic fixation (a response to the element of frustration inherent in seduction).

land without evil is 'a place of abundance where it is not necessary to sow crops, where arrows go hunting by themselves, where men enjoy a life of feasting, dancing and drinking'. But 'in order to reach this utopian land where there are no taboos, *one must completely abandon real society, its territory, its cultures, its marriage rules and its established truths* (compare Chasseguet-Smirgel, 1985). Man was born to be a god, but he has become trapped in

> social constraints (work, law, power); by liberating himself, he can over-come old age and death, and recover the absolute freedom promised him by his divine nature. The collective dream came to an end ten years later in Peru; only 300 survivors reached that country. (Castres, 1976)

In order to trace the dialectic between the monad and pre-oedipal and oedipal conflict within analysis, I must first mention one peculiarity of the unconscious which has led to psychoanalysis being accused of pansexualism, male chauvinism and, above all, monotony, given the frequency with which we come across sexual themes in the analytic material. It is true that analysis is a process which constantly brings up the phallic image in one form or another, but that is the result of a certain polysemy. In Chinese, for example, a single sign can, depending on where the stress falls, have a number of very different meanings. Similarly, the phallic image simultaneously signifies sexuality, the energetic expression of sexuality, oral, sadomasochistic and genital castration and self-castration. In short, it can signal any manifestation of psychosexual life and – more importantly – the accomplishment of the narcissistic project, its vicissitudes and both its positive and negative forms. In order to make a distinction between these two worlds we can speak of the penis and the phallus, but given that both are represented by the same figurative sign, misunderstandings or even errors are inevitable when it comes to interpretation. When certain analytic material, particularly dream material, comes up, it may be necessary to *retranslate*, so to speak, the symbol of the penis as a phallic symbol, as a symbol of the narcissistic factor. Here is an example.

I once had a young patient – let us call her Olivia – who came into analysis because of the specific problems she was having with identity and identification. Her mother was Jewish but her father was both a non-Jew and an anti-Semite, and the vicissitudes of life constantly brought this problem to the fore. Yet when the analysis began, it did not arise. That this should happen so often in similar cases is a testimony to the autonomy of the analytic process. We began the analysis, and some material did emerge, albeit in what can only be described as a rather monotonous manner. Various modes of castration and self-castration were expressed in sexual terms, but the analysis itself seemed to be vanishing as water vanishes into sand. One day, she recounted the following dream:

> A woman with the same name as me (Olivia) is lying on a couch (like this one) . . . no, she's not actually on it, she's lying alongside it. She gets up and goes, gets up and goes. Then the room is full of people, a whole procession of them. The room is no longer empty.

She then produced the following association: 'I don't like seeing myself in the mirror, but I do like multiple images.'

I will ignore her other associations and go on to describe my interpretation: I pointed out the reduplication of the central figure (a woman with the same name), the repetition of 'she gets up and goes, gets up and goes', which she interpreted as the in-and-out rhythm of coitus. I then interpreted her dream as follows. She and I (she and the analyst) formed a double unit, and the void had been filled (in other words, I saw the sexual aspect of the dream as masking a narcissistic aspect bound up with the monad). I have just been reading Martin James's article on Winnicott, where he describes (James, 1962, p. 74) an event which he heard of from a colleague's analysis:

> This man fifteen years after termination of his training recalled most vividly from his analysis not any interpretative work but one single incident overwhelmingly and irrationally moving. This was when the analyst and analysand at opposite ends of a corridor turned two-way switches so simultaneously that the corridor light remained as it had been. Evidently the emotion belonged to the mutuality of 'two minds with but a single thought': an evocation of primary narcissism.

This experience seems to me identical to the experience I took as an example of the monad. When the analyst's interventions coincide with what the analysand is already consciously thinking, they have the same 'monadic' power and are usually the source of an intense narcissistic gratification.

All this reminded Olivia that she and her sister had once formed a couple, rather as though they were twins, and that she would have liked a similar relationship with her mother, but her anti-Semitic father was in the way.

At the end of the session, Olivia got up and, to my surprise, told me: 'I'm sorry about what I'm going to say to you; you have been a great help, and I want to thank you.' All this was said in very inspired tones, rather as though she were talking to a guru. And then the analysis began. I think that up to that point the entire analysis had been devoted to the construction of the monad (beside the couch, initially) and that she had experienced its construction as an act of penetration (filling a void). Once the monad had been constructed, the next phase in the analysis, which dealt primarily with sexual conflicts, was narcissistically valorized and could be integrated.

II Perversion: persistence of the monad and expression of monadic frustration

Perverts regard their sexual activities as normal, or even as representing the only sexual norm, and they value them more highly than the sexual life of so-called 'normal' people. Moreover – and this is typically narcissistic – they claim to be superior to others whose sexuality ('making love like Daddy') is dirty and ridiculous, whereas their sexuality is beautiful, pure and innocent. Freud himself (1905b, p. 171) seems to confirm them in their view and to justify it by stating: 'The disposition to perversion is itself no great rarity but must form part of what passes as the normal constitution.' He also writes (pp. 161-2):

> It is perhaps in connection precisely with the most repulsive perversions that the mental factor must be regarded as playing its largest part in the transformation of the sexual instinct. It is impossible to deny that in their case a piece of mental work has been performed which, in spite of its horrifying result, is the equivalent of an *idealization* [emphasis added] of the instinct. The omnipotence of love is perhaps never more strongly proved than in such of its aberrations as these. The highest and the lowest are always closest to each other in the sphere of sexuality: '*vom Himmel durch die Welt zur Hölle*' ['From Heaven, across the world, to Hell': Goethe, *Faust*].[2]

I see Freud's reference to the 'omnipotence of love' primarily as a reference to narcissistic omnipotence.

Whilst the pervert's claims to being pure might, at first sight, be justified in that the narcissistic component does have its part to play in perverse actions, the highly aggressive component justifies the way in which members of human society react with horror to such anomalies. As we shall see, their

---

2 It must have been the illusion of purity (a narcissistic triumph over matter) and a hostility that awakens a certain feeling of disgust in the nonpervert that inspired the homosexual novelist Dominique Fernandez to write *Dans la Main de l'ange* (Fernandez, 1982). The book is based on the life of one Pasolini, and the cover note (presumably written by the author himself) sums up its theme as 'Christ or Devil? Saint or bandit?', a phrase which reminds me of a book devoted to another homosexual – Sartre's *Saint Genet* (1952). When one of my colleagues asked a pervert who enjoyed being anally penetrated by his partner to describe what he really felt when he was undergoing what is, objectively, a very painful experience (the perversion in question is known as fist-fucking, or anal penetration with the fist), his patient spoke of a 'deep, exhilarating feeling of communion, a sort of complicity, filled with fervour and love'. This highly spiritualized feeling does, however, have a more sinister aspect: betrayal, which is commonplace in the shady world of the pervert. For a description of the 'delights' of betrayal, see Genet's *Journal d'un voleur* (Genet, 1949).

reaction cannot be explained in terms of the survival of certain 'prejudices' (which should be rooted out). It has a much deeper basis.

Like many of the nosographic notions used by psychoanalysis, perversion is part of the heritage bequeathed to it by psychiatry, which classified the sexual anomalies and thus provided a framework which has proved inadequate, outdated and over rigid over since.

Krafft-Ebing (1892, Case 52, p. 138) has no hesitations about making forced interpretations of his material in order to make it fit a schema that has been established once and for all. He describes, for example, the case of a man whose mistress urinates on his face and makes him 'drink of the voidance' as an instance of 'sadism in woman' [sic], and thus confuses the subject of perversion with its object. It is possible to get round the difficulty by including the case within the category of sadomasochism, and it would not be wrong to do so, but that tells us nothing about the specificity of the perversion in question, as in my view its essential motivations lie elsewhere. In order to promote a better understanding of this case, I propose the hypothesis of the monad. It will, I believe, shed some light on a group of perversions which have not been classified, or have been forced into a catch-all category.

I have already described the case of Laura (Grunberger, 1983) in a context which is as limited as that of the present study.

Laura went into analysis because she was suffering from severe depression and frigidity (this had become apparent during coitus), and only when the analysis had reached a fairly advanced stage did I learn of the existence of a perversion (the perversion was old, latent, but often reactivated). The fantasy centred on a little girl 'having to pee', and being prevented from doing so (which resulted in sexual arousal and orgasm). I use the word 'pee' deliberately, as the use of that specific word had a decisive importance for her. For Laura, there was something charming, impulsive and amusing about 'peeing', whereas she had a horror of 'urinating' because it was crude and dirty. She took great care over her appearance and her clothes and, according to her own account, spent an enormous amount of time on housework and hated coming into physical contact with anything dirty (drinking out of a glass which was not perfectly clean, for instance), but when she began to associate around her perversion, we also learned that her pleasure coincided with the fact (and the corresponding fantasy) of being prevented from peeing, but eventually having to do so and wetting herself or wetting her pants. She greatly enjoyed having manual or lingual contact with mucous or cutaneous surfaces covered with sexual excretions. She felt completely at ease lying naked amongst men as they masturbated, to say nothing of the narcissistic satisfaction she derived from the homage they paid to her beauty.

We are obviously dealing with perversion in the true sense. But although Laura had an extremely strict, even sadistic, superego (she had in fact once suffered from a serious obsession, but that crisis had been resolved), when she indulged in perverse acts, her only feeling was one of pure, innocent elation. She reminded me of Danaë, who was made pregnant when Zeus descended upon her in a shower of gold.[3] Laura also displayed a number of other 'minor' perversions, if I can put it that way. Amongst other things, she enjoyed lying on her stomach with her husband's powerful thigh crushing her waist.

In constructing my monad hypothesis, I draw upon the work of Phyllis Greenacre (1941). In a rather different context, she reminds us of something that is presumably no secret to obstetricians: amniotic fluid is far from crystal-clear. On the contrary, it is discoloured by organic matter and probably gives off a powerful odour. Moreover, 'The foetus moves about, kicks, turns around, reacts to some external stimuli by increased motion. It swallows, and traces of its own hair are found in the meconium. It excretes urine and sometimes passes stool' (p. 29). In other words, the uterus (the monad) is at once a heavenly, radiant source of bliss and a chamberpot – not that the two are mutually exclusive: on the contrary. It is well known that children enjoy playing with their excrement and smearing themselves with it, but such ludic activities differ greatly from those of the true anal stage, which is a source of tension and conflict. There is a transition from one dimension to the other, and a fundamental change occurs during that transition. Infants also like to wet themselves, and begin to cry only if the liquid in which they are wallowing begins to get cold. The consistency and density of the content of the womb, or the liquid environment, tends to be slimy. As a result, the child ascribes a positive value to this environment, and what is known as 'toilet training' may therefore be a difficult matter, though it is not in fact merely a question of bowel training. This explains why Laura enjoyed playing with the sexual excreta her partners left on her mucous and cutaneous surfaces (and on their own): they became slippery. She loathed handsome young men dressed up to the nines and with perfect creases in their trousers, as they reminded her of the difficulties she had had in tolerating the constraints of toilet training.

Freud (1905b, p. 150) expresses his surprise that kissing (contact between the mouth and the entrance to the digestive tract) should be held to have such charms. He overlooks the liquid in which the participant organs are bathed, and the fact that it is a reminder of the substance in which the foetus splashes around. That this particular form of affectionate contact is perverse can be seen from the fact that the puritanical English see it as such; if that were not

---

3 Freud remarks (1905b, p. 161): 'We cannot escape from the fact that people whose behaviour is in other respects normal can, under the domination of the most unruly of all the instincts, put themselves in the category of sick persons in the single sphere of sexual life.' It is only with strict reservations that I would now subscribe to that view.

the case, they would not project 'French kissing' on to their Gallic neighbours.[4]

To return to the case of Laura: we have no knowledge of the mechanical impulses to which she was exposed in her mother's womb (apart from the usual motor excitation). In the course of her analysis, which lasted for a long time, we did, however, learn that the numerous accidents that occurred during her mother's one pregnancy had made surgical intervention necessary, and we can assume that there was a connection between those pressures and tensions and Laura's predilection for having certain parts of her body compressed. We do not know how the foetus comes to terms with what happens to it, but contacts with perverts do teach us that they derive considerable pleasure from pain (which suggests that we have to look again at the erogenous origins of masochism). The perversion known as 'fist-fucking', for instance, must, by any objective criterion, cause intolerable pain, but it sends its adepts into ecstasy.[5]

I have described elsewhere (Grunberger, 1983, pp. 931-2) the shock Laura experienced when she met my wife in the hall. She had just begun her analysis and was apparently making a passionate 'transference'. She had in fact constructed a monad deriving from the prenatal narcissistic regression she had 'transferred' on to the analytic situation. The monad has to support the analytic situation, and then historic transferential situations; it assists in the integration of object conflicts, and finally of genitality and the Oedipus. As I have already said, the timing of this process is important and it must not be suddenly or prematurely interrupted. That is what happened when Laura met my wife at precisely the wrong moment: the trauma caused her to regress to primary narcissism, to the bipolar ego; and her regression destroyed the transference, which was bound up with the monad.[6]

There was, however, something peculiar about Laura's regression: its effects were in fact inverted. Rather than regressing to a delusional narcissism and to a deep aggressivity which could be turned outwards and projected, she concentrated all her narcissistic cathexis on me (turning me into an adored idol) and all her archaic and Anubian aggressivity on to herself. This

---

4 For the record, I will also mention the perversion of the *soupeurs* [diners], as they are known in the Bois de Boulogne, who hide in the bushes, watch couples making love and, once the act is over, rush forward to lick clean the sexual organs of the participants. There are other variations on this perversion and even though, as in fellatio, we do find components from different origins, it is useful to take into account the monadic origins of these marginal perversions which, in my view, are still ill-defined in nosographic terms.

5 Cf. Freud (1905b, p. 203): 'it is easy to establish, whether by contemporary observation or by subsequent research, that all comparatively intense affective processes, including even terrifying ones, trench upon sexuality.'

6 Laura herself said as much when I attempted to analyse what had happened in the transference. She remarked: 'No transference lasts; that's the truth of the matter.'

manifested itself in a total and ominous inhibition, and an extremely pejorative self-image. She merged with the imago of the bad archaic mother – at least, that is how she saw herself – and her self-image produced a very specific feeling of unease. What, then, could have caused this inversion?

The analysis left no doubt about the origins of her panic; she was afraid of the aggressive component involved in the introjection of paternal phallus (an important nodal factor in any analysis, whether the analysand is a man or a woman). She had begun to introject, with support from the monad, but the shock of seeing my wife had shattered the monad and she had suddenly begun to regress. The woman she met in the hall was far from being her oedipal rival; she was her own regressive image, that of her identification with the Terrifying Mother.

I would like to end this exposé by giving a brief account of a well-known perversion which conforms, essentially, to the monad hypothesis.

There is now a vast literature devoted to Hitlerism and to Hitler himself. It includes descriptions – and some attempts at a psychoanalytic explanation – of his perversion, by which I mean the specific perversion to which he had to resort in elective fashion in order to reach orgasm. Revelations on this point were made as early as 1943 by well-known individuals who were close to him (Otto Strasser, Konrad Heiden and his friend Haufstäugel) and by three of his victims: Renate Müller, Inge Ley and Angela Raubal, all of whom were later driven to suicide. According to the authors of *Hitler's Psychopathology* (Bromberg and Small, 1973), which contains the relevant documentation, a total of seven women were driven to suicide by the practices the dictator forced them to indulge in – or so we may assume.

Bromberg has also published a study of 'Hitler's character and its development' (1971) which inspires me to repeat my earlier comments on Krafft-Ebing's nosography. According to Bromberg (1971, p. 300n): 'The only way in which he could get full sexual satisfaction was to watch a young woman as she squatted over his head and urinated or defecated in his face.' Other descriptions of the act seem to suggest that it was preceded by a detailed visual examination, but Hitler did not leave matters there, and that is therefore no more than a secondary detail. Another author (Dr Langer, writing in 1943; cited by Bromberg and Small) defines Hitler's behaviour as an extreme form of masochism. That is no more than a partial truth and it expresses the wish for a hasty and superficial categorization, though given the subject there is some justification for haste. The case can be made even more banal if we refer to it as 'coprophagy', but that tells us nothing about its deeper meaning.

Given the narcissistic nature of prenatal coenesthesis, omnipotence is, as we have already seen, part of that experience, as is the elational position and the feeling of perfection. Hitler was pure; he was obsessed with purity, and his entire racial theory was based on that notion. He was vegetarian, and his hypochondria was also centred on the purity of the body and of corporeal functions. As I have said on a number of occasions, there is no contradiction between a certain form of anality and the obsessive illusion of purity. On the contrary, coprophagy can coexist alongside very high ideals of purity and innocence: Luther was a coprophage. Freud also notes (1905b, p. 155n) – though he was by no means the first to do so – that strong smells play an important role in the perversions. The smells in question may be those of excrement or, more simply, of *organic* matter which recalls the content of the uterus. Without going into a detailed analysis of shoe-fetishism, for example, it is immediately obvious that leather, the perversion's raw material, is an organic substance, and that the smell of dirty undergarments, another object of perversion, also has organic origins.

In the case of Hitler – and the reader will no doubt already have reached this conclusion – the sexual perversion, defined in the strict sense, is less important than the boundless aggressivity, which took on modalities and dimensions with which we are only too familiar: I refer to the extermination of an entire race, to the 'Final Solution'. And as Claude Lanzmann, the film director who made *Shoah*, understood only too clearly, the solution to the enigma has to be sought in the technology of extermination. The real question that has to be asked is not *why?* but *how?*. This brings us back to the perversion's physiological support, and it is now apparent that there is a direct link between perversion and its support. Indeed, they may even partake of the same essence.[7]

When I speak of primal narcissistic nuclei, or of Narcissus and Anubis, I am assuming the existence of a deep, archaic aggressivity which is almost indistinguishable, so to speak, from the complete metabolization that occurs in the digestive tract. I have spoken in that connection of devourment and aggressivity, of a cannibalistic and vampirish attempt to appropriate the outside world, of digestive combustion and of expulsion. I would suggest that

7 Cf. the ongoing controversy in Germany between Jürgen Habermas and the historian Ernst Nolte (and his supporters), who has been criticized for reducing the specificity of the destruction of the Jews to the technology of the process ('*Auschwitz schrumpft auf das Format einer technischen Innovation*) [for an account of this controversy, see Howe, 1989, trans.].

My own view is that the 'innovation' is not to be interpreted as a detail, and that we must not attempt to minimize or play down its effects. On the contrary, it is an indication of the deeply regressive character of the 'final solution'. This 'detail' (the term used by the far-right leader, Le Pen) is an expression of the very essence of genocide, and the song the Nazis sang at the 1936 Olympics – and even as early as 1935 – shows that they, or their unconscious, were well aware of the fact: '*Wenn die Olympiade vorbei/Schlagen wir die Juden zu Brei*' ['When the Games are over/We will crush the Jews to pulp']. Anubian aggressivity results in inhumanity, which is why no one – above all, the Jews – could believe what was happening; identification was impossible.

we have here a phylogenetic element which recapitulates the aggressivity of all the species, and that man is their heir.

Hell is modelled on the digestive tract, with its heat (combustion), its sulphurous odours, its gases; and individuals who are subjected to ordeal by fire, and to torture, are so many objects which undergo the projection of human aggressivity. And hell, like heaven, has a foetal anchoring point; the two have a common origin in the bipolar ego of the pervert. The Final Solution is a perfect copy of the digestive system, which makes use of everything so as gradually to transform it into excrement. The victims are hunted down, captured and thrust into the institution-organ which the commandant of Auschwitz called the *Anus mundi*. It gradually breaks down its prey (pre-digestion), crushes it, homogenizes it (numbers, tattoos, uniforms), faecalizes it or atomizes, using industrial and administrative techniques to create a world apart (the work of digestion takes place in silence and darkness; *Nacht und Nebel*) which resembles an extrojected digestive system.

Hitler's career (and his perversion) should be studied in relation to his anti-Semitism, which begins with the banal phenomenon of projection on to the Jews and ends with the Final Solution. There is much to be analysed; that analysis cannot be undertaken here. But we can make one important point by stressing the final phase in the process: *regression to projection on to the Terrifying Mother and, at a different level, identification with her.* The violence of the projection reflects the violence of the projected element – or in other words, the aggressivity which results from the accumulated narcissistic frustrations that lie behind it. The ultimate degree of regression takes the subject from ontogenesis to phylogenesis, back across the frontier of humanization. This sudden insight explains why certain perversions horrify us, and no doubt it also explains why Hitler's seven partners recoiled in horror and plunged into the void.

This essay merely outlines a possible study of the catastrophic consequences of the unleashing of extreme aggressivity, of the failure to establish a satisfactory post-uterine world – or, as I call it, a monad.

Chapter Six

The anti-Semite
and the oedipal conflict

THE STUDY of anti-Semitism, touching as it does so many aspects of psychic life, appears to me to be at the crossroads of individual and collective psychology: crossroads with so many avenues of approach that it is necessary to make a choice. I shall attempt to clarify the problem in the light of certain fundamental psychoanalytic concepts without the least pretension to present an exhaustive study of it. I shall not attempt to examine certain well-known aspects of the problem which to me lack the specific validity which alone is important. I have in mind, for example, sociological, political, economic, ethnographic, and other arguments which explain certain limited and superficial aspects of anti-Semitic manifestations but in my view are inadequate to account for them fully.

The remarkable continuity and constancy with which anti-Semitism reappears, in spite of radical differences in environmental factors, show us in effect that these factors are of account only as attendant phenomena or rationalizations wherein the pretended causes may be revealed as the consequence of much older elements and of a deeper psychological nature.

In considering the object of our study, we should not be satisfied with defining an 'anti-Semite' as 'one who is against the Jews'. In fact, anti-Semitic behaviour may take many forms, and from a topical viewpoint conceal very divergent and even contradictory motivations. Anti-Semitism varies from

This paper was read at the 23rd International Psycho-Analytical Congress, Stockholm, 1963. It was first published in *International Journal of Psycho-Analysis* 45, 1964, translated by Sidney Stewart. Copyright © Institute of Psycho-Analysis.

pure and simple sadism to very complex attitudes involving every form of individual relationship, and with each successive manifestation tending to be more specific and more arbitrary. It is my intention to approach the problem by trying to answer the question: Why the Jew?

Regression

The core of the anti-Semite's projections holds a privileged place within his ego and as such is irreducible. It is a section of the ego which is more or less radically isolated from the rest of the personality, but attracts to itself a considerable portion of the libido, thereby warping the remainder of the personality. The ego is immature, as though split and menaced with disintegration, and in any case succumbs to intense castration fear.

The anti-Semite lives according to the primary process and is unaware of reality, at least with regard to his specific nucleus. He lives in his fantasy, and any reference to reality tends only to irritate him and is rejected. He is in no way embarrassed by the contradictory character of the accusations he hurls against the Jew.

The lack of homogeneity in the ego affords us some degree of understanding of the anti-Semite, who, despite his role as a sadistic persecutor, may at the same time be a good member of the community, an affectionate husband, and an exemplary father.

The specific regression also affects his superego, which is an incomplete construction based on different superego formations, each corresponding to a different and overlapping phase in its development. The principal part is played by a precociously formed superego which is based not on the introjection of complete objects but on their educative function. It pertains to a *training role*, which is represented in the unconscious by the introjection of an anal phallus as a part-object. The pregenital superego is characterized, as we know, by its severity, and does not lead to a real identification. It is made up only of commands and prohibitions, and as the German saying has it: 'Whatever is not forbidden is obligatory.' Moral principles are replaced by formulas, rules and ethical values by a pseudo-morality, which can be expressed only as a system of respect for force.

One who depends on a regressive superego of this type will have introjected only the respective strength of certain superegos, independent of their intrinsic value and content, and this tends to explain why the German masses accepted a Hitlerian in the place of a Communist superego, inasmuch as it seemed to represent an incarnation of greater power. This enables us to understand how the Nazis would excuse themselves in the face of the terrible accusations brought against them by replying that they merely obeyed orders. It might be thought that this was mere subterfuge and fallacious reasoning, whereas in fact they were only obeying their *pregenital superego* and could not really understand how they could be blamed, since with respect to that superego they were innocent. All reproaches were in a dimension beyond their superego, and therefore their ability to understand.

When Eichmann listened to the enumeration of the monstrous crimes of which he was accused, he remained unmoved; for him they were obviously mere words without any real sense or content. But when reminded by the judge that he should stand when addressed, he offered embarrassed apologies, stuttered, and reddened with shame (Kessel, 1961). In this at least he felt himself guilty, since for a moment he had forgotten the rule of respect for superiors which had been taught him throughout his training. Such morality is formalistic, and the Nazis were surprised that their presence in Paris could be found irritating when their behaviour had been impeccable. Had they not helped blind men to cross the street, and never failed to offer their seats in the Métro to ladies?

Since anti-Semitic projections are formed under the pressure of a pregenital superego, the various accusations brought against the Jews betray their pregenital origin, and their stereotyped form reveals their archaic and regressive character. We know the time-worn accusation which turns up in different guises, but always has the same significance: 'The Jews have poisoned the wells.' The oral–anal character of this accusation is as evident as in that of ritual murder, a projection of oral aggression against the mother. In the unconscious of the anti-Semite there is also a certain equivalence between the Jew and the witch, the phallic, all-powerful and dangerous mother. According to some writers the witch hunts of the Middle Ages have been directly replaced by the persecution of the Jews, and the chronological succession of events confirms this hypothesis.

With regard to the anal sphere, the frame of reference is even clearer. The Jew is diabolical, the very incarnation of evil. As we know, the Devil represents anal components, endowed with guilt, whose home is the lower regions of the body. The Devil, with his colour, his odours and his manners, represents the excremental world. As for hell, region of darkness, place of eternal combustion where a torrent of sulphur burns away the very rocks while pursuing the destruction of the sinner (the bad object), it would seem to be the very projection of the digestive organs, mainspring of the last phase of the anal–object relationship, as I have shown elsewhere. The anti-Semite prides himself on his ability to smell a Jew a hundred miles away.

The anal allusion is sufficiently clear. The anal struggle *in toto* is projected on to the Jew – not only as regards dirtiness and all that concerns money, but also all the forms of aggression and treachery, culminating in the paranoiac fear of anal penetration. ('The Jews are everywhere, mingling with everything, corrupting all they touch, hatching dangerous plots', etc.) The anal components of sexuality are also projected upon the Jews – lewd monsters who rape innocent German girls in order to pollute the race.

The anti-Semite's specific regression is most clearly seen in his representation of the Jew. This follows the line of destroying his individuality. The Jew is denuded of all personal characteristics (the Nazis obliged the Jews to place before their names the epithet 'Jew', and finally in the concentration camps they were designated only by numbers. When the question of destroying some of them arose, the director of the operation merely verified their numbers without any consideration for their identity, a typically anal-sadistic process but serving a purpose opposite to that of the sadist. It is not a question of power, but a means of reducing guilt, though of course the two may be equally implicated.)

Anti-Semitism and narcissistic integrity

The anti-Semite presents a picture of specific regression affecting the ego in a selected manner but nevertheless touching the whole ego with respect of its homogeneity and the relationship between the introjects of which it is formed. The anti-Semite does not wish, or is unable, to employ the usual neurotic mechanisms. If they are used, they appear insufficient. As we have seen, he seeks to replace these mechanisms by projection on to the Jew, and seems to be at least partially successful in this, for he hides behind a topical constellation which is apparently healthy but nevertheless betrays his weakness and absolute dependence on his projective mechanism.[1] In fact, as long as this collaboration continues to function, the anti-Semite enjoys an apparently perfect equilibrium, even a euphoric sense of well-being. This leads us to the simple statement: 'One is anti-Semitic because it gives one pleasure to be so.'

Frédéric Rossif used in his film *Le Temps du ghetto* (1961) a series of photos taken by the Germans in the Warsaw ghetto. The Jews are shown as horribly deteriorated by the regime imposed upon them by the Nazis, which led to their total degradation. Certain shots showed the photographer himself (photographed by a friend) focusing his camera on a group of Jews who realized that they were going to be shot even as they posed for these souvenirs. I was struck by the expression on the face of one of the photographer-killers, which was beaming with pleasure and contentment. There was no trace of sadism, but rather a look of innocence and amused satisfaction. The soldiers on whom these photos were found were taking a great risk, but they had been unable to part with these compromising documents which apparently had an inestimable value for them. What does this prove to us?

The anti-Semite's profound satisfaction flows from the fact that his ego is in

---

1 J.-P. Sartre (1946, p. 33): 'The anti-Semite has the misfortune to have the vital need of the enemy he wishes to destroy.'

perfect harmony with his ego-ideal. Having made his projection on to the Jew, he has found his Manichaean paradise: all that is bad is thereafter on one side – the side of the Jew – and all that is good on the other side where he himself is. The photo carries the proof. The ego-ideal is narcissistic, and the satisfaction is that of perfect narcissistic integrity recovered through the projection on to the Jew.

The anti-Semites are recruited from among the weak and erratic, the complainers, the shiftless, and the immature victims of an intolerable narcissistic injury. They project the cause of their weakness upon the Jew; it is he who is responsible, thereby covering the wound left in their narcissistic integrity. All this is banal, but what matters is to show the tie that exists between narcissism and the oedipal situation itself.[2]

Collective anti-Semitism

During the course of psychoanalytic investigation we inevitably go back to earliest childhood, and we cannot do otherwise when it is a question of a collective social group. This would take us back to that early period in the history of mankind which directly preceded the advent of monotheism. The most superficial study of the religious life of that epoch teaches us that pagan religion was in a sense pregenital – that is to say, appealing to protective divinities whose cult was directly linked with fertility, especially the fertility of the earth which nourishes its children and whose love and protection it was necessary to ensure. There were maternal divinities, and without referring here to the question of matriarchy we find the figure of the 'Magna Mater' present in all primitive religions. But this relation with a maternal divinity or divinities must have had a deeply reassuring quality, and it is certain that in spite of the early frustrations arising from the oedipal relationship and of the marked early conflicts of that relationship, the narcissistic fusion with the mother constituted an ideal state that man seeks constantly to renew. (We shall leave aside the immense narcissistic radiance which the Pantheon of the pagans secured for man by filling the universe with his deified narcissistic projections.)

So much having been said, if we ask ourselves about the origins of anti-Semitism, we always find the opposition between Jewish monotheism and

2 I must wait for another occasion to discuss oedipal guilt and the confusion of that guilt with the feelings of inadequacy, which is narcissistic injury (and even lack of narcissistic integrity – castration). I quote from Freud (1921, p. 131): '... the sense of guilt (as well as the sense of inferiority) can also be understood as an expression of tension between the ego and the ego-ideal.' Here we see that Freud established (i) an equivalence between guilt and the feeling of inferiority; and (ii) that the basic conflict of this guilt corresponds to the existence of a margin of difference between the ego and the narcissistic needs of the subject (ego-ideal). The forbidden is not only the forbidden object but also that which it has not been possible to accomplish.

paganism, an opposition which has lasted a very long time and in a sense still continues. We have no space here for an analytic study of the different theologies, but we may state without fear of contradiction that *if paganism gives a very great place to the maternal elements, Judaism presents itself as above all a worship of the father*, a severe, omnipresent, omniscient father, an implacable judge: in a word, the superego. For the worship of the father is not limited to reactivating the Oedipus conflict, which is as old as mankind, but in addition has interiorized the punitive element and as such has presented humanity with something it is not prepared to forgive.

We may assume that the innovation presented by Jewish monotheism consisted not only in institutionalizing a superego sanctified by religion which favoured the repression of oedipal guilt, but also the transformation of that partly conscious guilt into deeply buried guilt. Monotheism, in cathecting the father as an object, has obscured religion and cooled it down. In taking away the maternal figure, as Freud has shown, religion has favoured spirituality, but has also removed that source of warmth and love, the mother. Christianity later repaired this frustration by deifying the maternal figure, but on a plane already transformed by the collective superego. This led to an exacerbation of the conflict in the Judaeo-Christian unconscious. *The Christian, the son, is in effect reunited with the mother,*[3] *the father having been deported to heaven*: an oedipal realization, one which has increased the Christian's guilt with respect to the Jews who have kept their fidelity to the father.

Briefly, the Jew, by introducing monotheism, has not only banished man from his intimacy with the mother (even with the Christian, the mother has remained the inaccessible Virgin) and from his narcissistic universe, but has installed within him a judge to persecute and punish him for his oedipal desires. *The Jew has therefore done exactly the same as the father. He has imposed the rule of the father, which explains why he particularly has been chosen by the anti-Semite for the abreaction of his Oedipus conflict.*

The Jew represents the father, and from that perspective we can understand the various aspects of the anti-Semite's behaviour. We understand, for example, why the Jew excites so much attention, why his conduct must be perfect, and why his slightest moral weakness is exaggerated by the anti-Semite who would remain utterly indifferent, even approving or amused, before the most shameful actions and moral turpitudes perpetrated by non-Jews. He reminds us of the adolescent at the climax of his Oedipus conflict, forgiving nothing in his parents and on the lookout for the slightest fault in their moral conduct; particularly with respect to the father, as though he would say: 'Look at yourself, you who preach

---

3 Cf. the pictorial representations of the Virgin mother and her child.

morals to me and wish to criticize me at every moment.'[4]

The Jew – all-powerful father and castrated father

The devil is a solitary traveller. (Montherlant)

We have seen that anti-Semitism, at least in one of its essential aspects, is a variation of the Oedipus relationship. It is vain to reproach the Jew for being a newcomer, for it is the ancestor in him that one strikes out against. Hitler first attacked the origins of the Jew, and consequently the father. Characteristically, anti-Semitism was first aroused in Germany when it was declared that graves and cemeteries had been profaned.

Freud has shown that the fear of ghosts has its origin in the Oedipus conflict. Much has been written on the manner in which the 'ghosts' of Jews from the concentration camps were welcomed, in general by the anti-Semites. We think of the adolescent whose oedipal rage sometimes leads to really criminal acts, even to parricide. In most cases it is not expressed except to be displaced on the Jews, of whom it is said: 'But they are indestructible, we shall never be rid of them.' The function of the Jew would seem to be to facilitate the Oedipus abreaction by permitting a dichotomy on the part of the anti-Semite. He divides his father into two (the paternal superego imago), and

4 Anti-Semitism is above all a collective movement, and it would be interesting to study the relation between anti-Semitic activity and the secret 'brotherhoods'. It is an established fact that anti-Semitism grows more readily in closed societies and that all organizations or groups tend spontaneously towards anti-Semitism in considering the Jews as a 'foreign body' and as a group hostile to assimilation. American anti-Semitism shows itself most strongly in this way. During the Middle Ages the secret brotherhoods (the corporations or early trade unions) excluded the Jews from nearly all trades, and if the Jews were sometimes protected it was always by certain isolated but powerful personalities, in a sense paternal figures, never by the brotherhoods themselves. A policy of Jewish exclusion exists in certain organized bodies and in certain Middle European countries. At some periods it has been easier for a Jew to become a minister of state than a janitor or postman.

It would seem that the relation between certain brotherhoods and the Jew reproduces that which existed between the prehistoric brotherhoods (as in the primitive hordes: see Freud [1913, 1939]) and the father. Brotherhoods banded together to fight the father's power. *As such the brotherhoods fight against the Jew as they have always fought, and still fight, against the father.* One might use this hypothesis in trying to understand better the youthful 'gangs' that give so many headaches to parents, police and teachers. It would seem that what excites so much rebellion against the father is consciousness of the fact that *their very union is charged with oedipal aggression*, which therefore increases their guilt. The anti-Semite projects that guilt on to the Jew by accusing him of forming secret societies and by speaking of mysterious Jewish plots with secret ramifications elsewhere, threatening the entire world. He cannot give up this projection, and even though all the courts in the world judged the 'Protocols of the Elders of Zion' to be a figment of the imagination, to him the validity of this document, invented by a masquerading police force to further the needs of their cause, was never in doubt.

abreacts his aggression on the Jewish imago while the positive sentiments remain fixed on the beloved father image in the form of God, ideals, country and fatherland, etc. These two images the anti-Semite forms into an indissoluble couple, since their constant association is a necessary requirement for the mechanism to function. Thus he can cry out in any language: 'Fatherland arise! Death to the Jews!'

The meaning of such a constant association is then: 'I beat only the Jews, the evil ones, who are my enemies and therefore my father's enemies; in contrast, I love and honour my father and want only his blessing.' In fact, as we can imagine, such an assertion is extremely ambivalent, and in spite of the dichotomy the anti-Semite cannot lose his repressed Oedipus aggression which resists all defence mechanisms and all reaction-formations. The anal-sadistic relationship which the anti-Semite maintains with respect to the father image finally obliges him to betray the father (he will always accuse the Jew of 'obeying a foreign power') and in fact behind the anti-Semite's patriotism he always works for the enemies of his country. We know of the assistance given to Hitler by the anti-Semites in each country he attacked and occupied, always under the pretext of patriotism.

We have seen that the anti-Semite operates a dichotomy and replaces one aspect of the father figure on to the Jew. But we also underlined the fact that this dichotomy is far from being a total success in that behind the ideal father there is always the hated father – in other words, the role played by the Jew with whom the anti-Semite identifies at a certain level of his unconscious. The double substitute object must therefore fulfil certain conditions, and it is a fact that these conditions are found in combination only in the Jew. We have seen that the role played by the Jew in the anti-Semite's unconscious is a superego figure, a powerful father imago, and in a certain measure an identification project, especially since it is given at the same time, owing to the projection, a powerful anal sexuality. In other respects it is the decisive factor that the Jew – according to the anti-Semite's criteria, which we shall examine – is an absolutely castrated being whom he may therefore attack without danger and without guilt. In the Jew we find combined the two contradictory characteristics which cannot be found anywhere else associated in such a way.

The father is both all-powerful and castrated, thus being, as Sartre (1946, p. 97) said of a Jewish Minister of State, 'at the same time His Excellency and an untouchable'. The Jew is castrated, not because he is circumcised but because he is cut off from the collectivity and therefore an 'outsider'. The anti-Semite is a regressed anal character, and for such characters only the organic insertion within an organized social system gives narcissistic importance to the individual, and only this form of narcissistic integrity is capable of giving him a phallus. The Jew, lonely wanderer, castrated and miserable, is as the anti-Semite would like to see his father, and is in a state in which the anti-Semite seeks to maintain the Jew.

The child who has known first the dual relationship with the mother later sees the father as an intruder, a foreigner – a foreigner, a term linked with the idea of distance. 'He should go back to where he came from', as the child will say about his new little brother, another intruder, and as the anti-Semite says of the Jew. And the Jew must not seek to free himself or to resist, for this only exasperates the anti-Semite, who finds therein a new reason to prove that the Jew is a criminal who does not play the game, an impertinent cheater. His aggression against the Jew is therefore increased, and we have in fact a secondary anti-Semitism caused by a frustration of the primary anti-Semitism.

This phenomenon, seemingly perpetual after twenty-five centuries, spanning so many social changes and resisting every attempt to eradicate it, is at last on the threshold of a radical change. I refer to the foundation of the state of Israel, which has brought the Jews to the Promised Land. It is true that this event, of such great importance, has not caused anti-Semitism to be forgotten like a bad dream. However, its tone has suddenly changed, and we now see the same Jew, who before had been despised and persecuted, now become for the anti-Semite a man like others, since he is now called an Israeli.

The Israeli is now possessed of a sovereign state, whose power, though objectively perhaps not great, represents for the unconscious a phallus like any other. The Israeli, by living in his own land, has thus refound the mother and forms with her a couple, as other peoples do. He lives, not in a vacuum like the Jew, but in a material[5] world that is governed and organized. He has suddenly become part of the system by adapting to a way of life like other peoples, with his own government, administration, and army. It may be that this painful problem, which has caused so much bloodshed and tears, cannot long resist the tangible reality of a simple little Jewish Customs inspector.

Postscript

This article ends on far too optimistic a note, and the realities of contemporary politics contradict it completely. In view of my obvious error, the reader may be tempted to refuse to accept the above study in its entirety. But I would point out that it is entitled 'The anti-Semite and the oedipal conflict': in that sense there is no contradiction between content and title. The title precludes the study of one essential problematic: narcissism. If that factor is taken into account, we should be able to arrive at a broader view of the problem.

---

5 As Freud remarked, the words *materia* and *mater* have the same derivation.

Chapter Seven

On narcissism, aggressivity and anti-Semitism

A T THE START of my training as a psychoanalyst, I was bold enough to attempt to analyse some of the criminals who had been committed to Sainte-Anne as mental patients. I began with a man who had killed several people, including his father. When I approached him, he naturally asked me about the purpose of the proposed analysis. In all innocence, I told him that its purpose was to bring about a profound change in his psyche. He could not believe his ears, and a fit of Homeric laughter quickly degenerated into uncontrollable giggles. He was not slow to inform me that he was perfectly happy as he was and that he recalled the murders he had committed with nostalgia; they had been unforgettably exciting moments and had given him an ineffable feeling of joy. He made no mention of the orgastic sexual aspect and in any case, for theoretical reasons to which I will return below, I insist upon the need to separate out the narcissistic component from the possible sexual sadistic component.

Hunters, including one woman, who have been in analysis with me have told me of the pleasure – or perhaps I should say joy or bliss – they gained from killing. They all made it clear that the supremely emotional moment coincides with *the moment when the fatally wounded animal suddenly falls to the ground*, preferably brought down by a single shot – in other words by an intervention reduced to a strictly ideal minimum.[1] The hunter's pleasure derives not from the illusion of omnipotence, which corresponds to a primary narcissistic

This paper was first published as 'Brève communication sur le narcissisme, l'aggressivité et l'antisémitisme' in *Revue française de psychanalyse* 4, 1984.

fantasy, but from a fulfilment of the wish for omnipotence, from the absolute superiority conferred upon him by the additional energetic component which allows him to fulfil his wish, albeit in a narcissistic mode. The hunter's assertion of his absolute power over his object allows him to share in an absolute omnipotence, or a total narcissistic self-assertion; *like God, he has power over life and death*.[2]

Narcissistic pleasure in absolute superiority, defined in the sense of acting under an energetic constraint, is equivalent to being sole master of the universe. But the illusion the enthusiast (and the very word hints at *thou*, or *god*) sustains at the expense of a single object representing all objects explains the romantic halo that surrounds transgressors, outlaws, great criminals, and even the sinner in certain orthodox sects. They thus become charismatic figures, and legends are embroidered around them, just as we embellish the image of film stars, who are also supports for projected narcissism. It also explains the increase in the number of fatal 'accidents' or unfortunate excesses, etc. The unconscious of narcissists pursues pleasure in such a way that they cannot resist the temptation of feeling, if only for a moment (a moment which holds out the promise of eternity), that they enjoy the privileges of the Divinity. We are dealing with a 'drive for mastery' in the service of cosmic narcissism.

Turning to the link between hunting and the third word of my title, I would point out that Jews do not hunt (though there are exceptions). There are a number of reasons for this, but the primary reason is that their religion forbids them to do so ('Thou shalt not kill', and permitted animals can be eaten only if they have been ritually slaughtered). Let us simply say, in terms

---

1 I did not undertake a structural examination of my murderer. Had I done so, I would no doubt have discovered a variety of unconscious material by analysing his drives, but the material would probably have been banal. Nor will I investigate the structure of the hunter; the results of such an investigation would be even less specific, as hunters are not very different from the rest of the population of France. The pleasure enjoyed by the hunter is not, as a rule, sadistic. Hunters claim to love animals, and once analysis had helped my woman patient to integrate her primary narcissism, she devoted her energies to breeding the animals which had once been her victims. Hunting is a feast, a choice feast; once the preserve of the aristocracy, it is still considered a *noble* sport.

2 A possible link between the pleasure of hunting and divinity can be found in the Old Testament, which describes Nimrod, the ancestor of all hunters, in a phrase which has passed into common usage. He was 'a mighty hunter before the Lord' (Genesis 10:9). Yet that phrase is meaningless to the believer; everyone stands before the Lord. As so often, the translation is faulty. The word *Liph'né* does not in fact simply mean 'before'; it means 'because of' (for the primary process, contiguity = causality) in the sense that every devout Jew says in his daily prayers: 'Because of our sins, we were driven out of our land' [*Liph'né k'hataénou galinou méartzénou*]. The Bible is thus alluding to the might of Nimrod, whose activities awakened in him a feeling of divine omnipotence.

that are as summary as they are provisional, that narcissistic and innocent cynergetic killing masks a representation of the oedipal-totemic murder, with its deeply regressive substratum, and that the function of the Jewish religion is to work through the guilt associated with it. It is an essentially oedipal religion, as opposed to Christianity, which is more narcissistic.

Whether we regard it as representing the rule of animism or that of polytheism, paganism is essentially narcissistic. The gods are mirror emanations of various human functions which have been 'deified' – that is to say, they take on a magnified and more perfect form, a form which is, narcissistically, more satisfying. At the same time, the pagan is prey to deeply primitive anxieties projected on to terrifying maternal imagos, and tries to appease them through self-mutilations and human sacrifices, to say nothing of the magical fertility rites (orgies and acts which are often incestuous or unnatural) which the Bible of the Jews preserves in the form of prohibitions.

This is the context for the outbreak of what might be termed the *Abrahamic Revolution*. Abraham, in fact:

1 attacks idolatry by destroying the fetish-gods his father Terah served ('A Jew is one who fights against idols'; the expression is Emmanuel Berl's, but the definition is much older);
2 enthrones the father, whose interventions provide him with constant guidance;
3 introduces symbolization by replacing human sacrifice with the sacrifice of animals (Isaac's place is taken by a ram), and thus comes into conflict with surrounding peoples;
4 uses the father to 'invent' the superego;
5 uses primary narcissism, in which man and universe fuse into one, to create the One God, who is invisible and omnipresent; he thus discovers absolute cosmic narcissism, which is immaterial and conflict-free, but from which man is cut off. One of the most important characteristics of Judaism is *havdalah*, or the strict separation of sacred and profane. In its disembodied form, narcissism is the preserve of God, as is projected narcissistic love. God is abstract, ineffable and unknowable, and His name (the tetragram) may not be spoken (a taboo which clearly expresses the need to keep the Holy Name pure of all sense elements; hence the commandment which forbids the making of graven images of God). God is, moreover, nonexistent in the modern sense of that term, as He escapes the criteria of evolution; the laws which govern the whole of life (and which Adonai legislates) derive from a very different and much more down-to-earth dimension, and the manual which summarizes them is known as the *Shulchan Aruch*: literally, 'The Prepared Table'. The Jewish religion is not

a form of mysticism but a set of instructions for living. God is the accountant who keeps the great ledger, and who once a year determines the fate of the individual on the basis of his merits. (This aspect of Mosaic law is often pilloried as 'sordid materialism', 'platitudes', 'lack of elevation', and so on, because this position undermines the illusion which sees it as an enemy; in May '68 one slogan read: 'You vomited on our hopes'. Those who cling to the illusion thus project all the archaic aggression that stems from their narcissistic frustration on to Jewish Law. Such criticisms may be addressed to the Jewish Law, but they are also applied more generally to the oedipal order and its derivatives.)

This second aspect of the Divinity is elaborated by Moses, the second founder of Jewish monotheism. Moses is a hero rather than a prophet, and he frees the slaves – Abraham's descendants. He organizes them, and becomes their judge and their leader in time of war. He confines them within a strict, obsessional framework of law which protects them and ensures their survival. After the destruction of the Temple, the rabbis reworked and greatly refined this code. The yoke of the Torah is harsh, but those who accept its constraints must find it to their advantage, as they remain faithful to it despite the price they have to pay so regularly.

Christianity appears at a point in the history of the Jewish people when, yet again, the pressure of events (Roman oppression) tests the strict discipline of the Law and reactivates a messianic faith. *The superego position becomes untenable*, and an idealized form of a return to the narcissistic illusion begins. Initially it attempts to synthesize itself with the religion of the Fathers. Ultimately, however, all the dominant and characteristic features of the religion of Christ – the unconditional love of God, the deification of man, mysteries, miracles, grace, the Kingdom, immortality (resurrection), the Immaculate Conception, etc. – *derive their affective charge from primary narcissism, and represent a challenge to reality and to the order of the Father*. The Father is, at least in theological terms, still present, but *this massive narcissistic cathexis* takes as its object the Son, and then the Mother. It is also important to note, finally, that the *economy of human sacrifice* reasserts itself, and becomes central (the sacrifice of Christ is re-enacted in the Mass).

These characteristics may be contrasted with the Jewish-oedipal ideal of equity, justice and morality, the Ten Commandments, the fear and love of God, the Law, which has an intrinsic logic based upon the real (*lex talionis* is simply the institutionalization of a quantitative equation between crime and punishment, or rather between the harm that has been done and reparation; reparation is evaluated in the form of fines), righteousness and unrighteousness, respect for an early life that is lived in the present tense, recognition and regulation of the life of the drives, the planned organization of good works, the protection of the poor, wage-earners and foreigners. The institution of the year of Jubilee, when slaves were set free, prevented the accumulation of wealth, protected the family patrimony and prevented people from being ruined by debt. This is an impeccably ethical, logical and rational system, but its strict application overlooks the narcissistic component and the sublime beauty of certain parts of the Scriptures (the Psalms, the Prophets, the Song of Songs). They constitute a separate domain because poetry is in a sense made secondary to the central corpus of the five books of Moses.

Man, born with a memory-trace of prenatal bliss (and therefore with a right to reclaim the Kingdom, given that he really did once live in it; it is his lot and must therefore revert to him), is destined to suffer a trauma (the frustration of his completeness) which might be called the 'existential trauma'. Initially, he continues to live in a state in which he can merge with the mother; that allows him to sustain his illusion and to rest assured that the absolute and spontaneous bliss of this union will be his throughout life. But he must become disenchanted and learn to reorganize his postnatal existence *by integrating his primary narcissism into his instinctual life, and therefore into his ego*. It is this oedipal development which is rejected by those who want to cling to the narcissistic solution. All sorts of artifices can function as substitutes for narcissistic completeness, but religion and ideology are the only ones which will be dealt with here. These formations allow narcissists to identify with a global narcissistic fantasy and to use the reactional aggressivity provoked by the cracks that appear in their completeness by attributing it to others and projecting it on to others (when I refer to religions, I am speaking of non-Jewish religions because ideally Judaism, with its oedipal structuring, allows guilt to be worked through internally).

Now, as we have seen, the narcissistic wish for omnipotence is absolute. This is why religions and ideologies will not allow themselves to be challenged; they are totalitarian and must use projection to rid themselves of anything that does not conform to their completeness. They therefore need scapegoats. And because it was the Father, with his laws, prohibitions and reminders about reality, who drove them out of the paradise in which they merged with the Mother, *they attack the first herald of that strict authority, namely the Jew*. No matter who committed the offence, it is the Jew who is held responsible. The narcissistic sons reject responsibility on the grounds that it is 'obscene' (a graffiti seen in May '68) and is incumbent upon the Father, his representative or his supporter. Constant propaganda spreads accusations which date from early times (spanning the pagan period) and have therefore been with us for 3,500 years. The same accusations are constantly being made, as the Jew has become a symbol implanted in the unconscious of the narcissist; resorting to it is almost a reflex action, particularly as intellectual laziness encourages the use of this convenient and familiar schema. 'The Jew' thus becomes a *category* which can quite naturally be applied to any enemy, real or imaginary ('Judaeo-Bolshevik', 'Zionist-Imperialist'); he is both the source of evil and a narcissistic wound, and he is a source of evil because he is a narcissistic wound.

Anti-Semitic propaganda is the product of religions on the one hand and ideologies on the other for the simple reason that *both stem from the same narcissism, and because the enemy is the contemptible paternal order symbolized by the Jew*. The divide is not between Jews and non-Jews but between the narcissist and the oedipal, and it can be seen within both parties, or even within the family. It is in fact obvious that the proportion of non-Jews who obey the oedipal order is probably the same as the proportion of Jews. Anti-Semites are recruited from marginal groups, from amongst those whose narcissism has been seriously wounded; the ranks of 'narcissism' therefore contain many Jews who fight against the order of the Father. Jewish anti-Semitism is a classic phenomenon which is found in all periods. There are narcissistic reasons for this, but there are also specifically oedipal reasons (mixed formations), as no one has more valid reasons for being anti-Semitic than the Jew who owes his Jewish existence, with all its implied uncertainties, to his ancestors. The same division runs through both the Catholic religion and Judaism, both being sites for a constant conflict between the oedipal and the narcissistic.

Hasty generalizations which are full of good intentions but erroneous can only be an obstacle to our understanding of the phenomenon of anti-Semitism, which has obvious links with Christianity. If there were any real truth behind all the talk of Judaeo-Christianity (with a hyphen) or behind statements such as 'We are all sons of Abraham', anti-Semitism would have disappeared long ago.

Chapter Eight

On purity

I

PURITY IS A NEW IDEA in psychoanalysis, if I may paraphrase Saint-Just, who was something of an expert on the subject. The absence of this concept from Freud's work can probably be explained in terms of the reasons that delayed the introduction of narcissism for so long. The demand for the narcissistic ideal of purity is so widespread that Freud could not see the wood for the trees, so to speak. The ideal of purity is universally recognized as an acceptable demand, but the motives behind that demand remain obscure. In his letter of 8 July 1915 to Putman, Freud (1961, p. 314) writes: 'What is moral is self-evident.' The fact that it is self-evident did not, however, prevent him from discovering the origins of morality (a question which philosophers have, of course, always debated) or the way in which it relates to the Oedipus complex. I think we are therefore justified in asking the following questions:

1 What is purity?
2 What is its origin?
3 What is its function within the psychic economy?

These are enormous questions, and one would have to write a whole treatise in order to answer them properly, but I have to restrict myself to an essay of conventional length. Without going into the multiple and far-reaching

This paper was read to the Société Psychanalytique de Paris on 17 January 1984 and first published as 'De la pureté' in *Revue française de psychanalyse* 3, 1984.

implications of a subject which goes way beyond our discipline in the strict sense, I will therefore restrict my remarks to points which are likely to be of both historical and contemporary relevance to us as analysts.

In a number of other papers read to the Society, or to other audiences, I have already attempted to pinpoint (if I may put it that way) the major difficulty which blocks certain analyses for a considerable length of time, sometimes for ever. I am saying nothing new in reminding you that the introjection of the father's phallus is governed by the integration of a certain aspect of the anal component. In certain cases it proves extremely difficult, or even impossible, to achieve this integration. The outbreak of the *preterminal crisis* (we can refer to it in this way because it occurs at the culminating point in the analysis, and indicates the possibility or probability that it is about to come to an end) forces the analysand to make a sudden retreat; he digs in his heels, and demands to break off the analysis because he is in the grip of apparently uncontrollable anxiety. We attempt in vain to trace its origins. We speak of guilt, of the Oedipus, of the fear of castration and so on, but we analyse in vain.

The important point to be noted in connection with the unfolding of this sequence is the overall nature of the reaction of the analysand, who stubbornly resists attempts to pursue the analysis. Not content with protesting at, say, some particular interpretation, as he did before the crisis, he suddenly wants to stop the whole process, to reject analysis completely. 'Too bad,' he says, 'I give up. The analysis is over as far as I'm concerned. I can't go on. It's impossible.' It should, however, be noted that he has no intention of carrying out the project he has described. He is in no sense rebelling against the analytic situation as such; merely against the revelation of a certain content. So he does not give up analysis; he rejects a certain technique or method and settles for an analyst 'of a different persuasion', one who offers a variation which allows him to remain in analysis but shelters him from the complications which gave rise to his panic. He chooses, in a sense, a purified variant of the content he wants to avoid. Unlike neurotics – and especially obsessional neurotics – who, in their flight from the Oedipus, regress to the anal stage and at the same time struggle against the libidinal and aggressive motions typical of that stage, the 'pure' flee anality and attempt to retreat back to a certain narcissistic stratum which usually coincides with an aspect of the analytic situation (its essential aspect) with which they feel comfortable, but which they defend against the integration of the drives in some way, transferential or otherwise.

We can now leave this individual crisis and look at a crisis which affects, to a greater or lesser extent, the psychoanalytic movement in general. It can take either acute or latent forms, depending on when it occurs.

Throughout its existence, our discipline has always come up against resistance movements, some covert, some overt; and they all converge on one central point: anality. One aesthete-analyst used to say: 'There are so many beautiful things to analyse without going into that.' As we have seen, the authors of the weighty tome entitled *Anti-Oedipus* (Deleuze and Guattari, 1972) are offended by what they call 'the dirty little family secret' (p. 49) and recommend, on purist grounds, that the doors of the consulting room should be thrown wide open to get rid of the nasty smell and to 'disinfect' (p. 50) it. Jung did not object to the *Vater-Komplex*, or the Oedipus, but he did thunder forth against '*rubbish* about infantile sexuality'. This polarization between a demand for purity and the instinctual aspect of the material can be seen throughout the history of psychoanalysis; it is a shibboleth which can be concealed or displaced, and take on many different forms. I am not, of course, saying that the Oedipus is not the 'nuclear complex' of the neuroses (Freud, 1908, p. 214), but I do think there is such a thing as a pretence of accepting it, provided that everything is dematerialized or *purified*, provided that the anal component is removed.

Freudian theory is a *Trieblehre* (a science of drives, and of defences against drives) and as we know, the notion of mobilizing the means to struggle against instinctual excitation is found throughout Freud's work. The concept of a 'barrier against stimuli' is a quantitative notion, but at a certain level the human ideal is one of absolute purity: 'And they were both naked, the man and his wife, and were not ashamed' (Genesis 2: 25).

We are in fact talking about primary narcissism, which is both a derivative and an expression of *prenatal coenesthesis*. It asserts itself *in opposition to the instinctual solution*, yet the instinctual solution is the human solution, and it is structured on the basis of our postnatal life. Primary narcissism has a tendency to go on existing in the form of an ideal of absolute purity, as does the primitive fiction of being able to achieve narcissistic completeness by means which are completely divorced from corporeal factors, and without having to turn for help to oedipal psychosexual evolution: *purity can therefore be defined as a narcissistic ideal of omnipotence and absolute sovereignty (well-being) that is completely free from the instinctual dimension*. It is a 'purely' theoretical concept, if I can put it that way, but we will continue to use it as it stands for the moment, as it allows us to make a fundamental distinction between this ideal purity and the purity demanded by the *superego*. The latter form of purity is bound up with the oedipal dimension, with quantitative regulation, and with corporeality itself. We can also make a distinction between this ideal purity and forms of purity which have been infiltrated by instinctual elements, and are therefore relative.

The pure narcissism which originates in coenesthesis is, in theory, gradually integrated into the ego, but it can take on a permanent and individual existence. It can thus exist parallel to the evolution of the central agency and can become divorced from – or even antagonistic towards – the process of ego maturation. Given that the narcissism can exist only if it has a minimal level of support from the drives, and given that such support goes against its very essence, it can survive only in the form of fantasy; but that fantasy will be supported by a *past which really did exist (prenatal life) and can therefore demand to exist again in the same form.*[1]

Before going any further, I would like to introduce a working hypothesis as to the functional modality of the narcissistic ideal of purity.

Narcissus is pure. We know that he rejects both hetero- and homosexual love and contents himself with worshipping the reflection of his face in the water. He and the image he admires thus form a double unit, and I think that the term *monad* gives an accurate description of a state which might be compared with the state of a foetus surrounded by something which, in its view, merges with it. That substance *is* its universe (cosmic narcissism), even though it does not *physically* merge with it.

The monad that is formed in this way is destined to shatter when the subject comes into the world – as we know, water also signifies birth (particularly as, although Narcissus does not know it, the River Liriope is his mother). Narcissus dies in his attempt to merge with his image, as he cannot accept postnatal life and the need for the intervention of the drives. But he does experience the process as an enormous frustration which begins with the awakening of his primal aggressivity (Grunberger, 1983) and the projection of that deep aggressivity transforms the initial image into a terrifying image. This is a tragic, almost nightmarish metamorphosis, and paintings from Pompeii (in the Naples museum) depict it by portraying the face of the dying Narcissus contorted in a hideous grimace, just like the grimace on Dorian Gray's face as he destroys the portrait that bears the stigmata of a life of unbridled passion (Wilde, 1891).

At the moment of birth, the mother does not exist as such, but her gaze (narcissistic confirmation) and her touch[2] may act as a substitute for prenatal bliss and may therefore compensate for the *basic existential trauma.* From this point onwards the child's narcissistic existence will be supported by the monad, which has now been re-formed (we know that a child which is being breastfed looks into its mother's eyes, not at her breast). Having been consolidated by this intervention, the monad can, given the right conditions, serve as a matrix for the ego (the monad can be found, in a transformed form, in love – and marriage – and in sublimation, etc.) but it can also live on in its

1 The notion of the 'purified pleasure-ego' corresponds fairly closely to what I understand by the notion of purity, but we have to add two qualifications: (1) purity cannot be purified because it is pure from the outset; (2) elational pleasure is a feeling of well-being, but it may reach an intensity infinitely greater than that procured by pleasure.

2 Certain parallels could be drawn with ethology here.

original form in various other circumstances. The subsequent mother–child relationship is also grafted on to the monad, as in the Kleinian duality of the good and bad mother, which is supported by *historical* images of the mother.

The monad functions for a certain time (three to four months) in this perfect form (narcissistic fusion), and then makes way for the 'instinctual solution'. It is essential, however, not to confuse the pure narcissistic demand with the instinctual (oral, anal, or even 'genital') demand; the child is in fact the first to protest at the equation of the two. It rejects the equation, and in the historical (and transferential) material this rejection finds its expression in ironic recriminations, many of them relating to food – the only thing the parent has been able to give the child. Even money, even sexuality itself, is a stopgap solution for the subject's insatiable narcissism. In this connection, it should be added that the failure of the primal monad which never functioned satisfactorily will result in a perpetual demand for its reconstruction and in a basic dissatisfaction which can take the clinical form of the depression felt by a spoilt child whose parents have given it everything but the one thing it really wants.

II

Purity is a force and a value in its own right, and it thus conforms to its original essence, stripped as it is of all carnal elements. It is an instinctual *void* – or, more simply, a material void. To take only one of the many examples provided by religion, Simone Weil, who was venerated as a saint by certain of her contemporaries, said: 'The soul is that which rejects the body'. Sainthood means the total rejection of the body. As the Gospel has it, 'If thine eye offend thee, cast it out.' And Raymond Cahn's woman analysand (Cahn, 1983, p. 1128), who had yet to reach the stage of sexual differentiation, says: 'What is a woman? What is a man? I could be either . . . For me, analysis was a mystical experience, an encounter; *it was as though the body and sexuality were an obstacle*' (emphasis added).

Sartre's Saint Genet realizes purity (the void) in a different dimension by eradicating the Oedipus and its derivatives, and through systematic transgression (Sartre, 1952). As for Buddhism, it realizes 'the annihilation of being' by 'freeing men from desire'. The doctrine of reincarnation is based on the belief that there is a higher degree of disembodied spirituality, and that it can be reached through *the gradual and repeated suppression of corporeality* (an ever more refined process of cleansing).

The ideal of purity implies elevation, or a movement away from reality. Achieving purity by suppressing instinctual urges (for example, the triple ideal of chastity, poverty and obedience) is not, however, merely a matter of using a mechanism to achieve narcissistic completeness. It is also the source, in itself and of itself, of an equivalent to instinctual pleasure, a sort of spiritual orgasm, and its adepts value it more highly than mere orgasm (this is also true of the drug addict's 'trip'). Mystics speak of 'ecstatic joy' or of 'beatific illumination', and the same flight from corporeality can be observed in certain alcoholics who speak of '*static* bliss' or '*disembodied* excitement'.[3]

Dreams of flying or levitation are probably an expression of the same fantasy of disembodied purity, and of a fantasy of omnipotence involving the phallic emblem, which would explain why they are interpreted as erection dreams. Not that the two interpretations are mutually exclusive: in the unconscious, the phallus and the penis are represented by the same emblem, and it is therefore quite logical to equate the two.

Purity is a sort of coenesthesis which subsequently becomes a state of *consciousness*; as we have seen, the fantasy has all the force of a lived experience. For structural reasons, this ideal of purity imposes itself as an absolute which must be preserved at all costs and by any means necessary – even if this entails *the destruction of anything that stands in its way*. The means used to achieve that end are themselves the object of a narcissistic cathexis, because 'to the pure, everything is pure'. This subjective conviction escapes the vigilance of the reality principle; indeed, it throws down a challenge to that principle. 'Love, and do as you will', said St Augustine. It is in fact Narcissus who 'takes away the sins of the world' thanks to a pure radiance which carries the believer up to the Kingdom of Heaven. The pure narcissist does not 'act'; he simply *is*. ('Where are you speaking from?' means 'Which narcissistic communion do you belong to, in which narcissistic radiance do you share?') And this narcissization of space provides us with a key to what might be called the *paradoxical purity* that is obtained through instinctual abreaction. One example is provided by the painter who used to masturbate before he crossed the threshold of his studio – a place of pure inspiration – in order to rid himself of all instinctual tension; and there is in fact no reason why instinctual abreaction in general should not give rise to a conception of purity. We say that we feel 'purified' after an instinctual discharge; in fact we return to a primal narcissistic state which no instinctual urge can sully – for the moment. And the well-known Latin tag '*post coitum...*' can only be a reference to a failed abreaction.

3 It is well known that it is quite pointless to try to convince an alcoholic who is lost in his regressive narcissistic elation that he should give up drinking because of the harm he is doing to his body. The enemy he is trying to destroy is in fact his own corporeality, and reality in general. The same could presumably be said of the 'consumption' which once carried off so many people; it was an illness that attacked young narcissists, young men in love, and poets, all of whom had romantic notions about purity. Even when they were dying they seemed quite indifferent to their fate, and it appears that the same indifference can be observed in people suffering from lung cancer. Both these illnesses affect the respiratory system, which does not become operational until after the child has been born.

III

Idealization simply casts a veil over the primitive instincts that dwell within us. We should note that idealism and human wickedness can coexist very happily. All around us, we see sincere and enthusiastic idealists who may well be vile, wretched creatures when it comes to their private lives. (Ferenczi, 1970, p. 30)

We have until now been examining purity – an absolute and autonomous narcissistic ideal. It is now time to recall that Narcissus and Anubis go hand in hand. The formula *pur et dur* ['pure and hard'; often applied to a 'hardliner' in politics], which is constituted by the juxtaposition of the two terms, expresses well the direct link *between purity and aggressivity*. If I may once more paraphrase someone who was an expert on the subject, I would say that purity brings cruelty just as storm clouds bring rain. Robespierre's words ('The Virtue without which Terror is harmful, the Terror without which Virtue is powerless') give birth to the *Terror–Purity pair*. The Incorruptible was a perfect incarnation of purity, and the term Virtue, as understood by the spirit of the times, may be considered to be synonymous with Purity. Dostoevsky was obsessed with the same pair of opposites: his works are populated (so to speak) solely by heroes who are abject scoundrels, and saints or Christlike angelic characters; one has the impression that the systematic contrast between Purity and Evil is the key to his aesthetics. In his *L'Homme révolté*, Camus (1951) speaks of the purity of Terror, and describes the Russian terrorists of the early twentieth century as 'delicate murderers', thus intuitively identifying the narcissistic origins of the pair (pp. 200–10).

The pure immediately come up against the fact that they are being frustrated by the real, and must either withdraw from reality (delusion) or opt for a regressive equilibrium in an attempt to re-create the narcissistic monad. Finally – and this is the usual solution – they may *project* the evil on to others, unless of course they turn their aggressivity against themselves. In so doing they provide the basis for a study of asceticism or even masochism, but I cannot explore that topic here.

> Life was filthy.
> We two alone were as pure as snow
> We two alone were pure.

In the last lines of his poem, the Hungarian poet Endre Ady invites his lover to commit suicide with him, and at the same time *faecalizes* the world by projecting. According to Sartre (1944, p. 92), 'Hell is other people', and one of Sadger's patients said: 'Anything that is not me is shit' (1921).

At the unconscious level, the double primal or archaic imago of the mother has in a sense already prepared this position; the absolute narcissistic nucleus necessarily coexists alongside the negative narcissistic nucleus, which is constituted by reactional aggressivity and has to be projected. The *purity–projection pair* can thus become a narcissistic ego-organization which seeks to attain an absolute dominance, as opposed to the oedipal ego, which remains stunted and fragile. The idea of a *bipolar ego*, if not the term itself, appears in Ferenczi's 'Confusion of tongues', where he speaks (1933, p. 163) of 'a mind which consists only of the id and superego' (and they crush the true ego, which is caught between the two).

This narcissistic bipolar ego does not, in its absolute form, take part in oedipal evolution, but it may live parasitically on it, and ultimately replace it. The battle that takes place within the child's psyche between the drives that threaten its narcissistic monad, but must eventually integrate and produce a new monadic structure, can become extremely violent, and may be projected on to historical objects or their precursors (part-objects), the whole process being dramatized by the appropriate primitive fantasies. The sound of this epic battle echoes through the unconscious, and it was discovered and described thanks to the genius of Melanie Klein. It is, however, in my view regrettable that the revelation of this archaic conflict, which enriches and deepens our clinical vision, should have become 'Kleinianism', which insists upon applying the content of this early period to the whole of psychic life.

Oedipal aggressivity as such cannot be described in such schematic and summary terms; the Oedipus integrates this primal aggressivity into the ego by applying the appropriate economic principles and by adapting to the successive phases of maturation. This is no doubt a simplified picture, but it does allow us to attempt a definition of maturity: a mature ego is *an ego which has given up the pure narcissistic solution because it is a vicarious solution to an oedipal development.* A child who has not integrated the Oedipus is not *responsible* and is pure in so far as it is not responsible and in so far as it continues, at least in a potential mode, to live, to a certain extent, inside the monad.

Kohut (1972) speaks of *narcissistic rage*, and in phenomenological terms it is certainly true that the narcissist's aggressive reaction has more to do with that affect than with a display of oedipal aggression.

The narcissist's aggressive defence may lead him to distance himself completely from the bearer or surface on to which he projects his anality, and that surface may therefore become nonexistent. *Contempt* is a typically narcissistic affect and it pertains, to some degree, to the anal component, which explains certain forms of the return of the repressed. The typical reaction of a narcissist faced with something which is 'impure' (because of the projected anality) is to mime his disgust by wrinkling his nose, but in Lyons someone who 'turns up his nose' (see Freud, 1985, p. 279) is antiphrastically described as 'a stinker'.

When it is not limited to aloofness, the aggressive reaction is crushingly violent, irrational and out of all proportion. The level of tension is at once very high and inhibited by motor immaturity (hence the occasional tendency to *delegate*, in *ad hoc* fashion, to someone who has reached a state of physiological equilibrium and has the corresponding desires). It is not dissimilar to the temper tantrums of a child, and the same classically nondirected outbursts of rage may be observed, as in some of the murder cases we read about in the press these days (paradise lost giving way to apocalyptic destruction).

Being an ideal characteristic of cosmic narcissism, purity often finds its expression in a religious faith or an ideology whose purity the believer has to preserve at all costs. I refer not to the purity of the content, but to the narcissistic cathexis which supports it. When it is threatened by the projection of anality, purity finds its confirmation in the destruction of the projective surface itself, and this Manichaean splitting supplies the proof *that once the source of the contamination has been removed, the ideal of purity has been restored* in a spontaneous and immediate mode which conforms to its essence. The mystical variant of purity therefore causes enormous damage; the statistics on wars – most of them wars of religion – drawn up by political scientists show that 'spirituality' has always had horrific effects. At the moment a number of wars are in progress, and they have been caused by sanctity and purity.

The pursuit of the ideal of purity can result in massacres, torture, brainwashing and the extraction of confessions, particularly in that a narcissist who doubts the purity of his convictions is forced to raise the stakes to prove that he is still true to his faith. Without its support, he could well collapse. In *Group Psychology and the Analysis of the Ego*, Freud (1921, p. 128) writes: 'Therefore a religion, even if it calls itself a religion of love, must be hard and unloving [*hart und lieblos*] *to those who do not belong to it*.' A few pages later (p. 131) he adds: 'It is unmistakeable that in this whole connection men give evidence of a readiness for hatred, an aggressiveness, the source of which is unknown, and to which one is tempted to ascribe an elementary character.' Pasche rightly notes that

> behind aggressivity in the true sense ... whilst its appearance may seem to be tardy, the destructive pressure that lies beneath it is no less primitive than the narcissism and its antagonist: it is in fact manifested even at the intercellular level (katabolism).

If aggressivity is the dynamic factor, purity is its detonator. The pure must fight the impure – which, by its very existence, sullies the cosmic integrity of purity. And as both sides demand purity, projection can work both ways. As the saying goes: '*Un pur trouve toujours un plus pur qui l'épure* [A pure man will always be purged by someone purer than himself].

97

As we have seen, analysands who do not succeed in mastering the anal component either abandon analysis or opt for a method which they hope will eliminate that obstacle, but the problem is posed in rather different terms for analysts who are in analysis and who intend to make analysis their career (the father of the training analysis is indeed Ferenczi). In such cases, the conflict may acquire a different depth and intensity. These subjects inevitably come into open conflict with analysis, and particularly with their analysts, because, we can safely assume, the narcissistic cathexis of psychoanalysis – and therefore the narcissistic trauma – is particularly intense. Moreover, their active involvement in the profession means that their relationship with the analytic phallus is called into question if they break off the analysis. As the original positive cathexis is transformed into a narcissistic wound, and as their aggressivity is therefore aroused, they feel a greater need to project their anality – or, in other words, to analize both analysis itself and the individual analyst, to transform them into dross. We now have sufficient hindsight to get a coherent idea of what happens. The list of dissidents (literally: 'those who sit down elsewhere') is long enough and varied enough for us to be able to draw some valid conclusions.

I therefore propose to discuss the case of Ferenczi, to take up the arguments put forward in an earlier essay (Grunberger, 1979b), and to engage in dialogue with Raymond Cahn, who recently produced a fine study (Cahn, 1983) of my illustrious compatriot – who is, as it happens, a focus of attention for both analysts and a number of those who gravitate around analysis.

In my essay 'From the "active technique" to the "confusion of tongues"' (1979) I adopted an oedipal perspective and attempted what Cahn (1983, p. 1116) calls 'a first-degree Freudian reading' (Cahn and I obviously trespass on one another's preserves!). I will now attempt to add a few complementary remarks concerning narcissism, and only narcissism.

As I said at the beginning of my earlier study (Grunberger, 1979b, p. 127), I have no intention of denying the value of Ferenczi's work. I regard him as a unique and dazzling genius, but even if Raymond Cahn does object (1983, p. 1116) to my classifying Ferenczi as a deviationist, we cannot ignore the fact that Ferenczi does make a complete about-turn, and begins to contradict his earlier statements. That is, of course, quite acceptable, and it is well known that only imbeciles never change their minds. It is also quite acceptable to believe – what am I saying? to state – that adults do seduce children and do lead them astray. It is also legitimate to note the fact that in terms of his psychic apparatus and his degree of physiological maturity, the adult is in advance of the child. Finally, it is legitimate to turn to Ferenczi's later writings for 'recipes' for technical variants, should classical analysis prove impossible.

The problem is that some authors (and I am obviously not thinking of Raymond Cahn) pick up the idea that children are totally innocent: as though children came into the world without any instinctual baggage of their own, and infantile sexuality had never been discovered. This is a Rousseauist vision of man. What I want to stress is that the last phase in Ferenczi's theory coincides with a fatal illness which seems to have resulted in a regression to the bipolar ego I have just been describing: *a search for purity on the one hand, and a projection of anality on the other.* In the same article, adults are accused of terrorism, sadism and perversion. We know that there are terrorists, perverse and sadistic adults, but it can scarcely be denied that the drives which result in such forms of behaviour have their roots in infantile sexuality.

It is no accident that the Ferenczi who has been put on a pedestal by recent commentators should bear no resemblance to the early Ferenczi, to the Ferenczi who proposed the formation of an International Psycho-Analytical Association to ensure that, as he himself puts it (Ferenczi, 1911b, p. 305), 'Freud's own psychoanalytic methods were being used, and not methods cooked up for the practitioner's own purposes.' He bears even less resemblance to the Ferenczi who wanted to force any analyst to refer to the IPA before publishing anything or before giving an interview – an authoritarian and paternalist position, to say the least! Yet the young Ferenczi did give psychoanalysis a number of articles which are important, rich and original: 'Introjection and transference' (1909), 'On the definition of introjection' (1912a), 'On transitory symptom-constructions during the analysis' (1912b), 'Stages in the development of the sense of reality' (1913a), 'A little Chanticleer' (1913b), 'On the ontogenesis of symbols' (1913c), 'On the ontogenesis of an interest in money' (1914), *Thalassa* (1924), etc.

Dissident analysts can be classified in two categories. There are those 'to whom psychoanalysis was never really congenial. After sojourning for a while in the chilly castle of psychoanalysis, they pass on to smaller, cosier habitations... They are people in whom the germ of psychoanalysis has never caught hold' (Malcolm, 1984, p. 27). I borrow these lines from Janet Malcolm's account, which is as serious as it is brilliant and well documented, of the Freud Archives affair and the quarrel between Kurt Eissler and Jeff Masson. Malcolm, who takes a very American view of things, gives the following list of dissidents: 'from Adler, Jung, Rank, and Stekel to Fromm, Sullivan, Horney, Alexander, and, possibly, Kohut' (ibid.). The second category consists of those who attack their own analysts. (Paula Heimann attacks Melanie Klein; Jones attacks Ferenczi; Tillman Moser [1974] writes a book in order to unmask his analyst [for a critique of Moser, see Gagnebin, 1984], or to attack psychoanalysis itself. Someone writes a book accusing Freud of having driven Tausk to suicide [Roazen, 1969]; someone else attacks psychoanalysis on the grounds that it is a Jewish psychology and ends up taking an anti-Semitic position; another critic denounces analysts who force their patients to live out their fantasies, and so on.)

At the same time it has become fashionable – and we have now reached the stage where the game is being played in a number of different circles – to play at being the first to discover the counterfeit coin in Uncle Joseph's pocket, or the flaw in Minna Bernays's virtue. Someone discovers that Freud made a mistake in interpreting one of his dreams, and concludes that his entire theory is false and therefore obsolete. Others criticize the theory of the Oedipus and of internal conflict (arguing that Freud invented it to defend the honour of his father or the honour of Fliess, and that the theory is designed to cover up the 'real' conflict). Neurosis is said to result from seduction, or from some other trauma that really was inflicted on the subject.

This is a return to the theory Freud put forward at a very early stage in his career (he also put forward other theories, and thought that *coitus interruptus* and masturbation caused neurosis, which prompts Malcolm to remark [1984, p. 24]: 'If Freud had continued his own efforts in this direction, he would have become the inventor of a better condom, not the founder of psycho-analysis'). He would in fact have turned psychoanalysis into a theory of trauma. In an interview, the psychoanalyst Leonard Shengold tells Malcolm (p. 83):

Let me say this about Jeff's trauma theory. It fits in so well with most patients' resistances – resistances not just to analysis but to the responsibility for one's own inner life: 'Look what they did to me!'.

Malcolm also cites a letter to Masson from Anna Freud:

Keeping up the seduction theory would mean to abandon the Oedipus complex, and with it the whole importance of fantasy life, conscious or unconscious fantasy. In fact, I think there would have been no psychoanalysis afterwards.

The seduction theory (and the theory that neurosis results from a specific trauma) regularly reappears in psychoanalysis as the *ne plus ultra* of research, for the reasons I have just outlined. And it often goes hand in hand with the accusation that adults and psychoanalysts rape and murder children (Roazen, 1969; Schatzmann, 1973).

Ferenczi, for example, speaks (1933, p. 160) of innocent children who want only 'maternal tenderness' being traumatized by the passions of tactless and capricious adults (the paper was originally entitled 'The passions of adults and their influence on the sexual and character development of children'; the same expression appears in the title of Cahn's paper), adding (p. 162) that the 'authority of the adult' paralyses them and 'makes them dumb and can rob them of their senses'.

I would like at this point to refer to the concept of the *monad* in an attempt to look again at the problem of the framework proposed by Cahn's study.

Birth destroys the monad and therefore threatens the very existence of narcissistic coenesthesis, which is projected on to its new protector. The monad can thus be re-created. I refer to the face or gaze of the mother, which becomes, in a sense, a substitute for the uterus. We can therefore say that the mother – or rather, the mother's gaze – is a source of *narcissistic confirmation*.

Ferenczi's references to pure or guiltless children who want only maternal tenderness, or narcissistic confirmation, should be understood in this sense. Failure to provide this confirmation (which is a way of making reparation for the real loss of prenatal existence) results in a basic existential frustration. *All other traumas are, in that sense, deferred repetitions* and, as Nacht (1948) puts it, 'the conflict is intra-psychical from the outset, because man is already divided against himself when he comes into the world'.

In theory, narcissistic confirmation is provided by the mother, who responds to the infant's demand with a narcissistic cathexis which is adequate, total, profound and, above all, exclusive. The child wants to own it all, and to be its exclusive owner. That exclusivity can be destroyed if the *libidinal* cathexis has to be shared (I am thinking here of the mother–lover conflict described by Fain, 1971). More importantly, it can also be destroyed if anything else is narcissistically cathected.[4] The creation of an atmosphere imbued with this extramonadic narcissistic cathexis is the responsibility of the child's parents. It may result from their attitude towards a charismatic figure or idea, should they worship a guru or be totally committed to an ideology. A similar atmosphere can be created if the father or mother represents an object which is narcissistically cathected by others (famous parents, leaders, politicians, etc.). We should not be surprised when we hear that the child of a celebrity is depressed, takes drugs or has committed suicide.

Certain kinds of problem are more likely to affect children in intellectual or cultured families than the children of parents from more modest backgrounds where the child is the primary beneficiary of narcissistic cathexis. (I once analysed a man belonging to a diplomatic family. Ever since he could remember, his parents had been involved in the social whirl and had attended numerous receptions and ceremonies, and the child had been left with an ever-changing and impersonal series of servants; the family was greatly influenced by the pomp and ceremony of the diplomatic life, and their fascination with and admiration for it had awakened feelings of frustration in the child. One evening, the house was full of prestigious guests. Although he was only just learning to walk, he slipped into the room that was being used as

4 The narcissistic cathexis of the infant – precocious eroticization, for example – is of course just as damaging, and as Fain (1971) shows, the *folie à deux* indulged in by mother and infant must also come to an end. It is all a matter of striking the right balance, and 'good enough' parents can do so spontaneously.

a cloakroom and, armed with a pair of scissors, snipped all the buttons off the coats of these demigods.)

The children of professionals and intellectuals suffer because the monad has failed and cannot support the instinctual changes that should be taking place (the saving intervention of a candid and loving nurse can sometimes make reparation – in extremis – for the deep narcissistic deficit caused by the mother who retains this cathexis inside her own economy). It is the children of the aristocracy and the upper classes who become Savonarolas and Robespierres, but they also become members of the Baader-Meinhof Group or of Prima Linea. They are children who have grown up in the conditions I have just outlined and never have any real opportunity to grapple with the anal component.

We can also apply the same criteria to the historical periods which give birth to generations of 'spoilt children' because of their opulence, their high technology, and so on.

Ferenczi grew up in a large family and was made to feel inferior to his older and younger brothers and sisters, and Freud was surely not mistaken when he assumed that his mother had not been able to give him the exclusive love he needed. The bookshop run by the Ferenczi family was a cultural centre, a sort of club or meeting-place for the intellectuals of Miskoclz; it was frequented by local and even national celebrities, and was no doubt narcissistically cathected by his parents. (Ferenczi re-created this milieu, so to speak, by spending his life in the famous literary cafés of Budapest, and using cafés and hotels as a home, presumably because he once felt that he was not wanted in his own home. He was in fact looking for the monad, especially when the final phase of regression set in.) He was dominated by the fantasy of a purely narcissistic monad, and consequently projected an aggression that was exacerbated by frustration. Not surprisingly, the theme he went to the Wiesbaden Congress of 1932 (the year of 'The Confusion...') to discuss was exogeneity, or the view that all evil comes from the outside. According to Ferenczi (1933, p. 162) this even applies to the feelings of guilt that adults instil into children; originally it is the adult who feels guilty, precisely because he has mistreated the child. Freud had little time for Ferenczi's 'maternal tenderness' [Mutterzärtlichkeit], and quite rightly criticized him for taking offence when others were not delighted by the way he played 'mother and child' with his patients.

In his 'Child analysis in the analysis of adults', written on the occasion of Freud's seventy-fifth birthday, Ferenczi writes (1931, pp. 136-7):

> One gives up all consideration of one's own convenience, and indulges the patient's wishes and impulses as far as in any way possible. The analytic session is prolonged ... The patient is not left to himself until the inevi-

table conflicts in the analytic situation have been solved in a reconciliatory way by removing misunderstandings and by tracing the conflicts back to infantile experiences. The analyst's behaviour is thus like that of an affectionate mother.

When Ferenczi fondled his patients he was in fact looking for something that was missing from the monad constructed in his infancy.

It is, of course, quite legitimate to use whatever therapeutic tools come to hand. After all, analysis is not a panacea; we find the classic indications for analysis in only a limited number of cases, and such cases are, it would seem, becoming increasingly rare, but that does not mean that we should ignore the analytic perimeter. It does in fact seem – but is it by chance or because of Freud's genius? – that the analytic situation is the best, and perhaps the only, means of triggering the process and the only thing that can support it. In my view, the analytic situation in fact reproduces the initial monad in optimal conditions, and may lead to a *Neubeginn*. It is the monad itself that is *transferred* in the analytic situation; the historical transference comes later (though not in all cases) and is *induced* by the narcissistic monad, a monad (the analysand and his reflection) which is silent but profound, is there from the beginning, and neutrally supports the process. In other words, it places it under the sign of purity. The monad is a matrix with which man merges in his paradisiacal innocence. It is at once the angel, man's combat with the angel, and the axis of his assumption of maturity.

Chapter Nine

Introduction to the study of the early superego

Foreword

IN ITS COMPLETE FORM, the internalized agency of the superego is 'the heir of the Oedipus complex' (Freud, 1923a, p. 36), or the 'moral conscience' which controls the moral life of the individual. The dissolution of the Oedipus and the emergence of the superego open up the path that leads to the socialization of the individual. There are, however, earlier forms of the same agency, ranging from the 'censor' described in *The Interpretation of Dreams* (Freud, 1900) to the precursors of the superego referred to by certain authors, and to Glover's 'nuclei of the ego' (Glover, 1930). Melanie Klein (1933) takes the view that the agency of the superego is based on the incorporation of part-objects. We also find a number of transitional superego forms, ranging from Ferenczi's 'sphincter-morality' (Ferenczi, 1924, pp. 266, 267) to Kant's 'categorical imperative', a philosophical concept which expresses the *transcendental* aspect of the agency.

The superego appears as a result of various identifications or introjections, but it also has a deep pregenital (and narcissistic) basis in the drives. In the course of this essay I shall emphasize the importance of this *intrinsic* factor, which plays a preponderant role in the formation and functioning of the early superego.

The moral agency sometimes seems to be charged with an irrational dynamism which is quite disproportionate to its content, and is often

This paper was written in 1972.

paradoxical. I will attempt here to explain that peculiarity in terms of the early roots of the superego. After all, irrationality, a lack of any sense of affective proportion, and an element of paradox form a triad which is characteristic of the phenomenon which depth psychology takes as its chosen object of study.

When he speaks of the superego, Freud (1929, p. 142) stresses that 'the mental processes concerned are actually more familiar to us and more accessible to consciousness as they are seen in the group than they can be in the individual man.' Whilst this comment does provide an insight into an important aspect of the superego, in my view it fails to take into account its early manifestations.

Freud's references to the censor and to the prohibition of incest, and his introduction of the ego-ideal (Freud, 1914), prefigure the notion of the superego, but we know that he does not really conceptualize it until 1923, when he assimilates it to the ego-ideal (Freud, 1923a, pp. 28–39). But the existence of certain dialectical situations, and the constant need to take into consideration the possibility or reality of their sudden appearance, means that we have to make a distinction between the ego-ideal and the superego. The origins of the ego-ideal are narcissistic, whereas those of the complete superego are oedipal. We therefore have to trace the course of their respective development, a process which is not always smooth and which may, depending on the circumstances, be marked by convergences or intersections between two sequences: the 'narcissism–ego-ideal–narcissistic wound and shame' sequence, and the instinctual sequence of 'drive–superego–fear of castration–guilt'.

We will then go on to investigate the anal-sadistic phase, which in my view begins with the introduction of an element of conflict – that is, at the point when the child can no longer use hallucinatory wish-fulfilment to overcome frustration. As we know, the child imputes the frustrations and traumas it experiences to its mother, and the introduction of this primal conflict allows it to perceive her as an object. In that sense, the object is 'born in hatred'. The hatred expressed by the child has anal-digestive repercussions, because according to my hypothesis it stems from the primal nutritional function, which is *cannibalistic and parasitic*, and because the primal biological force lends its energy to the aggressivity aroused by frustration. Simmel (1946) formulates the hypothesis of a gastro-intestinal organization that predates even the oral stage, arguing that it is the source of aggressive drives in so far as they are an emotional expression of the digestive tract's ability to devour.

The situation of overt conflict between the child and its mother (and care-takers in general) finds its expression in a particular mode which is held to be specific to the anal-sadistic stage, and is usually associated with sphincter training (not to mention the early Oedipus, which is beyond the scope of this essay). The anal stage in fact begins long before this and any disturbance of the child's narcissistic well-being may trigger its aggressivity (for a certain length of time, the child spends its life alternating between periods of narcissistic regression and phases subtended by conflict). Driven out of its prenatal paradise, the child attributes its postnatal existential regime to its mother, who watches over its life functions. The child sees her as having appeared after its prenatal solitude, and as having introduced it to a regime over which she presides; ultimately, it is possible to argue that the child's essential complaint relates to its exile from a state of primal prenatal bliss in which it had an invisible but permanent source of nutrition which was at once autonomous and automatic. The appearance of its mother's breast (the apple in the Garden of Eden) interfered with that state. Narcissistic feelings of being unique, omnipotent and 'without sin' would appear to originate in the prenatal coenesthesis of the 'cosmic ego' (Federn, 1953, p. 242n) – or, in other words, in a period preceding the change of regime and the conflicts that result from it. Certain depressives give voice to the same complaint: 'Is that all you can give me?' (meaning food), not to mention anorexics or others who refuse food, or those babies who have to be persuaded to eat spoonful by spoonful ('one for Mummy, one for Daddy'), and so on.

The child will experience any interruption of its narcissistic peace as a trauma (which does not, of course, prevent it from using a wide variety of sources to develop its erotism, or even from cathecting a benevolent maternal image), and this will inevitably lead to a build-up of aggressive tension; the slightest contact or unwelcome touch (or lack of contact at the right moment) may result in a high degree of aggressive tension. The disturbance is equivalent to a threat of annihilation which is perceived in a heightened state of sensitivity (a sensation which might be compared with the more absolute, and therefore more terrifying, feeling of 'being skinned alive' to be observed in those adults who are categorized as 'sensitive paranoiacs'). We find, then, a build-up of tension which, in the absence of a psychologically viable outlet, can only exacerbate a feeling of unease that can scarcely be mastered by an ego-structure which exists only in an outline form, and oscillates between a state of total calm and a state which brings it close to annihilation.

A child with an ego which scarcely exists as such, which cannot be perceived or recognized in its totality, cannot channel the emotional mass that is reactivated by the introduction of conflict – it lacks the necessary supports – and its only solution is to eject anything that is a source of unpleasure (see Freud, 1925c) and to attribute it, together with the unorganized and elementary aggressivity which has been reactivated by the trauma that overwhelms it, to its environment – in other words, to its mother. The mother therefore provides a first sketch for the superego.[1] She is a source of absolute constraints, and the child recognizes her as possessing – in a displaced form – something of its own prenatal narcissistic omnipotence. She provides a

107

functional framework in which the content of the superego can be inscribed in accordance with the modalities we shall be examining below.

The introduction of conflict into the primal bundle of drives known as the child results, then, in a phenomenon of '*assimilation-identification*' which will induce both the process of the differentiation of the ego and the id, and constitution of an object which appears to be assimilated by the child. But at the same time, the child is plunged into a state in which it is dependent upon that object. Object and primitive ego appear together; they are at once split and bound up together, and this triggers a process which will at once release the child from its conflict-ridden cacothymia and allow it to recuperate both its narcissistic omnipotence and its primal aggressivity. This recuperation is made possible by projection, but projection is also the price the child has to pay. *The primitive ego will submit to the superego and will identify with it*, but that identification will take different forms as a result of the dialectical interplay characteristic of the anal-sadistic stage; the early superego is born, and exists, within a framework in which the protagonists in that dialectical interplay are always and necessarily involved in a struggle over the balance of power.

These remarks apply to the first part of the anal stage, which is eminently passive. Its very passivity exacerbates the aggressive tensions felt by the child and their unbridled virulence (the ego, which will eventually be able to censor them, does not yet exist) and the primal aggressive, cannibalistic fantasies in which they find their expression (here the reader is referred to the work of Melanie Klein). Other images of the mother do of course also appear in the child's psyche at this time; they are reassuring and benevolent, and they too enter into the final structure of the superego, but they do not share in its specific dynamic which, being a product of the anal-sadistic stage, functions solely in terms of quantities of energy.

It might be useful to recall at this point that a screaming baby is caught up in a relationship of power, and is powerless in the face of a giantess who is terrifying because the child's aggressivity has been projected on to her, who forces him to obey her will and brooks no opposition. By obeying her, the child likens itself to this absolute force and thus comes to possess her omnipotence. By attributing the huge aggressive charge to its mother it can, so to speak, be enriched by it without having to take its weight. Once it has submitted to the mother-superego, it has no cause to fear that its own

---

1 As for the term 'identification' (and the idea, introduced by Anna Freud [1936] and Spitz [1953], that 'identification with the aggressor' is the basis of the early superego), I tend to agree with Nacht that the term 'assimilation' is more appropriate in as much as it indicates that we are dealing with the stratum of the elementary unconscious. He is also right to point out that assimilation transforms part of the id into the ego.

aggressivity will retaliate; the terrifying object therefore becomes reassuring (we will come back to the conflictual aspect of this situation, which exists *in nuce* from the outset).

The early superego therefore functions as

1 a mechanism which preserves the child's primary narcissism (omnipotence);
2 a mechanism which defends the child from its own aggressivity, which is projected on to the mother and then recuperated by the child as it identifies with her as superego.

It will already be apparent that we have here a paradoxical situation. The child is both a subject who can assume its drives in a certain mode, and an agency which issues prohibitions. As we shall see, this gives rise to complex positions. Moreover, the child becomes the seat of a diversity of emotional currents which are, in theory, mutually antagonistic: I refer on the one hand to narcissism, and on the other to pregenitality and the drives.

The constitution of this *passive maternal anal superego* is of particular interest inasmuch as in certain circumstances it would seem that the early superego attempts to establish its presence definitively, *but in its original form*. Thanks to a process of regression, it attempts to take the place of the complete oedipal superego, and it also infiltrates the oedipal superego so as to imbue it with its essential characteristics. We shall therefore now attempt to find a specific explanation for these developments, which are possible, and to a certain extent (in the case of the second possibility) unavoidable.

When it has really begun, the active anal stage, or the second part of the anal-sadistic stage, to some degree puts an end to the child's total dependency on its mother, as the child can now rebel against her: not only as a result of his developing self-control, but thanks also to a defensive tactic based upon a satisfactory identification *with the father* supported by the unconscious fantasy of the anal introjection of the father's phallus. This fantasy is typical of the anal-sadistic stage, and an integral part of it. The child thus assimilates its anal-sadistic component. Behind this assimilation we can see, in outline, both an inversion of its imago position and a corresponding redistribution of its projections; this already provides an indication of the respective positions they will occupy within the future oedipal superego.

Let us assume, then, that all goes well and that the child is able successfully to abreact the successive anal phases thanks to its mother, who narcissistically confirms both its passivity and its activity and thus allows it to assume itself in the same way during both these phases of its development. If that is the case, the child will be able to consolidate its anal control, and then enter the phallic-narcissistic stage and the real oedipal struggle thanks to its paternal identification. Once the oedipal struggle has been integrated, the definitive constitution of the superego can begin. The superego is the heir of both the Oedipus complex and its dissolution.

In cases where all goes well – and I have, of course, described them in very schematic terms – the successive identifications reappear in the final superego (which will inevitably reveal traces of all the earlier versions). It will also include archaic and early elements, but these will, by definition, play only a secondary role in the constitution of the post-oedipal agency. But what happens in atypical situations where things occur in a different way?

We have of course all experienced the primacy of oedipal material, both at the beginning of the analysis and throughout the treatment. The same oedipal problematic will therefore appear in all the successive modes that correspond to the pregenital phases, but most of the analytic work is concentrated upon the oedipal conflict. This, however, is not always so, and in an increasing number of cases we find it necessary to undertake a pre-oedipal clearing-up operation, so to speak, before we can deal with Oedipus in *a dynamically valid manner*. Narcissism also has to be sufficiently integrated to incite the ego to undertake its own reorganization, but not to an excessive degree, for then the ego might be tempted to cathect itself once and for all (the regressive narcissism of an overfragile ego is another major obstacle to analytic investigation). Moreover, this pre-oedipal clearing-up operation – leave aside the question of narcissistic developments – is sometimes done very badly; before long we realize that something is blocked, and that the explanation lies in the anal strata because the corresponding phase has been poorly integrated; we are then faced with what can be an insurmountable obstacle.

Without going into a detailed discussion of the possible effects of this complete block, let me add that we are talking about predominantly narcissistic subjects who refuse to introject for two reasons. As we have just seen, the decisive sequences in the process of integration occur during the anal stage. These subjects do not reject this phase of object-metabolization simply because it has visceral connotations which they cannot assume (the homosexual aspect of anal introjection frightens both male and female subjects who have introduced an element of conflict into their identification with *the mother*; maternal identification remains in abeyance). They also reject it because it offends their narcissism: the narcissist, or rather a certain type of narcissist, wants to remain what he is and as he is, and refuses to introduce anything into his ego – unless he has complete control over it. We know that this is a transitional position and that whilst narcissistic opposition to analysis is the most banal form of resistance, there is another type of narcissism. As we have seen, it is impossible to settle into analytic treatment without that form of narcissism. (Similarly, fear of homosexuality can function as a defence against introjection, just as an exaggerated eroticization of the anal component can be used to resist identificatory introjection.)

The refusal to identify (the narcissist is 'no one's son', he is 'like no one else') can be based on an extremely precocious elementary attitude, in which case we find ourselves faced with subjects who cannot complete the process of maturation because their early identifications were unsatisfactory. Because they have not integrated the Oedipus, they react to that position by making a show of indifference, negation or disavowal; they hover around the oedipal problematic, but at the same time they disavow it with an exaggerated and compulsive intensity. There is, however, never any question of involvement in the Oedipus; the Oedipus is systematically avoided. The point is not to compete with the father, but to show that he does not exist, that one does not have to identify with the father, with any of his derivatives or, indeed, with reality itself. These 'aging adolescents' have yet to reach the Oedipus, and some analyses end in complete and definitive failure because of this obstacle.

The block does not, however, always occur at the same point; this allows us to identify, and try to analyse, its cause. It occurs in the transference, at the point when certain anal material begins to come to the surface, either directly or in a disguised form. Anxiety is triggered, and a crisis begins. The analysand finds it difficult to tolerate. Some analysands can overcome it; others try to do so in vain, and eventually the analysis comes to a complete stop. There are cases in which the break occurs suddenly: some obstacle provokes so much anxiety that it cannot be dealt with, and the analysand runs away.

The subsequent evolution of such subjects, is, however, of considerable interest, as it often takes a particular form. These analysands either turn to an analyst belonging to a dissident school (the function of dissidence is to conjure away the visceral aspect of maturation, and therefore the maturational process itself) or to para-analytic doctrines. They may surrender to a certain eclecticism (acceptance of the validity of *all* scientific opinions is one way of escaping the scientific domain) or even to some overt form of mysticism; or they may adopt an ideology. Having reached a certain threshold, they attempt to avoid the exploration of the *individual* unconscious and place themselves under the protection of a *collective superego* which, because it offers them an *ad hoc* construction – whose meaning will be discussed below – makes further exploration pointless.

That is a perilous undertaking, and it is obviously beyond their affective capability; I say 'affective' because they are intellectually interested in analysis, and even launch into extremely subtle conceptual constructs using this superficial narcissistic game as a defence against the lived experience of analysis. The very word is enough to provoke their sarcasm. They accumulate analytic 'knowledge' and cathect it because it reassures them, and because it is a substitute for a dynamically valid commitment to the analytic process.

If we turn to the family constellation of these subjects, we frequently find a certain homogeneity. We also find that historical factors are often reinforced by the corresponding fantasy projection.

Broadly speaking, we can say that their families are usually well-educated and prosperous; the father is usually dominated by the mother, and plays a minor, insignificant role. The analysand sees his mother as omnipotent, and the absence of the father is reminiscent of Alexander Mitscherlich's 'Society without the Father' (Mitscherlich, 1967). The patient is 'spoilt' by his mother, who does indeed confirm every stage in his psychosexual evolution and may even cathect certain of her child's motor and mental activities in an exaggerated fashion because they flatter her own narcissism, but she strongly repudiates his pregenital (anal) activities. Those activities are of crucial importance, but certain of their negative aesthetic qualities offend her 'sensibilities'. I am thinking in particular of an artist who was in analysis with me. Both his parents were nudists and he recalled that as a child he had danced naked with his mother, who was also naked. On the other hand, she carefully cleaned her son's penis with eau de Cologne when she found traces of night pollution on his sheets, and sternly warned him about his 'dirty habits'.

I think I can venture a comment on this boy here: I have the impression that he was saved *in extremis* by his father, who – no doubt in order to get his own back on his wife, who constantly snubbed him – decided to 'make a man' of his son in his own peculiar way: when the boy was five, he would teach him a new 'dirty word' every morning as they performed their ablutions together in the bathroom.

Whether or not things happen in precisely this way does not seem to matter very much, as fantasy activity does to a certain extent compensate for historical realities. Moreover, the role of the early superego can be played by an obsessional or even paranoiac father who manipulates the child and exercises strict control over the sphincter. In other cases, the obstacle to the integration of the anal dynamic is not parental opposition but excessive permissiveness. As we are now beginning to find out, this conjuncture represents a challenge to the psychoanalytic interpretation of instinctual freedom; children can be made to feel guilty because there is no obstacle to the satisfaction of the drives.

Before going any further, let us stop for a moment and look at the problem of the distinction between the superego and the ego-ideal, and at its theoretical and clinical value. Although there is an essential difference between the oedipal superego and the narcissistic ego-ideal (and that difference has been spelled out with luminous clarity by Chasseguet-Smirgel, 1985), the complete oedipal superego is a product of the synthesis of two mutually antagonistic components and represents the culmination of a series of stages, of successive degrees of maturation. The transition from one stage to the next is a dialectical process. But what happens if, for some reason or other, it proves impossible to achieve this synthesis? What happens if the maturational process is simply blocked? What happens if the defence used by the subject takes the form of a deliberate avoidance of the oedipal evolution, or of regression?

What happens is, of course, that the superego cannot be constituted, or that it is badly constituted; in its place, we find all the elements that were present in the conflict over narcissistic frustration: frustrated narcissism on the one hand, and the sadistic component (a reaction against frustration) on the other. They are still intact, and they are isolated from one another. I say that they are intact, but in fact they function in an exaggerated mode and with a primitive, archaic force that nothing – except a superficial attempt at rationalization – can temper, because at this phase in a battle from which the subject never emerges, the subject acts on the register of the primary process. We also find the imperious presence of primal sadism and narcissism: one acting as a primitive superego, the other as an ego-ideal. These two factors are still mutually antagonistic, but the ego attempts to build a bridge between the two (rationalization), rather as though it were an agency that had been inserted into a complete ego. This paradoxical situation allows us to account for certain characteristics of this hybrid and immature agency, which appears to be complete and homogeneous.

The early superego is, as I have said, structured like an anal maternal superego, and in a sadistic mode, but its *ad hoc* content can be borrowed from any model or object of identification. It may even merge with the narcissistic ego-ideal itself. Had the maturational process been integrated into the complete ego, and had the primal contradictions been resolved, we would now have a complete oedipal ego. But the narcissistic and sadistic components subsist in their primal state, are still mutually antagonistic, and are outside the ego, which uses the narcissistic ego-ideal as an alibi and a disguise, whilst the conspicuous presence of narcissism permits both the negation and the free, justified and guiltless abreaction of the sadistic component.

One of my mature patients provides a good example of this immature superego position. He had spent his life fighting for every social ideal and had been involved in (among other things) a propaganda campaign to have the death penalty abolished. In his opinion, similar views should be inculcated into children by teachers trained to spread humanitarian ideas. 'And what if some of the teachers were to disagree?' asked the interlocutor. 'They should be shot', came the reply, and he was certainly not joking. The absolute narcissistic demands made by the corresponding component of the early superego must be attributed to immaturity, to a failure to integrate the real, and above all to the extreme violence of the sadistic component, because whilst the ego can use that agency as a crutch, it can brandish it like a club.

And anyone who dares to disagree calls into question the validity of the mechanism.

The clinical experience which provided us with our starting point means that we are now in a position to gauge the discrepancy between the magnanimity and moral elevation of certain of humanity's benefactors and the openly sadistic manner in which they behave to their families, those close to them, and in particular to their subordinates and their servants.

The early superego is based on identification with the sadistic mother, but this identification dates from a very early stage in the development of the ego, where affects are far from stable and where the underlying anal component is not constructive but reactional and superficial. It is not a structuring anal component, nor is there anything constructive about the narcissistic component which strives to cathect it but can never overcome its own hesitations. Anality continues to operate at the level of fantasy, or even illusion. It is this which allows sadism and narcissism to merge in a purely artificial manner, even though they are essentially antagonistic; they meet in the domain of the imaginary. Rousseau, the prophet of the natural goodness of man and of Mother Nature, the man who inspired every executioner who has ever cut off heads for love of humanity, handed his own children over to a foundling hospital in the name of morality. This coexistence of sadism and a lofty moral ideal provides the basis for what is now a widespread structure within ideological movements where the 'pur et dur' [hardline] attitude prevails. This idealist 'intelligentsia' has adopted Alphonse-Donatien de Sade as one of its intellectual masters (as an anal maternal superego). In the light of the above comments, the very fact that he is known as 'The Divine Marquis' is in itself worthy of attention. While he was imprisoned in the Bastille, de Sade listed his narcissistic and instinctual desires and sang the delights of fantasy. As Belmor says to Juliette:

> Oh Juliette! The pleasures of the imaginary are so delicious. In such delightful instants, the whole world is ours; not one creature resists us. We destroy the world, and repopulate it with new objects which we then immolate anew; we have the ability to commit any crime, and we can unleash a hundred horrors. What we are doing is no more than an image of what we would like to do.

This significant passage combines a megalomanic narcissism and sadism at the level of fantasy and hesitant desire, but the real point of interest is that the author of the *120 Journées de Sodome* (de Sade, 1785) claimed to be a moralist, and that his latter-day disciples still regard him as such.

In his brilliant film *La Main dans le piège*, Leopold Torre-Nilson portrays a sexual relationship between a sadistic uncle and his niece. This relationship takes the adolescent to the brink of psychosis. One detail is of particular interest: the film-maker depicts his hero's sadism simply by showing him undressing in a certain way before he consummates the act. Locked in a greenhouse with his niece, he carefully folds each article of clothing, taking his time and looking for the right place to put his watch, rings and cufflinks: 'everything in its place'. The meaning of Torre-Nilson's brilliant insight is obvious: 'Provided that I respect all the rules my mother taught me to obey, no one has grounds to criticize me.' The fact that the act, which is perpetrated in a peculiarly incestuous context, has a traumatic effect on the girl can thus be overlooked.

I have already pointed out that a child who has difficulties with the Oedipus cannot construct a superego – the heir of the Oedipus complex – because there can be no superego unless the Oedipus has been integrated. We have, however, seen that there is such a thing as the early superego. If the child – though in my view this is more likely to happen with 'aging adolescents' – now fails to integrate its active anal component, the only remaining option open to it is regression to the one form of superego it has experienced. The path that leads to the construction of other forms of the superego is blocked; the aggressive component which should be used to create the superego ceases to evolve and is therefore restricted to its primal form. I refer to the anal maternal superego, which reflects the child's early training, and that alone. In German it might be termed an *Ober-ich*, as opposed to the *Über-ich*, or the Oedipal superego.

In his study of psychoanalysis and nuclear war, Fornari (1964) cites Money-Kyrle, who served with the German Personnel Research Branch of the Control Commission in 1946. The object of the commission was to select suitable Germans as leaders in the new democratic Germany. They were given psychiatric interviews to assess their reactions on being told about Nazi atrocities, Money-Kyrle (1951, pp. 11–12) comments that those who denied the existence of the concentration camps displayed

> no conscious guilt at all; but its unconscious presence was clearly betrayed by the vehemence with which it was repudiated and projected on to others... They were obsessively loyal to whatever authority they served. The authority itself could be of many kinds.

Money-Kyrle therefore classifies them as 'authoritarian' types. This is very important because, given that the content of the superego inevitably has social, moral and political implications, its effects can be far-reaching, particularly in view of the immense quantity of aggressive affect it may contain. It may attempt to justify aggressivity (not to mention the fact that the superego functions not only as a source of prohibitions but also as a support; a subject who is loved by his superego is sheltered from oedipal guilt;

moreover, the institution of the *ad hoc* constellation we will be studying later gives him a feeling similar to that of narcissistic completeness). But that content – and this is where the danger arises – is of no importance to the anal superego. It can be anything, even the content of the oedipal superego. All that matters is absolute obedience: obeying and being obeyed (we will come back to the Janus-like nature of this superego).[2]

Total submission is *pure*. In other words, there is no need to compromise: we thus have total, unquestioning and unconditional obedience.[3] The outcome of the religious 'disputations' in the Middle Ages was decided in advance, and Jews were handed over to the 'secular arm' regardless of the objective content of the discussion. In a *corrida*, the bull is condemned in advance and dies in a ritual which is applied as strictly and as implacably as a real death sentence.

It is in fact out of the question for a very young child to do anything but obey its mother, and as we saw earlier, the only solution available to it is to share her power by identifying with her. We know that strong governments have a fascination for the masses, quite independently of the slogans they use to dress up their sadistic attempts at seduction. This power does not have to be represented by anything real (it might even be said that the cathecting of the materiality of power presupposes that a developed ego has already integrated the anal component to some extent); it can be represented by an ideal, an idea or an ideology which implies both a narcissistic value and the idea of constraint. And this fascination is irresistible to the weak, who are ready to submit completely to a powerful government because they feel that it will protect them. The concept of absolute obedience or of *Perinde ac cadaver* (the motto of the Jesuits) appears whenever individuals congregate together and place themselves under the protection of a tutelary mother (in, for example, an army or a Church, to mention only the institutions described by Freud,

---

2 The early superego demands absolute and *strict* submission, just as the Primal Mother requires absolute submission on the part of the child. This form of submission must be duly signed, or formally recognized; the agreement lasts for ever, and there is no appeal. When the believer makes his confession to a priest, he begins with a self-accusation: *Pater peccavi*; he thus both indicates his submission and identifies with his superego by accusing himself of having sinned.

During the Moscow trials, the accused had to sign statements which had been prepared in advance by individuals who had nothing to do with the actual trial (they also had to accuse themselves of having committed crimes). Their submission was total, as was the sadism of the judges.

The hero of *Venus in Furs* (Sacher-Masoch, 1886) also assures the archaic mother of his absolute submission by *signing a contract*, but the contract is unilateral. (The symbolic fur symbolizes both the phallus he ascribes to the archaic mother and her primal, animal character.)

3 This superego component is, however, necessary, and I have no hesitation in saying that a parent who never makes a child do something without giving a reason – at a certain stage in its education – is making a mistake.

1921; I, however, tend to see the leader as representing an archaic mother rather than a father).[4]

Absolute obedience is the rule in the ideological groupings which tend to dominate our epoch; doctrines are handed down, either by the coercive apparatus of the state (which may lead to dissidents being interned in psychiatric hospitals) or, in the free world, by the pressure exerted by an absolute intellectual terrorism which uses projective mechanisms and then complains about repression.

The early superego (or the *Ober-ich* which feeds on the pre-ego cannibalistic aggressivity of the infant) therefore demands blind obedience; conversely, *anything that is blind can command absolute obedience* because it reminds us of the archaic mother who is its source, and because of the aggressive charge that supports it. *Obscurity in itself has power* because it reduces the subject to absolute dependence on the archaic mother and to identification with her; the child does not in fact have any precise understanding of its mother's intentions, but it does know, or feel, that blind obedience to her is of crucial importance. Its lived experience is one of identification with omnipotence – not because it understands what it is being ordered to do, but because its lack of understanding reassures it as to the *absolute* nature of its dependency, and confirms that it is dependent (and because omnipotence is essentially totalitarian, the child can participate in it).[5]

We have in France a movement which claims to be psychoanalytic (or even Freudian in a very exclusive sense) and owes its undoubted success to the incomprehensible style of its leader. In the present climate, everything – art, literature, psychoanalysis – has something to gain from being incomprehensible because the archaic mother, like the Sphinx, is worshipped precisely because she is shrouded in mystery. The very conditions of success themselves have changed, and so have value criteria. The content does not matter; all that matters is belonging to the circle that sits at the feet of the omnipotent mother who allows her children to share in her 'mana'. In extreme cases (see Crémant, 1979) the very same content can be despised and

---

4 It is said that discipline is necessary in any army, and in most cases this does seem to be true. Yet in an ideal army there would be no need for strict discipline, as such an army would not act under the pressure of constraint, but under the influence of a shared paternal leader: this leader would be readily obeyed on the grounds that he was *primus inter pares*.

5 Sibylline language is fascinating because its meaning is hidden (and this opens up the possibility of narcissistic regression, because 'anything is possible'). So too are the reasons behind the behaviour of the omnipotent mother. Coming into contact with something that is unknown simply because it is unknowable is like watching a blank screen: there is nothing behind it, but anything can appear on it. It is a reminder of the mother we were afraid to contradict: 'I don't understand anything of it, but I will have to read up about it before I express an opinion. The last thing I want to do is to look like a child' (who understands nothing).

ridiculed, or praised to the skies, depending on whether or not its author 'is one of us' and does or does not share in the 'mana'.

Given that the unconscious experiences the archaic mother as a massive and irresistible force, anything which can assert itself forcefully enough can, by virtue of that quality alone, attain the dignity of the early superego because training is based primarily on a balance of power (real or imaginary).[6] This is why the dynamic of training is so very different from that of education, as defined by the true superego. It is at once more superficial and more profound. It is more superficial because the narcissistically cathected ego does not play any role as such, and it is more profound because its focus is an ego which is purely energetic, primitive and relatively undifferentiated from the id. This is the key to its specific power. We know that it is not possible to train an animal after it has reached a certain age, and that for a child's education to be effective, it is essential that it begins in time. Toilet training acts directly, so to speak, on the sphincter, and the child's whole education will be structured accordingly, even if rationalist-inspired methods are used at later stages.

We can also use the same criteria to examine the power of fashion and of 'the done thing' in various domains. In French, something that is fashionable is said to be '*dans le vent*' [literally, 'in the wind']. The very expression is an allusion to anality (wind = flatus) and the constraints imposed by fashion in fact derive directly from sphincter training. The origins of fashion, and of what is fashionable, are usually somewhat obscure, rather as though fashion were imposed by forces which are as incomprehensible to the public as the intentions of the archaic mother are to the child. Even though we know that fashion is created by dress designers (maternal images with a female function, and a number of male homosexuals take up the profession), they themselves cannot explain what dictates their decisions. According to the perspective I am adopting, the important point is that choice is compulsory: Thou shalt (where and when I say) and Thou shalt not (where and what you will). It is impossible for a society woman not to be fashionable, in the same way that no matter what a given author publishes it will always be rejected by certain members of the public, irrespective of the rectitude or otherwise of his views, because he does not dress fashionably – in other words, does not express himself in fashionable language.

We also know that in North America men are supposed to wear a particular type of hat on one particular day of the year, and that if anyone dares to

6 Ferenczi (1913d) thought that the methods used by a famous Hungarian horse-breaker represented the action of a sort of mixed (maternal and paternal) transference, and attributed the man's success with horses to his ability to strike the right balance between gentleness and firmness. On the other hand, those characteristics might also be seen as an expression of two different maternal images (as for the secret of training horses... we will have to ask the horses).

venture out into the street wearing something else on his head, children will immediately run up to him and knock it off. Their behaviour must surely reflect the power of the primal mother with whom they identify.[7]

We can now sum up the characteristics of the early superego, as opposed to the complete 'oedipal' superego. (I am referring to the primitive superego, not to a paternal superego transmitted by the mother; it is in fact usually a mixed formation.)

The early superego is the result of the training the child receives at the hands of its mother, whereas the complete superego contains all humanity's moral values. As Freud (1933, p. 67) puts it: ·

> Thus a child's superego is in fact constructed on the model not of its parents but of its parents' superego; the contents which fill it are the same and it becomes the vehicle of tradition and of the time-resisting values which have propagated themselves in this manner from generation to generation.

The primitive maternal superego has – in its pure form – a dialectical aspect which makes it hostile to the oedipal superego; as a result, various conflict-ridden positions may emerge; we are all familiar with the tensions that can result from an oscillation between obeying the dictates of the collective

---

7 We are currently witnessing a certain convergence between fashion in the true sense of the word – clothes (and hair) – and cultural trends which are being forced upon us, to the exclusion of all others, on the grounds that they are 'modern', as though that were a convincing argument in itself. Hence the claim: 'That's the way you have to be *nowadays*.' It is tempting to believe that the real point about these trends is that the style of dress they impose is an expression of a basic affective position.

Sartre's existentialism was a fashion too (and Sartre denounced it, just as Marx, presumably for similar reasons, denied being a Marxist), but the father of existentialism omitted to invent a style (a fashionable way of writing). Existentialism became a fashion, not because of its alibi-content but because of the way its devotees dressed. It came to mean an extremely untidy way of dressing (to adopt a euphemism) and a particularly impressive display of hair. Such styles represent an infantile reaction against the early superego ('Get washed and tidy yourself up'). At the same time, it became a fashion thanks to identification with the superego as the source of prohibitions (or orders, which amounts to the same thing).

It might be objected that we all follow fashion in that we all tend to wear similar clothes, and that this is a banal phenomenon. Of course the early superego is part of the superego, but it is no more than a secondary part and does not 'normally' create problems. It was integrated long ago, has its rightful place in a primal stratum of the psyche. Its current unconscious motivations do not have the force of law. Young people have been known to commit suicide because their parents refuse to let them wear their hair long. The heroes of *Easy Rider* – which is, as it happens, a very fine film – die because they want to force the world to accept their freedom to dress as they like. They become a focus for conflict because they are so provocative (one of them wears the American flag as a shirt). No one dies in arguments over clothes unless their clothes represent a deeply conflict-ridden position.

superego and then one's own moral conscience (the influence of the collective superego tends to make the oedipal superego regress back to being a primitive superego). In certain periods of deep regression we therefore see the appearance of a true 'counter-superego' [*Umwertung aller Werte*]. In today's society we find, for instance, that notions such as liberty, justice and honesty no longer have a place in the superego framework, and that they have been replaced by very different notions. The content of the former superego is, moreover, pilloried and ridiculed.

The early superego results from a double identification with the mother: an identification with the primal sadistic affect which is projected on to the primal mother and subsequently reintrojected; then an identification with the content of the child's training. The latter undergoes minor modifications, and is the focus of a secondary identification. The early superego consists of projected moral commands and judgements: it will be used as a stick to beat the oedipal superego with, if not the entire paternal world, and will serve as a defence against the oedipal problematic in general ('avoidance' of the Oedipus).

The maternal superego functions with reference to a well-defined object, which can be represented in material terms (the mother, the written law, rules, dogma and specific concepts) and is always bound up with a 'system' or an ideology ('I have no conscience; Adolf Hitler is my conscience', as Goering put it). It is not a supreme agency which is valid in its own right, or over and beyond contingencies, but a coercive *hic et nunc* with a tendency to become generalized within the present–future dimension. The past, in contrast, is simply evacuated. The early superego is impulsive and coercive; it is implacably sadistic and strives towards the absolute; whereas the oedipal superego, being bound up with the adult ego, has a wealth of experience, develops a sense of the *real*, and therefore becomes more flexible. We can therefore put forward the following proposition.

The early superego performs tasks relating to the present, but claims to be absolute; whereas the oedipal superego *is* absolute, but amenable to a certain relativism. Despite the brutality with which it asserts its authority, the early superego remains superficial (it can be tricked or even corrupted), whereas the complete superego tends to be integrated into the overall personality of the subject.

The early superego does not affect the whole personality, and its authority is restricted to that sector of the ego which was once subject to training. The complete ego uses the partial dependency of the superego as an alibi ('I have done my duty, and no one can criticize me for anything'; 'I play Brahms and Schumann; I have sublimated my anality, I am a sensitive man and whatever else I do is beyond criticism'). It knows only the appearance of reality, its external surface and the lived experience of affect, and nothing of objective reality or causal relations (it belongs to the primary process and has no understanding of the contradiction between the reality governed by the primitive sector of the ego, and the reality that is lived by the complete ego).

Behind the oedipal superego we can glimpse a distant but narcissistically cathected paternal imago for which the subject is willing to sacrifice its life; the primitive superego, on the other hand, incites the subject to murder: either the murder of the other through projection (killing one's own drive in the other) or the sadistic murder of the ego (punishment by the superego). In fact the early superego can neither overcome its fears nor give up the projection that will – or so it imagines – free it from its guilt. The subject will spend its life being torn between two constraints, steering between the Scylla of superego tension and the Charybdis of the tendency to project. The oedipal superego is an internal support and a narcissistic achievement. In that sense, its development merges with the goal of life itself: achieving a moral ideal is indeed a source of narcissistic satisfaction.

Inside the oedipal superego we find, then, the narcissistic ego-ideal (and it should not be forgotten that narcissism was originally the sadistic component's antagonist), but in the case of the early superego, only the sadistic affect is cathected. The complete superego thus has two origins – one narcissistic, the other instinctual – but its essential characteristics pertain to the narcissistic dimension which is, as I have stressed, *essentially prenatal*. Like the foetus itself, the oedipal superego is therefore autonomous, independent and eternal, because (again like the foetus) it has no notion of time. It is ubiquitous and has a universal validity because it is the heir to a foetal coenesthesis which knows no limits, as the foetus merges with the world as a whole. At this level, perspective value-presentations merge with the expression of primal narcissistic coenesthesis (prenatal elation). That coenesthesis provides both the supreme image of perfection and a feeling of total bliss. It will subsequently reappear in an abstract dimension as the aesthetic or the ethical, as the world of the good and the beautiful.

As the foetus ignores considerations of time and space, and as it is infinite, omnipotent and omniscient, it will endow the superego with those same characteristics and thus gives us a psychic reality which will inspire revolutionaries with the notion of the Supreme Being and which religions will elaborate into the concept of divinity.

Chapter Ten

The struggles
and the failure of
Don Quixote-Narcissus

The mere presence of the everlasting idea of the
existence of something infinitely more just and happy
than I, already fills me with abiding tenderness and –
glory – oh, whoever I may be and whatever I may have
done! To know every moment, and to believe that
somewhere there exists perfect peace and happiness for
everyone and for everything, is much more important to
a man than his own happiness. The whole law of human
existence consists merely of making it possible for every
man to bow down before what is infinitely great. If man
were to be deprived of the infinitely great, he would
refuse to go on living, and die of despair. The infinite,
immeasurable is as necessary to man as the little planet
which he inhabits. My friends – all, all my friends: long
live the Great Idea! The eternal, immeasurable Idea!
Every man, whosoever he may be, must bow down
before what is the Great Idea. Even the most stupid man
must have something great. Peter, my boy – Oh, how I
wish I could see them all again! They do not know –
they do not know that the same eternal Great Idea
dwells in them too! (Dostoevsky, 1871)

I

THE HYPHEN that links the two names that go to make up the title of this
essay indicates that Quixotism and narcissism are almost the same
thing, and it is my intention to interpret both the history of Cervantes's
hero and his failure, which coincides with his death. The concept of
narcissism which I will be applying to the case that concerns us is one which I
have been elaborating and expounding for many years; as for the death of the

This paper was read to the Psychoanalytic Association of Madrid, 23 February 1985.

Knight of the Sad Countenance, I will try to show that the novelist's understanding of it coincides to the letter with my own description of the mechanism of the 'Suicide of the melancholic', to use the title of a study written some twenty years ago (Grunberger, 1966).

My thesis, which I feel obliged to summarize rapidly, consists in attributing the manifestations of primary narcissism (and its derivatives) to a prenatal coenesthesis which provides the matrix for a number of characteristics which we normally refer to as narcissism: self-love and self-esteem (in both their positive and their negative forms), the feeling of omnipotence (and related disorders such as megalo- and micromania), the 'memory' of and nostalgia for a particular elational state, and their revival in different conditions, an awareness of being complete and perfect, lordly forms of behaviour, the conviction of being invulnerable, pure and special, the fantasy of being free of all limitations, of being eternal and immortal, and so on. All these characteristics originate in the foetus's special conditions of existence.

This way of looking at narcissism has been criticized, and I intend to take the opportunity to reply to those criticisms here. Reference has, for example, been made to the undeniable fact that the foetus does not always enjoy the blissfully calm and unchanging state that I have described; to the fact that it is often exposed to disturbances of varying severity and that they may cause it pain. In reply to that argument, I would remind my critics that the being which is about to be born may be assumed not to have a complete ego in the metapsychological sense of the term, and that its foetal lived experience is 'recorded' in some way without being 'perceived' or remembered. I refer to the various impressions that are inscribed in the nuclei of the ego, either successively or in parallel. In my more recent writings, I have in fact modified my original thesis by introducing this basic polarity.

It has also been objected that the postnatal individual has no memory of this state of bliss. Yet those who refer to 'primal repression' or to an 'inscription' which leaves no conscious mnemic traces (which would explain, at least in part, why the newborn child continues for a while to live in a state of 'infantile amnesia') overlook the fact that folklore, myths, fairy tales, literature, religions and, at a different level, soteriologies and utopian ideologies, all provide so many indices of this particular lived experience that it has to be taken into account, at least as a hypothesis. Moreover, the notion of absolute bliss, which I attribute to prenatal coenesthesis, is incompatible with the act of remembering in any psychological sense of that term, as we can remember only if we distance ourselves from what we remember, just as it is only at the moment of awakening that we can remember a dream (as Freud writes to Fliess in his letter of 6 December 1896 [1985, p. 208], 'Consciousness and memory are mutually exclusive'; the same notion reappears in the 'mystic writing pad' 1925b, pp. 227-8). Memory necessarily puts an end to the calm and unchanging elational state, as memory presupposes *difference*, and therefore frustrations which distort memories. As in all foetal metabolisms, the instinctual factor introduces a multiplier coefficient into this narcissistic lived experience and supports it (and this is not to be confused with the 'drives' of metapsychology). If the foetus did *perceive* that factor, it would of course detach itself from it.

Don Quixote lives in such a way that nothing – reflection, thought, awareness of obstacles or even perception – comes between his fantasy and its external projection. He lives the elational aspect of the regressive coenesthesis he projects on to the outside world by attributing any irruption of the real that might disturb his vision to the work of 'enchanters' – of whom more later – or to his squire Sancho Panza.

Don Quixote tries to transform his fantasy into action, and he believes in his illusions. This is another form of narcissistic elation. Fairy tales are full of similar situations in which wishes are immediately fulfilled, and magical formulae such as 'Open Sesame' are simply compromises with the secondary process. Compromises may be necessary if we are to designate the content of a wish, but the foetus does not need to compromise as it has no notion of 'content', and its wishes are satisfied (for the same reason) even before they are expressed as wishes.'[1]

Memories are concerned with the past, whereas elation, which originates in prenatal life, contains an element of futurity precisely because it is incomplete. This is one of the reasons why it is so seductive, and it is made more attractive still by the gentle feeling of nostalgia expressed by evocations of, for example, the 'good old days'. But it is only the implicit reference to the future, or to the Christian 'Kingdom of Heaven', that makes them 'good'. We see here an expression of a narcissistic *project*, of man's attempt to regain the state of absolute completeness he once experienced, which was interrupted by his premature birth, by his neoteny. His project is an attempt to repair the damage that has been done to him.

---

1 It is well known that we all see what we want to see (and do not see things we do not want to see). It should also be recalled that there can be something 'grotesque' about transference (Freud, 1916-17, p. 442), that love is blind, and that eye-witnesses rarely agree with one another. Any 'committed' person sees reality in terms of his commitment, to say nothing of the various other forms of suggestion that may be at work. Any 'faith' can in fact be regarded as a form of illusion. But beliefs are, to a greater or lesser extent, fragile, which is why they have to resort to sacramentalization. Theologians can get round the problem of doubt only by making it a precondition to the true faith. The true faith overcomes doubt and magnifies it by throwing down a challenge to reality: *Credo quia absurdum*. The secondary process gradually undermines faith, but a nucleus persists because it is rooted in the primary process ('Yes, I know, but . . .'). This is why Don Quixote is committed to an endless struggle: he is defending his faith against his own doubts (which he projects on to a Sancho Panza and others). And that in turn explains the intensity of his struggle and his ultimate defeat.

Ontogenesis equals phylogenesis, and we know that the evolution of the foetus is a recapitulation of animal embryonic forms; the process thus has deep biological roots. The animal which lives on in the human foetus and in the neonate is narcissistically perfect in the sense that there is no interval between the triggering of an instinctual demand and its fulfilment. When the human being is born, there is a huge discrepancy between its narcissistic demands for immediate recuperation and its real *Hilflosigkeit* (helplessness), but it is also born with an assurance that it will be able to return to its primal state, with an ineradicable *hope* that feeds on primitive antenatal forces. Hence the peculiar intensity of primary narcissism. It is this hope which inspires man to attempt to make up for his loss and to transform his wounds into a very positive asset (humanization).[2]

II

Dostoevsky provides us with descriptions of regressive narcissistic bliss in his accounts of the epileptic aura (the author himself suffered from the *morbus sacer*). The following passage is taken from *The Idiot* (Dostoevsky, 1869, p. 258):

> He was thinking, incidentally, that there was a moment or two in his epileptic condition almost before the fit itself (if it occurred during his waking hours) when suddenly amid the sadness, spiritual darkness and depression, his brain seemed to catch fire at brief moments, and with an extraordinary momentum his vital forces were strained to the utmost all at once. His sensation of being alive and his awareness increased tenfold at those moments which flashed by like lightning. His mind and heart were flooded by a dazzling light. All his agitation, all his doubts and worries seemed composed in a twinkling, culminating in a great calm, full of serene and harmonious joy and hope ... 'What if it is a disease?' he decided at last. 'What does it matter if it is an abnormal tension, if the result, if the moment of sensation, remembered and analysed in a state of health, turns out to be harmony and beauty brought to their highest point of perfection, and gives a feeling, undivined and undreamt of till then, of completeness, proportion, reconciliation, and an ecstatic and prayerful fusion in the highest synthesis of life?'

2 A certain halo surrounds great criminals because the public cathects them narcissistically. (Freud [1914, p. 89] speaks of the criminal as being narcissistic.) This too can be explained in terms of the persistence of the foetal mode of their narcissism. Like the foetus, the criminal is autonomous; a law unto himself, free from social constraints. He lives in a world of his own, but is a parasite on society, just as the foetus is a parasite living off its mother. Dostoevsky was fascinated by two types of men: saints and great criminals. Both are structures on to which man can project his idea of narcissistic completeness.

A similar description occurs in an account of a dream in *The Devils* (Dostoevsky, 1871, p. 695). The dream concerns Claude Lorrain's 'Acis and Galatea', which the dreamer had seen in a gallery in Dresden; he refers to it as 'The Golden Age':

A corner of the Greek archipelago, blue, caressing waves, islands and rocks, a foreshore covered in lush vegetation, a magic vista in the distance, a spell-binding sunset – it is impossible to describe it in words. Here was the cradle of European civilization, here were the first scenes from mythology, man's paradise on earth. Here a beautiful race of men had lived... A wonderful dream, a sublime illusion! The most incredible dream that has ever been dreamed, but to which all mankind has devoted all its powers during the whole of its existence, for which it has sacrificed everything, for which it has died on the cross and for which its prophets have been killed, without which nations will not live and cannot even die.

These texts are typical ('the cradle of civilization', 'a sublime illusion', 'paradise on earth'), and it is because we find a similar passage in *Don Quixote* that I place such emphasis on this literature. I refer to the episode of the meeting with the goatherds (Cervantes, 1604–14, pp. 85–6):

Happy the age and happy the times on which the ancients bestowed the name of golden, not because gold, which in this iron age of ours is rated so highly, was attainable without labour in those fortunate times, but rather because the people of those days did not know those two words *thine* and *mine*. In that blessed age all things were held in common. No man, to gain his common sustenance, needed to make any effort greater than to reach up his hand and pluck it from the strong oaks, which literally invited him to taste their sweet and savoury fruits. Clear springs and running rivers offered him their sweet and limpid water in glorious abundance... the careful and provident bees formed their commonwealth, offering to every hand without interest the fertile produce of their fragrant toil.[3]

The inspiration behind this passage is the same that inspires the passages cited from *The Idiot* or *The Devils*, the difference being that here, prenatal bliss is represented primarily by oral-narcissistic autonomy (compare the biblical reference [Matthew 6: 26, 28] to the fowls of the air and the lilies of the field). If I may digress for a moment, it seems appropriate to comment on Don Quixote's age (and that of Cervantes) more generally. In so far as he is a

3 Dostoevsky himself (1869, p. 219) refers to this passage in his account of Myshkin's letter to Aglaya: 'Next day she took it out again and put it into a thick and strongly bound volume... And it was only a week later that she happened to discover what the book was. It was *Don Quixote de la Mancha*. Aglaya burst out laughing – what at, no one knew.'

fanatic, Don Quixote is a monk, but in so far as he lives on the margins of society, it is tempting to see him as a 'high-class' tramp, so to speak. He is like many irresolute people who dabble at being students or at various other activities, and live from hand to mouth. If they go into analysis, we find that their classic neuroses and depressions mask a strong narcissistic component, which explains their characteristic behaviour: the narcissist chooses his solution, and the illusion of narcissistic completeness replaces the process of oedipal maturation. Fantasy takes precedence over the despised pragmatic element, and the notion of time is completely absent[4] because, given that he has the whole of eternity before him, the narcissist can afford to wait. We know that Don Quixote lived as a bachelor on what was left of his fortune, that he enjoyed hunting and that his favourite pastime was reading books of chivalry – in other words, indulging in fantasies. Goncharov's hero Oblomov (Goncharov, 1858) and, closer to home, Fellini's film *I Vitelloni*, are other examples that come to mind.

Don Quixote is a narcissist who lives a lonely and marginal life, rejecting the love of men and women (his adoration of Dulcinea will be discussed below) and dreaming of winning worldwide fame and eternal glory. One day, he resolves to make his fantasies come true. He is his own sovereign, is dependent upon no one, and has no qualms about ennobling himself (Don) by taking sonorous names, promising himself an empire, and offering to make his squire the governor of an island. It is a truism to say that Don Quixote is a narcissist, and the point has often been made in the vast literature devoted to him. It is when we attempt to fit that characteristic into an overall pattern that the difficulties begin. In her essay on Don Quixote, Helene Deutsch (1937) describes the history of the knight errant as one of narcissistic overcompensation. In her view, then, his narcissism is a *secondary* factor (a compensation for something else) and his narcissistic hypertrophy is the result of its compensatory nature. She writes (p. 220): 'All cathexes, from the most primitive instinctual drives to the energies which bring the ego into contact with reality, are withdrawn and become agglomerated within the ego into a single narcissistic force.' For my own part, I am convinced that the narcissistic factor is primary and that the entire clinical picture results from this overriding primitive orientation. At the same time, however, narcissistic hypertrophy is brutally frustrated and therefore becomes traumatic (existential crisis).

4 Cf. Prince Myshkin's description (Dostoevsky, 1869, p. 259) of the narcissistic aura that precedes his epileptic fits: 'At that moment the extraordinary saying that *there shall be time no longer* becomes, somehow, comprehensible to me.'

III

Man is narcissistically frustrated at birth, but at the same time he inherits certain characteristics of prenatal life, including a peculiarly strong primal instinctual vigour. We find one of the many indices of this archaic strength in the famous *grasping reflex* which paediatricians always find so astonishing, not to mention the strength of the neonate's vocal chords, which it exercises in response to excitations it cannot master (in terms of the psychic economy, I attribute great importance to screaming). But as certain experiments demonstrate, this energetic precociousness is short-lived: when they are only a few weeks old, young babies can swim quite spontaneously, but they soon lose their almost innate ability to do so.

In the light of the above comments, I now feel obliged to give a brief account of the relationship between psychosexual development and narcissism. This will inevitably involve some repetition, for which I must beg the reader's forgiveness.

We may assume that from the outset psychosexual development takes place on two levels: one instinctual (oedipal), the other narcissistic. This initial duality will be resolved by a gradual synthesis of primary narcissism and the palaeo-aggressive and sexual dimension, with both components undergoing quantitative and qualitative modifications as they are integrated into the ego. If, however, this process is for some reason disturbed or blocked, my schema takes on a very different aspect or is, rather, replaced by another (I stress that I am of course sketching nothing more than a schema).

In the earliest stages of life, narcissism, which originates in prenatal existence, merges with what I term the 'monad'. The monad is constituted by the newborn child and the narcissistic confirmation it receives from his mother's touch and gaze. At this point the mother is, of course, neither a sexual object nor even an oral object; in other words, she is asexual, and during the transference certain patients compare her to a *landscape* or a familiar *atmosphere* which can support primary narcissism. (My description of this aspect of the monad – a primal positive 'transference' – owes a lot to a German-speaking woman patient who spoke of a *Mutterlandschaft* [maternal landscape] and coined the adjective *mamamässig* [conforming to Mummy].) Such terms relate to experiences that predate the establishment of object relations. This narcissism is, however, immediately traumatized (absolute narcissistic regression or fixation can result only in psychosis) and the trauma results in the formation of what I call the *double narcissistic nucleus*: one nucleus being the expression of pure narcissism, the other the expression of a certain reactional aggressivity with special characteristics of its own.

If we accept that this psychic formation exists – and if we further accept that there is a parallel and oedipally orientated process of evolution, which is inevitably fragile and results in a stunted ego – we arrive at the concept of a *bipolar* ego in which palaeo-aggressivity and primary narcissism coexist. However, *both factors retain their original characteristics.* The *pseudo-ego* which emerges from this formation does, even so, assert its ascendancy. Indeed, it does so all the more brutally in so far as its very existence is threatened precisely because it is so intrinsically conflict-ridden (aggressivity and narcissism). Because involvement in the oedipal problematic might imperil the primarily narcissistic character of the pseudo-ego, it adopts a *pseudo-oedipal* defence – in other words, it resists that development and the paternal principle itself, with all its derivatives (the Oedipus, the sense of reality, causality and pragmatic reality in general). Reality becomes an enemy to be combated, and the need to combat it strengthens the narcissistic illusion which is attempting to assert that it is equivalent, or even superior, to oedipal maturity. A constant *challenge* is offered to the real, and is supported by the *denarcissization*, or contemptuous devalorization, of the Oedipus and its derivatives.

The bipolar ego consists, then, of a twofold primal nucleus (see Grunberger, 1983), and its component elements are in conflict. On the one hand, Don Quixote enjoys a narcissistic omnipotence; he fights giants, fells them with a single sword thrust, then reconstitutes his own body, which has been cut in two, with the help of a magic balsam, simply replacing his trunk on the lower part of his body. At the same time he has to fight reality, which fights back in the shape of *enchanters*, who are also essentially the products of narcissism. The result is a bipolar ego, both of whose contradictory aspects are narcissistic. The adventure of the enchanted boat contains (p. 661) a good description of this polarity:

> 'Enough', said Don Quixote to himself. 'It would be preaching in the wilderness to try and induce this rabble by prayers to do any virtuous act. Two powerful enchanters must have met in opposition in this adventure, the one frustrating the other's designs. One provided me with the boat, and the other threw me out.'

Narcissism cathects the myth, and aggressivity protects it. Don Quixote is a valiant knight who possesses every virtue – that is to say, all the content of the narcissistic ideal of his day (an ego-ideal): he frees the oppressed, rights wrongs, defends the poor, widows and orphans; but at the same time he occasionally adopts a perspective which is that of the *Raubritter* [robber-knight] rather than that of the Crusader.

We know that narcissistic fantasies have to be absolute, and that they must be stubbornly defended against any adulteration. The narcissist is by definition a fanatic and whenever he becomes involved in a discussion, even over an apparent trifle, he is in fact defending his Salvation because, in defending it, he is defending himself against his own doubts about the absolute value of his narcissistic phallus. In so far as it is a narcissistic fantasy, an ideology is constrictive, absolute, total and highly cathected; the whole of the subject's libido must be mobilized to support its cathexis, and to throw down a challenge to the real.[5]

In his battle against the oedipal principle of reality and causality, the narcissist tends to elevate the narcissistic principle, which is supported by the Primal Mother, above the paternal principle. I take literary descriptions of the golden age, and in particular Don Quixote's description of it, to illustrate my point, and in order to show that he is not only expressing his nostalgia for prenatal regression, but wants to force others to share his vision. He tells his squire (p. 158): 'You must know, friend Sancho, that I was born by the will of Heaven in this our iron age to revive the age of gold, or the golden age.' He thus becomes a Redeemer, the Saviour of mankind. Don Quixote needs others to confirm him in his narcissistic expansion and assumption, and the Christlike element in his behaviour has often been noted.

But Quixote is not fighting in the name of Christ. His goal is to establish a solid reputation and to win glory for himself, and Dulcinea, the Lady of his heart, provides him with both a symbol and a projective surface. She is *a narcissistic ideal who has to be kept apart and protected from any hint of carnal desire.* She is also a highly idealized projection of his *ego-ideal* (her name betrays her maternal origins, as it suggests *dulce* and *dulzura* ('sweet', 'sweetness'), and perhaps the *dulzura* of milk. Don Quixote tries to confirm to himself that he has accomplished his narcissistic project by getting others to recognize the absolute validity of his image (by recognizing the image of Dulcinea, who is in a sense a repository for his own image). And that absolute necessity is the real object of his quest; he fights solely in order to achieve his own object. As for the obsessive nature of his quest, its violence stems from the subject's own doubts about the uniquely wonderful beauty of Dulcinea and from his desire to force others to share his faith, despite his doubts (and in fact he knows full well that the said Dulcinea is in reality a fat, ugly village slut

---

5 Space limitations preclude an analysis of ideology, and I cannot go into the question of the content of ideology and the value of its content here. I will, however, mention the *function* ideology plays within the psychic economy. Before doing so, I would remind the reader of Raymond Aron's (1955) distinction between *ideology* and *ideothèque*. An *ideothèque* contains a certain number of ideas, each of which has an *objective* value, and those ideas are used by the ego, whose economy is governed by the secondary process. The *ad hoc* content of an ideology, in contrast, is subordinated to a narcissistic ideal (a bipolar ego controls the whole ego; affects control mental activity), which has the function of establishing a narcissistic agency that can capture affectivity and function in a regressive mode. The most minor element in this formation's content has its effects on affectivity, and this may result in certain characteristic disorders at the level of thought. Don Quixote is convinced that his delusions are real, and that reality (in the shape of the windmills, for example) is the work of enchanters – or, in other words, of fantasy.

with a moustache and a special talent for preparing pickled pork. His *alter ego* Sancho says so out loud).

Don Quixote sets off, then, to bring about the triumph of the reign of narcissism, and his veneration for his idol is a means to an end. He calls upon those he meets to pay tribute to the wonderful and unique beauty of Dulcinea, to confess to her beauty. Similarly, during the Moscow trials, Stalin was obliged to make his Communist comrades confess, as they were the one object on to which he could successfully project his own doubts. The Inquisition did not persecute Christians or Jews; but it did force confessions from 'new Christians' – in other words, from converted Jews, whose faith in Christianity was supposedly less than perfect. Lapsed believers have to be rooted out to preserve the purity of the faith which is projected on to them, or on to the 'purity of the race'.

A narcissist who comes up against oedipal conflict can, then, resolve his conflicts by adopting the 'narcissistic solution'. This can be either a fantasy construct of his own or one which others have constructed for similar purposes. The construct has the value and function of a fetish because it is narcissistically cathected and because its value can put an end to conflict or act as a *substitute for the equilibrium which the oedipal subject tries to find by harmonizing his internal agencies.* Don Quixote adopts the literary creations he finds in books of chivalry; they are full of charm and possess every possible virtue, and he can thus attain a higher degree of ideal narcissistic accomplishment. But in order to do that he has to return to a regressive level. He must become an ascetic, as the instinctual component has to give way to pure narcissism. But as he does, after all, have a body, he must, so to speak, transpose his pure narcissistic ideal on to an ideal figure who exists only at the level of fantasy:

> You clod, you ignominious vagabond . . . You viper-tongued villain, who do you think has conquered this kingdom and cut this giant's head off . . . if it is not the might of Dulcinea . . . She fights and conquers through me, and I live and breathe and have my life and being in her. (p. 264)

The violent tone of the remarks addressed to the poor squire reveals not only the presence of the element of conflict, but also that of the palaeo-aggressivity of frustration, which can be discharged only through projection. Whilst aggressivity can be overcome by projection, sexuality, too, must be warded off. Greedy though Don Quixote may be for purely narcissistic success (worldly, poetic and heroic success), his response to even the slightest erotic approach is an energetic *Noli me tangere*, to use another biblical phrase. His ideal image will be reflected, as though in a negative mirror, and thrown into relief by Sancho – who displays, in contrast, a lack of panache, a lack of courage, a lack of ideals, a lack of culture and an absolute lack of spirituality. Anality also finds expression in the wealth of vulgar proverbs which Sancho Panza repeatedly drops into the conversation like so many little turds. Having rid himself of all its dross, Don Quixote is now in a position to offer a major challenge to reality, which he begins to see as a veritable source of provocation. When, for example, the merchants from whom he is trying to extort a declaration as to the unique perfection of his idol insist on seeing a portrait of Dulcinea, he becomes aggressive, couches his lance and charges: 'If I were to show you her ... what merit would there be in your confessing so obvious a truth?' (His comment is reminiscent of the Lord's remarks to those who asked him for a sign.) He goes on: 'The essence of the matter is that you must believe, confess, affirm, swear and maintain it without seeing her. If you will not ...' (p. 51). Anyone who dares to contradict him is not only ignorant but a 'traitor', and the 'knight' (the innkeeper) who asks him for money is a 'discourteous knight'.[6]

Don Quixote tries to preserve his illusion to the bitter end, and throughout the adventures that befall him during his quest he indulges in constant speechifying in an attempt to defend his point of view. The book, which might be seen as the ancestor of our comic strips, thus becomes a long series of speeches, or rather an interminable dispute between fantasy and reality, between the superego and the ego-ideal; and the moral agency eventually becomes a caricature of itself. We will look at the outcome of the dispute later.

IV

I have no intention of analysing Cervantes, or even the mechanism of sublimation, as to do so would distract me from my theme. But the creator and creation are so intimately linked that it does seem useful to draw certain comparisons between Cervantes and Don Quixote, particularly since the book does contain a large number of autobiographical details – indeed, it would be surprising if it did not.

To begin with, we know that Don Quixote is a late creation, as the author died only two years after the publication of Part II of his novel. In qualitative terms *Don Quixote* has, moreover, a very special place in Cervantes's literary *œuvre*; it brought him fame and, so to speak, a second lease on life. Don Quixote also acquires a second lease on life when Alonso Quijano or Quixada,

---

6 We find the same idea in Dostoevsky's description of the dream of the golden age (1871, p. 695). The dreamer accuses himself of having betrayed it by introducing elements of reality into the ideal society of the golden age, and of having destroyed the happiness of its inhabitants. The narcissistic adolescent who measures everyday life by the yardstick of narcissistic perfection also has a tendency to describe adults as traitors, and even to see himself as having betrayed his ideals as he grows older.

a minor provincial squire, becomes the knight errant known as Don Quixote de la Mancha.

We know that Don Quixote spent his life reading 'books of chivalry', and that he developed an insatiable passion for them. He reminds one of those adolescents who, when confronted with the oedipal problematic, plunge into an oral-narcissistic regression and into fantasy. Initially, Don Quixote's fantasy is non-elective and personal ('His brain dried up and he lost his wits': p. 32), but he then limits his choice of fantasies and finally adopts a specific, complete fantasy whose *ad hoc* content provides a set framework for his narcissistic hypertrophy. When fantasization reaches this point, we can speak of a myth or a system of beliefs, or of an ideology. In the case of Don Quixote, we find a personal variation on the myth of the gallant knight: the myth of the knight errant. That myth is, in part, determined by fashion, but the fashion in question is out of date, and our hero revives it for his own purposes; the myth is a product of the collective unconscious, and it has a stable nucleus which allows it to plunge into the depths of the collective unconscious and then re-emerge.

Cervantes was, in the last analysis, what is known as a failure (a poet who aspires to military glory is one thing, but a tax collector employed in provisioning the Armada is another), as are so many creative artists, and as was his hero. Both aspired to gain honour, or even fame, and in their own way they fulfilled their ambitions.

The narcissist lives his life as though he were immortal, and will risk his life without hesitation ('nothing can happen to me'). He also wants 'everything at once', but in certain circumstances he can wait: time is on his side, and he is expecting a miracle.[7]

Both Don Quixote and his creator are neurotics. The poet from Alcala had a stammer, and in sexual terms he appears to have been somewhat inhibited, to judge by the very well-documented book Byron (1988) has recently devoted to him, to say nothing of the other authors who have made the same point. As for Don Quixote, he lived the life of a virtuous bachelor, vegetating in what was left of his family estate. He was also an insomniac and Cervantes makes much

---

7 The narcissist lives his fantasy as though it were real – and that is his problem. He believes that he has been promised an apotheosis, that it is his due, and that its fulfilment has nothing to do with reality. The adventure of the Afflicted Waiting-woman (Cervantes, pp. 726–35) is a good example. Don Quixote mounts Clavileño, a wooden horse which is faster than thought, flies above the clouds (he is in fact a victim of a trick played on him by the Duke), and then finds himself precisely where he was before he set off on his imaginary ride. As the parchment found in the garden puts it (p. 732): 'By the mere attempting of it the illustrious Don Quixote has finished and achieved the adventure of the Countess Trifaldi, otherwise called the Afflicted Waiting-woman. Malambruno [his opponent] is completely content and satisfied.' Malambruno's admission confirms Don Quixote's narcissistic triumph.

of this symptom (p. 32), which he sees as the source of the 'madness' which, thanks to his passion for reading, made him set out to look for adventure. There is evidence of depression in both cases, and whilst Cervantes's defence against that was to lead an adventurous life, to say nothing of sublimating, Don Quixote invents a new life for himself. In his fantasy life, he wanders along with the typical gait which we see in the work of every artist who has illustrated the story of the Knight of the Sad Countenance. Cervantes's genius lies not only in his creation of a literary figure who has brought him unrivalled fame down the ages, but also in the accuracy of his diagnosis of his hero's illness and of his in-depth analysis of the final stages of the illness which led to Don Quixote's death. The entire diagnosis coincides with the broad themes of my own study of the suicide of the melancholic (unlike my colleagues Josip Bea and Victor Hernández (1984), who put forward the interesting idea that Don Quixote was cured before he died, I reach a more pessimistic conclusion, as we shall see).

Throughout his many adventures, Don Quixote succeeds in sustaining the illusion that his fantasies are real; their veracity is confirmed by the real and personal proof he produces in support of them. The inevitable doubts that arise are projected on to Sancho Panza, and at one point his convictions are corroborated by the Duke, who is delighted to have such a gallant knight as his guest. As he enters the castle, Don Quixote silently thanks heaven (p. 667), for 'This was the first time that he was positively certain of being a true and no imaginary knight errant, since he found himself treated just as he had read these knights were treated in past ages.' The past comes to life again, and reality coincides with fiction, or vice versa.

Yet before long, it is also possible to detect signs of the melancholia that is to come (Don Quixote's earlier reaction might be seen as an expression of the manic phase of a cyclical illness) and indications that the narcissistic current is about to dry up because it has been exhausted by the earlier manic outburst: 'Yet in the midst of those highly spiced banquets and snow-cooled drinks I seemed to be confined within the straits of hunger' (p. 387).

Even at the banquet itself, the intervention of a guest described simply as 'the Ecclesiastic' provokes a similar reaction. Turning to the Duke, he criticizes him for playing such cruel tricks upon our hero (p. 673):

> 'Your excellency, sir, will have to account to our Lord for this good man's doings. This Don Quixote, or Don Fool, or whatever you call him, cannot be such an idiot, I imagine, as your Excellency would have him be, seeing the opportunities you put in his way of carrying on with his fooleries and nonsense.' Then, turning to address Don Quixote, he said: 'And you, simpleton, who has driven it into your brain that you are a knight errant...'

Don Quixote replies at length, and in order to help sustain his illusion, the Duke really does grant Sancho the governorship of one of his islands. But the rot has already set in. As he leaves his hosts, Don Quixote is thrown to the ground and trampled by a herd of bulls, which he recognizes for what they are. Is this a step on the road to cure? On the contrary: things are beginning to get worse. This is certainly the first time Don Quixote has behaved normally, that he has not tried to blame enchanters or his clumsy horse for his failure and subsequent humiliation; but, given that he cannot use disavowal or projection to mask his narcissistic wound, it reappears, and the resultant aggressivity and frustration turn against the ego, which becomes denarcissized. Don Quixote goes off in a sorry state of mind, and refuses to visit the Arcadian shepherdesses he charmed during the banquet at which he was given the place of honour.

We have now reached the point of no return, and death is inevitable. Don Quixote is well aware of it; he says so and goes on saying so (p. 847): 'Let me die a victim of my thoughts and of the force of my misfortunes... When I expected palms, triumphs and crowns, I have seen myself this morning pounded by the feet of unclean and filthy animals.' Finally, another classic symptom of melancholia appears: 'I think I may let myself die of hunger, the most cruel of all deaths.' A violent and vulgar altercation with Sancho ensues. In narcissistic regression, the negative nucleus eventually gains the upper hand by cathecting anality. The crisis takes the form of a long dispute over how many lashes Sancho has to inflict upon himself in order to disenchant Dulcinea; the blows are in fact converted into money, and the rate of exchange fluctuates as the discussion proceeds.

It is at this point that Don Quixote falls into the hands of bandits. Once again, he recognizes them for what they are and does not resist. On the contrary, he surrenders (p. 856): 'They found Don Quixote on foot, his horse unbridled and his lance resting against a tree; in short, being utterly defenceless, he thought it best to fold his hands, bow his head, and reserve himself for a better occasion.' His identification with the negative narcissistic nucleus now becomes even more clearly marked: he makes friends with the bandit leader, who offers to guide and protect him on his way to Barcelona.

In Barcelona he is fêted by the bandit's friends and, after a splendid supper, the dance begins. But this time, the knight simply looks ridiculous. The narcissist who never let slip an opportunity to mock the representatives of the paternal order now turns his scorn against his own ego: 'It was a sight indeed to see the knight's form, tall, lank, lean and sallow, tightly encased in his clothes, so awkward and, even worse, by no means nimble' (p. 872). The final collapse occurs when the Knight of the White Moon challenges Don Quixote. He hurtles into the poor knight with such force that he knocks him to the ground, and Don Quixote is forced to say 'in a low and feeble voice... "Drive your lance home, knight, and rid me of life, since you have robbed me of honour"' (p. 890).

The Knight of the White Moon is in fact none other than Carrasco, the bachelor from Don Quixote's home village who, together with a few other neighbours, has staged this farce with a therapeutic aim in mind. But it is too late, and their psychodrama has the opposite effect (to that extent, this episode reminds one of those inclined to somatize: the analyst cures their symptom, but in so doing removes the obstacles which prevented them from inflicting terrible injuries on themselves). Had the Knight of the White Moon allowed himself to be beaten, Don Quixote's contrived victory might – perhaps – have had a therapeutic effect. But the proud hidalgo's defeat is the final straw. Don Quixote loses his strength and has to take to his bed. He then sets off back to his village, 'Don Quixote unarmed and in travelling clothes, and Sancho on foot' (p. 895). They begin to talk about the future, and our hero takes the opportunity to return to his fantasy of the golden age, although in more modest terms than when he set out, and his timid daydream is in fact a deceptive sign (the plan is now to become shepherds: 'we will wander through the mountains, woods and meadows, singing here, lamenting there...': p. 902). Quixote may well seem to have recovered and to be behaving as a sane and sensible family man, but that merely disguises his unconscious decision to do away with himself, and it is because he has taken that decision that he can act so serenely.

Sancho has by now whipped himself in order to disenchant Dulcinea, and as they approach the village, Don Quixote is confident that he will see her on the road. She never appears. Her admirer's narcissism is no longer there to create her, irradiate her and idealize her, and she has been precipitated into the void. Don Quixote is seized by a fever and forced to take to his bed for six days. His friends try to cheer him, but to no avail. His dejection persists, and the doctor tells him to look to his soul's salvation, since his body is in danger. His housekeeper, niece and squire weep, 'as if he already lay dead before their eyes' (p. 935), but he makes a brief recovery, calls them to his bedside and tells them that he lost his reason because of his continuous reading of books of chivalry, which he now describes (p. 935) as 'detestable'.

When a narcissist decathects his object, he rejects it and begins to despise it because it has suddenly been analized once more. When Rimbaud decathected his poetry, he called it 'dishwater'; it became rubbish, and he wanted nothing more to do with it. The belated wisdom of Alonso Quijano, once known as Don Quixote, is simply the expression of this massive withdrawal of cathexis. When Don Quixote dictates his will he shares out his modest possessions, forgetting no one, but he makes no mention of Dulcinea. It is as though she had never existed. Don Quixote has no illusions left, but one final and supreme narcissistic act remains to be performed: he must shuffle off a mortal coil that was the bearer of a double narcissistic nucleus which has been drained of all its cathexis. He plunges into the void, as did the Sphinx when she was defeated by the paternal principle (the riddle of the three ages of man) represented by Oedipus.

Chapter Eleven

On fetishism*

This essay has a threefold aim:

1 to provide a critique of the prevailing theory of fetishism;
2 to relaunch the debate on fetishism;
3 to outline a new approach to the problem by replacing the key
   words in the theory – castration, denial and splitting – with the
   words regression, narcissism and anality.

THERE IS obviously a feeling that the way psychoanalytic doctrine deals with this perversion is somewhat inadequate, and that the feeling is expressed even by those who use that doctrine and make it the cornerstone of their theorization. Pontalis, for instance, writes (1970, p. 70):

> Besides, one must admit that, since Freud, the clinical experience of psychoanalysis has not always been able to specify the peculiarity of the fetish object and the anxious desire which precipitates its quest: it could be said that any strongly invested subject, which one 'cannot do without', could be considered a fetish... Was his [Freud's] hesitation caused by a conceptual lack, or can one see in this something which could be related precisely to the very nature of the object?

The fact is that whilst the definition mentioned by Pontalis (something 'one cannot do without') does conform to our day-to-day clinical practice, it

This paper was read to the Société Psychanalytique de Paris on 18 November 1975 and was first published as 'Essai sur le fétichisme' in *Revue française de psychanalyse* 2, 1976.

cannot be regarded as a truly scientific definition because, quite apart from its lack of precision, it is a negative definition. Freud himself defines the fetish-object in the same mode: as something which, whilst it is necessary, has no sexual characteristics in any real sense; the paragraph devoted to fetishism in the *Three Essays* (Freud, 1905b, p. 153) is subtitled: 'Unsuitable substitutes for the sexual object – Fetishism'.

Most authors pay homage, so to speak, to the theory of fetishism, and then ignore it and allow themselves to be guided – in, for instance, their diagnoses – by their clinical instincts, and in most cases this proves perfectly satisfactory. Masud Khan (1965, 1979) is no doubt right when he labels a homosexual who is obsessed with foreskins a 'fetishist', but according to the theory of disavowal, the foreskin should mean the maternal phallus. Naturally enough, the author resists the temptation to find it there.

When it comes to a differential diagnosis, the hesitation noted by Pontalis is even more pronounced: thus the perverse Jacob who figures in Sidney Stewart's remarkable study (1972) does indeed have an enema-fetish, but he could also be classified under the rubric of masochism (he himself thought he was a sadist), not to mention his scopophiliac tendencies. The list is far from exhaustive as we also encounter homosexual fetishists, transvestite fetishists, and so on.

It should also be remembered that the father of masochism (which is named after Sacher-Masoch) was a fur-fetishist, and as for Jean-Jacques Rousseau (1782), we will never know which gave him more pleasure: exhibiting his buttocks or being whipped as a result (I leave aside the other facets of his exhibitionism).

Freud's theory of fetishism is initially expounded in the *Three Essays* and in a number of other texts written at much the same time (*Delusions and Dreams in Jensen's 'Gradiva'* [1907], *Leonardo da Vinci and a Memory of his Childhood* [1910a], The 'Rat Man' case [1909b] and 'A case of foot-fetishism', the unpublished paper read to the Vienna Psycho-Analytical Society in 1914). These texts provide all the elements which matter from the clinical point of view, but, as often with Freud's texts, they also contain material that has yet to be exploited. Unfortunately, Freud – no doubt surrendering to a pessimistic impulse[1] – then abandons those elements and develops a different perspective, particularly in 'Fetishism' (Freud, 1927). Psychoanalysis therefore in fact has two separate theories of fetishism; we will now examine both sides of the doctrine, which are separated by a caesura.

1 Sadger (1921) reports Freud as remarking that even an author who claimed to have elucidated the role of the fetish could not put an end to fetishism. The reference is no doubt to the unpublished paper on 'A case of foot-fetishism' read to the Vienna Society in March 1914 (Cf. Jones, 1954, vol. 2, pp. 342-3).

Freud initially (1905b, p. 154) ascribes the formation of the fetish to 'an after-effect of some sexual impression, received as a rule in early childhood', and speaks of 'a symbolic connection of thought'. But he also notes, in connection with foot- or hair-fetishism, that it is not always possible 'to trace the course of these connections with certainty' (in a footnote added to the text in 1910, he specifically states that the 'shoe or slipper is a corresponding symbol of the *female* genitals': 1905b, p. 155, n 1). In a second footnote, also added in 1910 (see below p. 145), he discovers the importance of the pleasure of smelling in the choice of a fetish, and of the 'coprophiliac pleasure in smelling' (and makes a distinction between pleasurable and unpleasurable smells; the latter relate to anal eroticism. Only a clean foot can become a fetish, and an opposition is thus established between fetishism and perversion), and finally identifies the basic and constitutive element in the theory: 'the foot represents a woman's penis, the absence of which is deeply felt'.

We will have an opportunity to return to this point, and we may therefore move on to the second period in Freud's theorization, a period characterized by the systematization of the concept of disavowal or denial [*Verleugnung*].[2]

You will be familiar with the arguments Freud uses to justify his theory of the disavowal of female castration; he bases them on the fear of castration and the horror inspired by the sight of the female genitals. To take fear of castration first: we know that this is a general phenomenon and, indeed, that it is too general to be invoked in this particular case.

According to Freud, the fetish overcomes the fear of castration, and thus provides the individual with a defence against castration; but we often encounter perverts who are both homosexual and fetishists. In theory, a fetish should also allow the subject to engage in normal coitus, but this is in fact rarely the case; on the contrary, the fetishist achieves orgasm without coitus. Finally, in clinical practice we frequently encounter cases in which the subject eroticizes the fear of castration, seeks it out, and – effectively – makes it his 'fetish'.

I am not referring only to the case reported by Angel Garma (Garma, 1956)[3] but to specific cases taken from my own clinical experience, such as the case

---

2 The most important text in this connection is 'Fetishism' (Freud, 1927). Freud does, however, make sporadic use of the notion of disavowal in earlier papers (1923a, 1924b, 1924c). Although it is now fashionable to split hairs over this, I insist that the German terms *Verwerfung* and *Verleugnung* should be regarded as interchangeable synonyms.

3 'Contrary to what is frequently stated in psychoanalytic writings, *his considering the female genital organ as phallic had by no means the aim of overcoming his castration-anxiety*, but quite the reverse... *His fantasies about a phallic vagina were analogous in form and content to those he had about the toothed vagina.* Neither of them relieved, but rather intensified his castration-anxiety' (Garma, 1956, p. 415).

of Otto, which will be described in more detail below. Otto regularly dreamed of having sexual relations with his mother by bringing their buttocks into contact; at the same time, he saw in his dream that he had no sexual organ, male or female, on the front of his body. Besides, the belief that women have a penis is not enough to explain the choice of fetish, the fascination it has for the fetishist, or the way he adores his object.

As to the *horror* that the female organ is said to inspire in the boy, it is difficult to understand why it should inspire such a frantic search for that very same organ. That search can be so frantic that Sadger (1921) can write that the fetish is primarily the whole female sex organ (pubic hair – hair, fur, shoe – a hollow organ, etc.). Virtually all the fetishists I have had the opportunity to observe were also *voyeurs* in the strict sense of the term. Even allowing for the fact that the interest they took in the female genitals might of course have concealed a certain anxiety, they seemed to be perfectly capable of mastering that anxiety (or of eroticizing it?). We therefore have to ask why they had to resort to the mechanism of fetishism, which would appear superfluous to their needs.

Garma (1956, p. 415) also says of his shoe-fetishist: 'What was primitive in him, prior to these conflicts, seems to have been the knowledge of the female genital and the pleasure at the sight of it.' All the fetishists I have had in analysis grew up in circumstances which permitted great intimacy with their mothers, who seduced them in such a precise and intense sense as to remove all possible doubts as to the anatomical reality of their genitals. The future pervert usually finds repression quite impossible, which is why his latency period is short or even, according to some observers, nonexistent. It is the neurotic, or even the 'normal' subject, who represses as a result of oedipal conflict, but we know that the pervert finds a solution which removes the object of the fear of castration – unless, of course, he deliberately actualizes it in order to eroticize it.

Even so, the female genitals can inspire a certain horror, either because male subjects project their own sadistic sexual tendencies on to them, or because it is a way of expressing the *narcissistic* contempt felt for them by men who fight their own homosexuality by rejecting any identification with women (the word 'horror' is in fact an expression of disgust in the sense that we can describe something despicable as 'a horror'. In German, the word *Abscheu* in fact means 'disgust', not 'horror').[4]

If the subject suddenly encounters sexuality without being adequately

---

4 We know that perverts narcissistically cathect their way of going about things and feel nothing but scorn for anyone who is so crude as to 'make love like Dad'. I once analysed a fetishist, an educated scientist, who was convinced that the most sublime form of love, the form most worthy of a man, was to ejaculate whilst smelling the dirty knickers of the woman he loved.

prepared for it, the encounter may awaken feelings that come close to 'horror' for reasons to do with the superego and the nonintegrated part of the drive which, precisely because it has not been integrated, becomes persecutory. Quite apart from rape, a chance encounter between a woman and an exhibitionist, or even an eminently conventional wedding night, may trigger a similar reaction, although it is increasingly difficult to imagine that it could have this effect in the present climate. But such cases involve the penis and not the vagina, although the unexpected sight of the vagina can of course produce a similar reaction in certain circumstances.

We can now examine the third element in Freud's argument: the problem of the localization of the fetish. I would remind you that according to Freud (1927, p. 155), it is 'the last moment in which the woman could still be regarded as phallic' that determines the choice and positioning of the fetish: 'Thus the foot or shoe owes its preference as a fetish – or a part of it – to the circumstances that the inquisitive boy peered at the woman's genitals from below, from her legs up.' Whilst it may have been possible to justify this argument in Freud's day, it no longer has any validity in the age of miniskirts, not to mention family nudity. Yet shoe-fetishism is as widespread as ever, if not more so.[5] Indeed, if this historical explanation did have any validity we would be at a loss as to how to understand the appeal of articles of clothing (whalebone corsets, knee-length boots...) which have long been out of fashion and which no contemporary fetishist ever saw in the dressing-room of his mother or sister.

As Katan (1965, p. 238) remarks, Freud's approach is based on the model he used in his studies on aphasia, where he notes that aphasiac speech remnants may contain impressions that preceded the lesion. I do not think that a pre-Freudian model applicable to the observation of an organic process can be unproblematically used in the study of a complex psychic phenomenon like fetishism.

We now come to the concept of splitting, which now tends to dominate the theory of fetishism and even to extend beyond that theory, given that it provides the basis for an overall conceptualization which purports to call itself psychoanalysis. Freud discusses splitting in the paper on 'Fetishism' (1927), and then returns to the subject in much later texts like 'Splitting of the ego in the process of defence' (1938) and in chapter VIII of the *Outline*.

I refer, as the reader will have realized, to the splitting that occurs when

---

5 I recently heard of a newspaper published in a Swedish town which devotes a weekly column to fashion in shoes. The paper in question pays a woman reporter to travel the world, to see what is in the shoe-shop windows, and to interview footwear specialists. Sweden, it is to be noted, is an area in which there has always been a degree of sexual freedom (whole families unashamedly take saunas together).

reality is both recognized for what it is and disavowed: 'This disavowal is always supplemented by an acknowledgement; two contrary and independent attitudes always arise and result in the situation of there being a splitting of the ego' (Freud, 1940, p. 275). Yet Freud began to study the phenomenon of splitting in a very different context (Freud, 1894), and he himself notes that the mechanism applies to 'other states more like the neuroses'. It is therefore not specific to the perversions.

The mechanism is in fact universal and present in all psychic manifestations, both normal and pathological. The whole of psychic life is governed by an incessant dialectical interplay between perception and nonperception (anyone who doubts this should try questioning a dozen people who all witnessed the same road accident), dream and reality, rationality and irrationality, an objective vision of reality and the narcissistic perspective – or, more succinctly, between the secondary process and the primary process. A child playing at cops and robbers really believes he is a cop or a robber, but at the same time he knows he is neither and that it is all make-believe.

Even the most well-balanced adult uses the same splitting mechanism, because on the one hand and at a certain level he knows that he is mortal (secondary process); while on the other hand and at a deeper level he is convinced of his immortality; if he were not, he would collapse under the weight of his finitude; if he arrived at a truly complete perception of his finitude, he would not survive for a moment. Some delusions are almost physiological, and the interplay between primary and secondary processes is the very basis of our psychic life. Splitting is in a sense unavoidable, and according to Melanie Klein, the absence of splitting is a cause for concern, at least during a certain phase in the child's development which, in my view, always persists to a certain degree. The splitting of the ego is a permanent phenomenon because the component elements that make it up are not all integrated to the same extent. Now that state of disequilibrium is, so to speak, permanent and unavoidable, as it is in the nature of those component elements to be both complementary and antagonistic, the narcissism–anal component pair being only one example.

The *analytic process* itself implies the release of a certain instinctual content; it takes us, that is, from the primary process to the secondary process, and thus reduces the extent of the splitting. And does not *transference* correspond to *a simultaneous conviction* on the part of the analysand, who believes simultaneously (and on two different levels; that is the whole point) that his therapist is Dr X, and that he is his father or mother. His position is illustrated by the well-known joke: 'My analyst is mad; he thinks he's my father.'

Having formulated these critical comments, we can now direct our research along different lines and begin to look at the enigma of fetishism.

I

In a note added to the *Three Essays* in 1910, Freud (1905b, p. 155, n 2) writes:

> Psychoanalysis has cleared up one of the remaining gaps in our understanding of fetishism. It has shown the importance, as regards the choice of a fetish, of a coprophiliac pleasure in smelling which has disappeared owing to repression. Both the feet and the hair are objects with a strong smell which have been exalted into fetishes after the olfactory sensation has become unpleasurable and has been abandoned. Accordingly, in the perversion that corresponds to foot-fetishism, it is only dirty and evil-smelling feet that become sexual objects.

By simultaneously raising the problem of dirtiness (and cleanliness) and the tendency towards cruelty, he brings together a number of elements which circumscribe the dimension we refer to as anality, defined in the broadest possible sense. This term designates a whole dimension of the psyche, and the role of that dimension is in my view essential to any understanding of the sexual deviation which concerns us here. We will begin our examination of foot- and shoe-fetishism in this light, with further reference to the relevant early texts by Freud. Freud himself establishes a connection between the two, and they can be regarded as providing the basis for the equation between container and contained. Feet and shoes are also connected with the *olfactory* factor, and we know the importance of leather and its particular smell, and the importance of smells in general, in all forms of fetishism, whether it concerns feet, gloves, mackintoshes, rubber or, of course, underwear. In a word, I am convinced that when Flaubert had his lady friend Louise Colet's slipper rushed to him so that he could use it for the obvious purpose, the parcel did not contain the lady's penis, but her smell: the smell of her feet.

But the foot is also the organ of locomotion and propulsion – that is to say, of aggressivity (anality); a kick is the aggressive gesture *par excellence*, and the expression 'a kick up the backside' describes the way the aggressive urge performs a veritable revolution (a circular movement) and combines, in an almost autonomous way, the source of the acrodynamic energy and the anus, which is the other pole of the same anal-aggressive impulse (acropathology was once a real medical doctrine). In French slang, shoes are sometimes known as 'shit-crushers' [*écrase-merde*], and the term takes on its full meaning if one thinks of the lack of hygiene to be observed in public places and in our streets, which have been strewn with rubbish for centuries. The case material supplied by one of my woman patients clearly brings out the pleasure of walking on turds ('partly by accident, partly on purpose'). She was both a phobic and a fetishist (we will come back to the association between the two), and it gave her enormous satisfaction to indulge in this activity outside a shoe shop; behind it there was a jeweller's shop, and she was particularly fond of the rings it sold (rings = anus).

Ignoring expressions that link anality with sexuality, such as *trouver chaussure à son pied* or *prendre son pied* [slang expressions meaning, respectively, 'to find a suitable wife' – literally, 'to find a shoe that fits' – and 'to enjoy sexual pleasure'], let me refer to the testimony of a colleague who works as a doctor in the suburbs. In his experience, men will do nothing to get rid of the characteristic smell of their feet, which they regard as a sign of virility. Their wives object to this, and complain about it to him. He then has to referee a real conflict over anal castration. Whilst we are still on this subject, it should be recalled that the faithful have to take off their shoes before they enter the mosque (during the 'Green March', the king of Morocco advised the marchers to keep their shoes on while they prayed so as to indicate that the march was – as we already knew – an act of war). The Algerians used to call French settlers (the aggressors) *pieds-noirs* ['black feet']. The Jewish custom of refraining from wearing leather shoes on Yom Kippur, the Day of Atonement, has the same meaning. And all analysts are familiar with those analysands who ask if they should take off their shoes before lying on the couch; it is usual to see this as an index of a particularly violent aggressivity that has been bottled up.

Quite apart from its sexual significance, we know that hair is bound up with dirtiness – and not simply when there is hair in the soup – and that there is something attractive about dirty hair, just as there is something attractive about the smell of wild animals. It should not be forgotten that our aseptic and deodorized civilization (and there are those who complain about these qualities) is relatively recent, and that the marquises of Louis XIV's day wore capillary edifices that were as complicated as they were enormous, and that they could go for months, if not longer, without combing them out. Nor should we forget the conflict that can break out between certain young people and adults over the issue of long hair, which can become a real *casus belli* (in certain cases, the conflict has resulted in murder or suicide). Were it not for the (unconscious) anal significance of hair, such conflicts would be incomprehensible.

According to the theory of depth psychology, phenomena are always overdetermined, and in that sense a definition provided by a woman shoe-fetishist I analysed ('A shoe has a point in front and a hole at the back for the heel') opens up horizons that are as broad as they are varied. But I will restrict the discussion to the study of a single factor. The notion of retention (anal mastery) can be applied to shoes, but also to any article of clothing which can take on a fetishistic meaning. We all know Abraham's description of the case of the schoolboy who derived pleasure from putting on a uniform that was too tight for him. Retention is an expression of anal mastery, and the object which is retained or constrained becomes an anal object. When it is immobilized in this way, the object is in a sense deprived of its own anality; the prototypical example is the retention of excrement by the anal sphincter. It is this that allows us to understand the fetishistic character of the object of the patient described by Masud Khan (1965, 1979). This patient had a foreskin-fetish. The foreskin is, in effect, a typical container which encloses the glans penis, and excessive contraction can result in the anomaly known as phimosis (a variation on the theme of *penis captivus*). The fetishist in question extended retention to the body ego in its entirety, presumably as a result of some fantasy.

A woman in analysis told me that her husband, a foot-fetishist, insisted that she must keep still during coitus (the act was rarely successful, and her husband achieved satisfaction without intromission). He said that she had to keep perfectly still, like a foot in a boot (an expression which I immediately associated with 'being under the heel of the enemy'). For this man, his wife's whole body obviously had the significance of an anal object which he could insert into his anus. All the articles of clothing which fetishists prize so highly correspond to this need – which explains the use of (for example) corsets, which have been out of fashion for a hundred years, but which allow a woman to be laced so tightly that she almost suffocates; or high-legged boots: it requires patience and care to lace them up, and the whole process can take half an hour, but they satisfy the same need for retention. A woman wearing boots and gloves, a helmet or a mask, and tight clothing, may seem to have numerous phalluses, but she is in fact an anal part-object imprisoned in a sphincter. Paulette Letarte (1973) tells the moving story of Esdras Lachance, who kept his doll-fetish in a suitcase and said: 'She can't talk, but I can make her say anything I like'. Jiri Kolar exhibits a painting entitled *Shoe Woman* (New York, Guggenheim Foundation): it depicts a standing woman who merges with the outline of the shoe that fits tightly around her; the shoe itself stands at the entrance to a sort of corridor with an obviously anal meaning.[6]

A woman who is dressed up in this way is completely imprisoned inside her clothes, and can represent a fairly common and extremely schematic fetish (this is true of all fetishistic accessories – they are all prototypes – and is a further agreement against the view that they are historically determined in any sense, as I suggested in my introduction). The fetishist reaches orgasm at

6 One female shoe-fetishist quite happily used tights, and told me: 'I like being dressed in a condom.' During her analysis she described how, at the age of eight, she had drawn a girl lying half-naked on a bed with an expression of perfect bliss on her face. Beside her, she drew a man putting on a suit and fastening a tie, his face contorted with the effort. She added: 'It could also be the face of a man making love.' I had no difficulty in showing her that as a child she had fantasized a penis being constricted by the anus, had projected her orgasmic feelings on to the man, and that her current style of dress expressed the same wish for anal contention.

the precise moment when the woman is completely imprisoned (transformed into an anal object). For reasons which I will explain later and which pertain to the very essence of fetishism, his actual orgasm is very discreet, almost secretive. The costumes adopted by fetishists are all very similar, and when you have described one you have described them all; this usually applies to perverse practices in general (Joyce McDougall used to say that all perverts had been to see the same film). It might therefore be more discreet to cite a literary text; as Freud (1927, p. 152) puts it: 'For obvious reasons the details of these cases must be withheld from publication.' The text in question is Renato Ghiotto's novel *Scacco alla regina* [literally, 'The Queen in Check'] (Ghiotto, 1967); the fragment quoted below is absolutely accurate from a clinical point of view. Chasseguet-Smirgel has also made use of the same text to establish a link between the fetish as described by Ghiotto and Wilhelm Reich's character armour, which she sees as a representation of a rectum enclosing a subject who has been reduced to an excremental state:

My costume is made of black leather and covers me completely; I cannot get into it unless Vittorina [the maid] helps me. It is a sheath that comes up to my neck, with long sleeves; it is attached at the waist to a pair of trousers which come down to mid-thigh level; both are made up of very supple leather which gives and fits like a glove. On top, I wear a polished leather corselet which hugs my body, a pair of long gloves and boots that come up to my thighs. The boots have high heels, and are laced from top to bottom at the front, so that they are moulded to the shape of my legs. It takes half an hour just to lace up the boots. A leather helmet covers my whole head, face and neck included; the front of it is a sort of mask moulded to the contours of my face, with two slits for the eyes and one for the mouth. I have seen myself in this costume; the most impressive thing of all is the beetle's head.

When Vittorina has fastened me into this leather sheath, and when I am standing on the carpet with my new black skin and a shape which looks like mine, but which no longer looks human at all, Margaret comes over and stands by me. I am so tightly laced up that I cannot bend over, but I could walk and move my arms; she wants me to stay still, and stands there watching me closely and breathing in the smell of leather and roses. Slowly, holding her breath, she places small padded lids, which are attached to the mask, over my eyes and my mouth and closes them; I cannot see anything, I cannot hear anything, and I cannot say anything; I breathe through the two holes under my nose. I am in a prison which has the precise dimensions of my body; I have difficulty in breathing, and I am so tightly fastened in that I begin to go numb; I no longer have any sense of sight, feeling, hearing, taste or speech [I will come back to this point]. Only my sense of smell is left; the smell of roses and leather tickles my throat; it smells like a stable or even a hearse.

The fetish is, then, a prison; some call it a *cache*, as in *cache-sexe* [a G-string], which does in fact correspond to a dialectic of showing and hiding, hide-and-seek. But in my view, it is a real *claustrum* which both defends and imprisons the subject, like the château in *Les 120 Journées de Sodome* (de Sade, 1785). One fetishist who had a very rich fantasy life realized the idea of the *claustrum* by constructing a wicker doll; the thorax was a cage shaped in such a way that two rats (which he caught himself) could be placed in the equivalent of the lower stomach and could pass through a sort of trap door to the higher storey, whilst an ingenious mechanism allowed them to come down again via a passage fitted with a sort of sphincter. The head of the doll was left incomplete (Francis Chabert described this case in a paper read to the Séminaire de perfectionnement in 1973).

Now it so happens that this doll closely resembles a painting by Magritte entitled *The Healer* (Collection of J. B. Urvater, Paris), though I have good reason to believe that the patient had no knowledge of it. The painting depicts a tramp-like male figure with a cane and a bundle; his trunk consists of a cage covered with a blanket, and in the trunk is a pair of white pigeons. Given that it is a work of art, I am inclined to see the pigeons as an expression of sublimation (freedom from guilt) and to say that the process itself (and the conflict) is masked by the construction, which is completed by a headless hat. The fact that the figure has no sense organs is a direct reminder of Sylvia (the slave in Ghiotto's novel) in her prison. All this is, of course, no more than a hypothesis. Even so, the absence of the head can only mean *deindividualization*, that being a typical feature of an anal object which is homogenized like excrement (see Grunberger, 1959, 1967). This is one of the essential characteristics of the fetish. (Animalization has the same meaning: being a phobogenic object, the fetish is similar to an animal, which testifies the depth of the regression. No doubt the same is true of totems.)

The fetish-object is primarily a deindividualized object, a generic object or a prototype – and not only because, as Pasche notes, 'Regression results in a sophisticated form of behaviour being replaced by a form which is more unpolished, more primitive and less psychic.' In my view this is primarily the result of anal regression, in which the object is homogenized or analized. It is manufactured in the sense that we speak of *bricolage*,[7] and it is artificial in two

---

7 Cf. the following description of the materials used in predicting the future in Cameroon (Garnier and Fralon, 1951): 'Pangolin scales, mysterious words (which the fetish-owner alone can interpret) drawn on the scales... Others use "magic" buffalo or antelope horns containing fragments of dead insects, nine pebbles, a piece of yob wood and tiny bones. The horns are fastened close with pieces of leopard skin.'

senses. The fetishist puts his creation *in the place of* the object he wishes to replace in accordance with his own absolutely sovereign will, and he creates the object from whatever comes to hand, preferably by using raw materials which were originally intended to be used for very different purposes. As Janine Chasseguet-Smirgel puts it, this is the typically *sadistic* aspect of the process (personal communication). In *La Maitresse*, Jules Renard (1896, p. 40) speaks of the feet of his beloved (whom he calls *maman*): 'Poets sing the beauty of the feet of women; and yet if you were to lose a foot and if it were to be replaced by a foot made of rosewood, I would still love you.' Once more, we find an allusion to roses; and their anal meaning (antiphrasis) is well known.

The fetish also corresponds – for the same reason – to a heterogeneous bric-à-brac, but its very heterogeneity is a source of deindividualization, and it is this that leads Masud Khan to say (1965, 1979, p. 164) that the 'fetish is built like a *collage*'. One female shoe-fetishist dreamed of making a shoe that could be taken apart and put together again at will (like excrement) – 'like a jigsaw puzzle', she added.

The fetish is often elevated to this status after being picked up or pilfered from somewhere or other (see Letarte, 1973), as that way of acquiring it gives it special quality, since the process of capture and retention is inscribed in it in absolute fashion from the outset. It has to be owned in a complete and absolute sense, and it has no counterpart; here we begin to touch on sadism and kleptomania, and on the mystical veneration of idols (during the Middle Ages the trade in relics was organized on a vast scale, and coveted objects were often stolen from abbeys in veritable raids organized for that one purpose, yet these organized thefts were tolerated to a certain extent, and were known as 'pious thefts').

The obviously anal character of the fetish-object becomes apparent if we look at a process which in itself reveals something of the importance of the economic viewpoint, and is a classic expression of the anal dimension. Sacher-Masoch, a masochist and fur-fetishist, initially falls in love with a marble statue, which might be regarded as his first fetish-object (Sacher-Masoch, 1886). But we know that he 'decompensated' (he died insane) and that in *Drama-Dschenti*, one of his last tales, the hero falls in love with the Amazon queen of an African tribe, a 'chocolate-brown Venus' (see Meyer, 1964). I see no reason why we should not establish a link between, on the one hand, the increased substantiality of fetish-objects as they come closer to the anal level, and on the other, an increasingly deep regression which makes displacement impossible and ends in a final decompensation.

In his film about Ludwig of Bavaria, Visconti displays a perfect understanding of the process of analization. Initially, we see the sick sovereign fighting his perversion (homosexuality), and then giving in to it. From this point onwards, we see the king parting his lips to reveal a rotting mouth full of decayed dents and stumps (an anal orifice displaced upwards) – a recurrent theme in Visconti's work. At the same time, we hear the clatter of wooden-soled shoes (shoes do not simply mean leather; they also mean tramping and noise). The quality of the music then declines, and Wagner is finally replaced by the tune of the *Schuhplättler* (more shoes) – the most vulgar dance in the world.⁸ The palace manservants dance frenetically. They are drunk, and a homosexual orgy ensues.

In one of the final sequences we see a table set with the most luxurious refinement (and roses, roses everywhere) topple into the cellar, where the kitchen staff greedily fling themselves on the royal leftovers, grabbing slices of pâté and lapping up the flowing champagne. Everything is transformed into a sort of monstrous dustbin, and we soon realize that it will not be long before the king himself ends up in it.

II

As we have seen, the fetish is an anal part-object, and as such it is a support for every dimension of anality. By that I mean that the fetish represents the container–contained pair at the anal level, or in other words the faecal stick in the sphincter; this is true no matter whether the actual fetish is a woman wrapped up in a mackintosh, the subject laced up in a corset or a uniform, or a leg laced up in a boot or covered up with a tight black stocking. The container contained bipolarity links fetishism to sadomasochism, from which it is inseparable – so much so that it is usually extremely difficult to make any distinction between the fetishistic elements and the sado-masochistic elements. But the fetishist obviously cathects the anal object with which he also identifies in a very particular way. If, like perverts in general, he sexualized anality, he would be a sadist or an anal pervert, but not a fetishist. In fact *he does not simply sexualize the anal object; he narcissizes it.*

Freud stresses (1927, p. 151) the dual nature of fetishism by stressing that whilst the fetishist *reveres* his fetish, it is also the object of hostility and destructive wishes. Evans-Pritchard (1956, p. 137) indicates clearly the coexistence of narcissistic and aggressive factors:

> A bundle of wood in which a fetish-spirit lives... It is before the bundle that he [the fetish-owner] makes his offering and it is the bundle that he points at the enemy he wishes the spirit to harm.

The fetish therefore means black magic, the casting of spells, death and destruction (anality) as well as cosmic love [*aimance*], adoration and ecstasy (narcissism).

---

8 The dance is performed only by men; as they dance they take turns in slapping one another's backsides with the soles of their shoes.

I will now transcribe some fragments of case histories described by Medard Boss (1953), an existentialist and former Freudian psychoanalyst whose accounts of fetishism place great emphasis on the tonality of the lived experience, which he interprets in an existentialist perspective. In my view, however, that tonality is the very hallmark of deep narcissistic regression.

The patient referred to by the author as Konrad is a leather-and-fur-fetishist; even as a child, he would sometimes stop in the middle of the street when he saw a girl (or little girl) he did not know, fling his arms around her and kiss her with great emotion [... *mit grosser Innigkeit*]. Contact with – or even the sight of – a woman's riding boot sent him into ecstasy:

> Suddenly, the whole world was transformed; everything about me that was banal and run-of-the-mill – my sterile and petty day-to-day life – suddenly vanished, and I was surrounded by a luminous splendour emanating from the leather. Yes, for me these leather objects have a strange halo, and its radiance outshines everything else around me. It's ridiculous, but I feel like a fairy-tale prince. An incredible force, a mana, emanates from these gloves, furs and boots, and it holds me in its spell.
>
> These shoes and gloves are an incarnation of the God Eros himself, or rather, he enters into them, and lives in them and nowhere else [the unique nature of the narcissistic object].
>
> For me, women's gloves, boots and furs are a vase sacred to love. It is only there that the pleasures of love, sensuality and grace, and my whole sensual being can take on a concrete form. This is the only form in which I can feel carnal love; only a glove or a shoe can bring the god of love down to earth for me and make him leave his heavenly dwelling to join me. And then it seems to me that he takes possession of me through the gloves and shoes, that he makes me tremble and crushes me in my orgastic ecstasy.

(The patient's language might be described as overexcited, overblown and naively mystical, or even prepsychotic, but that does not mean that we have to dismiss what he says, as fetishism does in fact imply all that.)

And then narcissism suddenly proves to be hostile to the drives:

> Naked women, a woman's hand or glove, or even a woman's foot (a naked foot) do nothing for me in the sensual or sexual sense; they look to me like pieces of meat in a butcher's [and here one thinks of Oscar Wilde's 'cold meat']. Yes, a woman's foot would disgust me, and so does nudity in general. It's rather unpleasant; I have the feeling that it is definitely hostile to me; I don't trust it; I loathe it ... I cannot imagine coming into physical contact with a woman without feeling guilty, as though I were committing sacrilege; but a glove, a fur coat or a shoe immediately elevates a woman above her limited personal existence ... It removes her from the petty and

evil existence she lives as an ordinary being and from her appalling sexuality, and makes her someone impersonal who is both more and less than human, someone who dwells in a universal divine radiance ... Yes, gloves and shoes do have a human form, but they are 'idealized' or 'stylized', and at the same time *there is something animal about them if they still have the animal smell of leather.* [emphasis added]

Boss's little book is full of similar examples, but it would be extremely boring to reproduce them all, as the affective tonality of the texts remains much the same from one case to the next. What I am trying to bring out here is the almost simultaneous appearance of the narcissistic component and of sadism: both are projected, one on to the woman and the other on to an object belonging to her (or even on to part of her body). That object is the fetish. But the object which receives the narcissistic cathexis in such an exclusive way also represents, in an equally exclusive manner, narcissism's antagonist: anality. The fetish-object is the anal object *par excellence*, and the fetishist himself is aware of the fact. The fetish in fact expresses, represents and, above all, materializes the *projection of an internal conflict* which corresponds to both the narcissism–anality antagonism and to its resolution through the creation of the fetish-object.

Before going on to attempt to describe the mechanism of the process itself, let me use a case of fetishism described by Boss to show the acute nature of the conflict. I again refer to the Konrad case, from which the above fragment is taken. In his dreams, Konrad constantly saw the rotting bodies of women crawling with worms and insects. Cats and snakes crawled out of them; the cats tried to seize hold of his feet and hands, and the snakes threatened to coil around him and strangle him. He claimed: *'The vermin's main aim was to destroy my spirituality.'* The persecutory aspect of all this material is obvious. He once dreamed, for instance, that he was making a great effort to complete a scientific manuscript (Konrad was a linguist specializing in Greek and Latin), but 'every page was immediately sucked into a gaping hole in the ground, sucked and devoured by magic'.

The case of Erika provides a further illustration of the attempt to use an elational and narcissistic aura to *transfigure anality*. Erika was a kleptomaniac, who began by stealing from her husband. I will transcribe only one fragment of the case history:

Once I had got over my feelings of anxiety and remorse, the feeling of excitement was indescribable. I saw a coin lying in the open drawer before my very eyes, just waiting to be taken. Shiver after shiver ran through me, a ticklish, trembling feeling flooded through my whole body, and suddenly condensed in the pit of my stomach, and then completely overcame me; I

have never known such a feeling of pleasure. Before my very eyes, the
silver coins shone as though they were pure gold, and as they glittered they
lit up everything with luminous rays. It was a miracle, I felt as though I was
drunk... complete ecstasy.

Otto is a pervert whose case raises the usual nosographic problems, but I
consider him to be a fetishist. For reasons of professional secrecy, I cannot
describe his perversion as such. That is unfortunate, as he is a rich and
picturesque character, and the case history is extremely instructive.

Otto's perversion – or rather, his perverse act – involves a number of
different phases corresponding to the unfolding of a fairly complex scenario,
as you will see.

Having reached a state of high excitement, Otto seeks out certain cinemas
where he hopes to have sexual contact – touching, exhibitionism, masturbation – with women. He usually, but not always, approaches women who are
alone. The danger of complications arising (being caught, being beaten up or
denounced), which is in fact slight, does not put him off at all. He is of course
acting as though under a compulsion, but at the same time he knows that all
this will not really satisfy him, and that it is a matter of preparation, a sort of
preliminary pleasure. Even if his partner does follow him to a hotel, he tends
to consider the act as a 'chance encounter'.

Then he continues his quest. He wanders along certain streets, looking for
someone who must meet certain very specific requirements. The man in
question must be poor, a virtual tramp who is dirty and scruffy and smells as
though he has not washed recently. Otto stresses that the individual he is
looking for must be a deadbeat: 'I need a bum, a wreck.' He invites him home
and stuffs him into his wife's bed; I will leave her out of my description, even
though she represents a problem which is of interest in its own right. I will,
however, point out that objectively (she once came to see me) there is nothing
repulsive about her – on the contrary. But at this point her husband tries to
transform her into an anal object, by cursing her, humiliating her and calling
her all sorts of obscene names (and he is able to exploit a wealth of slang and
obscenities). He accuses her of every crime and vice he can think of,
criticizing her for being in a situation into which he has got her and which she
passively tolerates.

While his wife is making love with her chance companion, Otto frantically
takes photographs of them from every possible angle. His photographic
technique is sophisticated, and he would like to achieve a certain artistic
perfection. For Otto, the film has a fetishistic value in itself; he has only to
look at the prints (he enlarges them himself) to obtain a certain pleasure. But
even this is a mere shadow of the greatest pleasure of all, which is still to come.
In order to describe that, I must mention his relationship with his wife, which

we have already touched upon. Although they have children, and although Otto is happy to be a father, he is on permanently bad terms with her. He continuously provokes dramatic scenes, and his behaviour takes on the aspect of a veritable perversion in itself because of its obvious libidinal component. During our analytic sessions, he constantly brings up the same complaints and criticisms about his wife; he does accept my interpretation quite happily and even with a certain intellectual insight, but he obviously needs to transform her into an anal object. That is the essential core of his perversion, and he seems quite unable to give it up.

To go back to the fetishistic act itself: he heaps the most filthy insults on his wife, constantly exacerbating the intensity of the process as his sexual excitement mounts. But the orgastic resolution occurs only in the final phase, when his behaviour suddenly changes and is reversed into its opposite. Otto is suddenly overcome by a sort of enchanted wonderment and discovers that his love for his wife is sublime, marvellous and unique. He feels that he is being carried away by a wave of tenderness, and is moved to tears by it. He would like to give his life for her, to sacrifice himself to her in an act of adoration which is at once exalting, ardent and chaste, and is swept away by a wave of narcissistic expansion, experiencing a state of complete bliss – and then it is all over: the gates of heaven close, the world becomes dirty, sordid and depressing. The world is so dreary that he wants to die.

And then the cycle begins again. Otto curses himself and turns up for his sessions begging me to rid him of his perversion because he is so disgusted with himself. That in fact proves impossible, and although the analysis does produce good results (which I will not describe, so as not to reveal the patient's identity), Otto still cannot give up his perversion: although it is now in the background, and has been appeased and controlled by the rest of his personality, the perverse relationship continues to serve its function; the conflict has not been resolved, but it has been circumscribed and put to better use.

In the Musée Cheret in Nice, there is a painting by Adolf Mossa entitled *Resurrection* (1907). It depicts a cemetery. A beautiful woman emerges from a pile of brownish objects; she is swathed in bandages (container and contained) and carries a cithara. She is an image of the narcissistic ideal emerging from a mass of anality. The fetishist lives his anality, but at the same time he uses the narcissistic component to cover it up. This explains both the hostility he provokes in those around him (who regard his 'solution' as an easy way out, and as the very opposite of their own) and the fascination he exerts over them. The triumph of narcissism over anality means not only an apparent liberation from the Oedipus and from conflict, but also a liberation from reality – or, in a phrase, from the human condition.

This is in fact an illusion which does not put an end to the conflict and does not change reality into its opposite. A fierce struggle is going on beneath the calm surface, and its effects can be seen in the fetishist's ambivalence and in the precarious solution he adopts. It is in fact impossible to narcissize anality, just as it is impossible to square the circle. There is only one way for the narcissist to persevere in his attempts: he must deliberately elevate the whole process to the level of a deluded omnipotence by means of a kind of *credo quia absurdum* which he assumes as such. That in itself is a narcissistic achievement. Yet the rot has already set in, because he knows that the process cannot really work and that his whole construction may collapse because it is so unbalanced. The hustler who works a three-card trick can prove to you that the queen you just saw is really a jack, and he fascinates you because of his magical ability to challenge reality. You come under the spell of his intoxicating power, even if it does cost you your last penny and even though, at a more superficial level, you know that he is a liar and a cheat. The words of the fairground barker, his gift of the gab and the gestures he makes to distract your attention are the shimmering, mysterious cover (*cache*) that hides the trickery (and there is a catch . . .), and that cover can take on the value of a fetish.[9]

Besides, who knows? After all, there was once a time when the real did not exist and you lived in a state of narcissistic bliss in an immaterial, infinite world. And life has denied you that bliss.

III

We have established the existence of a certain link between anality and narcissism; in certain conditions, the former may trigger the emergence of the latter. We have advanced the hypothesis that this pattern of action (anality) and reaction (narcissism) constitute the armature and content of the fetishistic object, and we have even suggested that there is a dialectical interplay between these two factors: that the process obeys a certain finality and that the narcissistic-orgastic conflagration also functions as a defence against the threatening tension of anality.

What is in my view certain – and all my clinical material proves it – is that anality tends to be integrated into the ego, to be metabolized by the central agency, and that *the quantitative and qualitative threshold at which this integration is achieved differs from one individual to the next*. Once that

9 The fetish may merge completely with the *cache*, which can be made in different ways and from different materials: its function is always to express and conceal anal mastery. Both this twofold action and its fantasy support are inscribed within the configuration of the fetish-object. The material existence of the fetish corresponds primarily to the fetishist's need to *project* the entire process outwards (we will return to this point) and to materialize it or, rather, to make it *visible*. In that sense, the fetish might be compared with the hypnogagic image; it too makes what is happening visible.

threshold is reached, one of two things happens. Either the process is blocked, or the excess anality is, so to speak, inscribed under a new sign. It takes a new object, and either flows back into the ego in a persecutory form or triggers *a sudden, deep narcissistic regression* on a large scale.

Coitus itself might be seen as the prototype for the process I have just described, especially if we look at it in the light of clinical studies of certain cases of *premature ejaculation*. Such cases show that there is a limit beyond which the subject cannot tolerate the increase in anal pressure required for erection and penetration, and that once he reaches the threshold of nonintegrated (and therefore inadequate) anality, he ejaculates prematurely (though we should in fact be speaking of premature orgasm) and reaches orgasm too quickly because the elational narcissistic component (release) has overcome the anal component. (Anal immaturity in women results in frigidity – sometimes they appear to be astonished by the anality of their partners, or by what they describe as the ridiculous contortions they indulge in. Alternatively, they may achieve rapid and repeated orgasms; but such orgasms are mediocre in quality, as they are in fact the female equivalent to premature ejaculation.)

The process whereby anal tension reaches a certain threshold and then provokes a narcissistic reaction might be identified as one of the laws that govern the destiny of civilizations – a certain anality (wealth, comfort, technology) is automatically followed by a mystical-ascetic period. But I will not go into that here.

I am of course aware that in outlining this process I have done no more than describe the fetishist's orgasm, or even orgasm in general, and have not taken into account the importance of the fetish-object itself and its indispensable presence. In other words, I have overlooked the important point.

We have seen that the fetish is 'entirely unsuited to serve the normal sexual aim' (Freud, 1905b, p. 153) and that it can be said to be marked by – and, more important, to reveal – a certain nonsexual *sense impression*. The fetish has been described as the source of a particular cutaneous sensation (Hermann (1970) discusses the importance of music in five cases of perversion, two of them involving fetishism), of the tactile pleasure mentioned by Clérambault (1908), who speaks of women's erotic passion for fabrics. Coming closer to our own day, Stoller (1968, p. 166) mentions 'the capacity for sexual excitement triggered by clothing of the opposite sex', whilst Payne (1939, p. 166) speaks of the importance of smell to a mackintosh-fetishist, as does Parkin (1964, p. 357). For his part, Pasche refers to 'sensorial qualities as a source of immediate pleasure . . . a shining, coloured object, a surface with a certain texture, the grain of the voice, etc.' It seems, then, to be an established fact that the involvement of the sense organs is essential to the structuring of the fetish, so much so that it is possible to speak of tactile, visual, olfactory or auditory fetishism. As we have seen, it also seems to be an established fact that the structuring of the fetish is based solely on anal erotism, or on the corresponding sense impression to the exclusion of all others. As for the nature of the sense impression, we find that its source is imprecise and that it is, moreover, ephemeral, coming into play only to disappear immediately and to give way to the triumphal narcissistic wave which submerges it.

The time has now come to stress the distinction between fetishism and perversion in the true sense of the word (and here, as I indicated at the beginning of this essay, we come back to Freud's basic insight). Whereas fetishism ignores the sense organs – with the exception of the olfactory organ – those organs are sexualized in a more lasting fashion in perversion (and, of course, in so-called normal sexuality). Thus, Freud speaks (1905b, pp. 204–5) of 'contrivances which bring it about that in the case of a great number of internal processes sexual excitation arises as a concomitant effect, as soon as the intensity of those processes passes beyond certain quantitative limits'. In this connection, it is worth remembering that Freud regarded the conscious mind itself as a sense organ; this reminds me of a woman analysand who, whenever we arrived at an insight – and especially if she had played an active part in the process – experienced not only intense narcissistic satisfaction but also a definitely sexual sensation in her vagina. The precise nature of the material that had been interpreted was irrelevant. The obvious thing about this woman, a hair-fetishist, was that her intellectual activity was invested with a highly anal cathexis, as is usually the case with certain intellectual functions. The distinction between fetishism and perversion tends to be somewhat theoretical, but it does have a certain relevance. As I indicated earlier when I made a distinction between the various perversions – but not between perversions and fetishism – and as we all know, we also find cases of mixed formations (perversion plus fetishism).

The fetishist is looking for a certain anal sense impression which is ill-defined and primitive, and probably dates back to an early moment in his evolution. At that point it was probably almost imperceptible, and there is every reason to think that the deciding factor in the choice of sense impression (and its fetishization) is that it is concomitant with the constitution of a certain quality of perception specific to narcissistic regression, which is midway between the recording of impressions that are not wholly perceived, and perception in the true sense. And anality plays a definite and decisive role in the constitution of perception. (It will be recalled that the Wolf Man had the feeling that a veil was being torn as he defecated: Freud, 1918, p. 75).[10]

The fetish, a visible, palpable object, is one of the forms taken by the primal anal object which has left the domain of narcissistic regression, but it also carries with it the sense impression characteristic of that stage of development, of the transition from one world to another. It is both a unique lived experience and an everlasting symbol (think of the word's etymology). The fetish-object perpetuates the mark of its early origins; it is primitive, clumsy, laughable, and awkward. The choice of object is often childish, and it often appears as such in case histories, but precisely because it is so archaic it allows the fetishist to make an easy transition through the 'strait gate' of selective narcissism, and to gain access to the dynamic unconscious – in other words, to prenatal bliss. The fetishist uses the appropriate sense impression and then discards it as he enters the elational state; a trivial object suffices because the 'descent into the abyss' takes place in a dimension specific to the narcissistic universe, a dimension which has no substance.

The fetish-object revives memories of an epoch in which nothing was perceived with any precision, when everything was blurred and had no boundaries. Hence the generic character of the fetish-object, which has no definite link with any specific trauma; this is why fetishes are interchangeable; one mackintosh is as good as the next, and it is almost possible to speak of dehumanization in this context (because of the depth of the corresponding repression). I have already stressed the *animal* character of the fetish; this is particularly obvious in hair- and fur-fetishism and in leather-fetishism, but the same could also be said of the phobogenic object, presumably because they both have the same deep origins.

As to the impact of the sense impression, it can be readily observed in cases in which sight appears to play a primordial role. I say 'appears' because even if the fetishist's scenario is designed to produce the dazzling appearance of the image of the object, the image cannot in fact be seen, precisely because it is so dazzling (the blurring of perception covers up the image and finally excludes it).[11] To illustrate my point, I will transcribe a description given by the 'cage'-fetishist I described earlier:

---

10 I am increasingly inclined to believe that infantile amnesia (which, paradoxically enough, concerns a period when the lived experience is at its most intense and has the most decisive effects on the structuring of the individual) is not a matter of 'loss of memory' (of memories pertaining to oedipal material which continues, despite the loss of memory, to have powerful effects) but a mode of registering perceptions which is all the more amenable to repression in that it is not consciously perceived. Although it is not perceived, this form of registration is absolute. In a sense there is something almost animal about it, as we can see from certain mentally effective psychopaths who have astonishing memories and can recite the contents of a telephone directory after reading through it once. No element of choice is involved, and nothing has been filtered by the ego.

11 Certain films (I am thinking in particular of Carmelo Bené's *Salomé*) in effect literally club the spectator by using images which are projected for a very short space of time (one-tenth of a second) before disappearing from the screen. At a superficial level of perception, the result is a blurred image in which nothing has a clear outline.

I wait in the bedroom while my wife gets ready in a sort of cubicle. It is purpose-built, and has almost transparent walls. My wife puts on the accessories, which I have prepared with great care. I cannot see her clearly, but I can follow the various stages of her preparations. She finishes putting on her make-up, adjusts her mask [one fetishist said of a mask that it was an arse on the face. The mask is the fetishist's own anus projected on to his face – this is a very important aspect of the fetish-object], and suddenly comes out into the light [in other words he is dazzled, and cannot see anything at all; he then goes on to add: 'I can see that she is surrounded by a halo, but I cannot make out her features]. I am now in a heightened state of excitement; in the grip of emotions that I cannot describe; and I ejaculate as though I had been carried away by a wave and been submerged beneath it.

Fetishism consists of an attempt to integrate anality, but at the same time it represents the triumph of narcissism, and I am very tempted to interpret Freud's *Der Glanz auf der Nase* (Freud, 1927, p. 152) in this sense, and to explain the fetishistic character of the object in terms of a combination of the same elements: the nose – the organ of smell – as anal object (displacement upwards), and the shine as a mask for narcissistic. I suggest, that is, that we retain the word *Glanz* in its German sense (shine) rather than the English sense Freud gives it (glance) – not that the two are mutually exclusive.

The process might be compared to the content of a dream, which may tell a long story. A whole lifetime can flash by in an instant once our head touches the pillow. The narcissistic factor always results in the erasure of substantiality, which is why all mystical experiences necessarily occur in an atmosphere of chiaroscuro: the dazzling quality of the light in a sense produces darkness (lack of clarity). The vocabulary of mysticism is full of references to the radiance of the light from heaven and to being dazzled. We find all these elements in Boss's case histories. As we saw earlier, for Konrad, leather, which smells strongly, becomes a source of luminous splendour (saints have halos, but there is also such a thing as the odour of sanctity). But the dialectic between anality and narcissism is always present: 'If a woman is wrapped in a piece of leather or fur, the disgustingly slender contours of her body disappear; everything becomes clear and light . . . I am in heaven.' And as Eugénie, another of Boss's patients, put it: 'I depend on my eyes for my sexual relations. The touch of the gaze is tender and chaste, but direct contact is as crude and bestial as sin.'[12]

12 Narcissism means hostility to the real materiality of things and to the sequence of cause and effect (generation). Black is the colour of anality, whereas narcissism is a dazzling light which blurs details, takes away substantiality and bleaches out colour. Anality is dense and stable; white light, in contrast, floods over everything, defying attempts to limit it, and spreads out to create a timeless feeling of boundless space.

IV

Fetishism, like the other perversions in general, means the adoption of a regressive position with respect to the Oedipus. Faced with the threat of castration, the subject retreats to the anal-sadistic stage, and that is the fetishist's fixation point. But we also know that the fetishist's regression takes him to a still deeper level, and President de Brosses, who wrote on the subject in 1760, regarded fetishism as a puerile cult which was characteristic of the earliest recorded history of mankind (Brosses, 1760). And what is phylogenitically true is also true from an ontogenic point of view.[13]

The fetishist's regression corresponds to a veritable vertical fall, and its effects will be felt throughout his history (and its various component elements, and certain historical events or remnants of conflicts, may reappear in a telescoped form in the structuring of the fetish-object itself).

What regularly emerges from the prehistory of fetishists is an early oral conflict of enormous violence which is rapidly analized and takes on a vampiristic savagery, and it can be assumed that the baby had difficulty in mastering it. Esdras, the fetishist described by Letarte (1973), was a 'vampire baby', and the fetishists I have observed regularly speak of their past as one of cannabilistic ferocity; the memory is perpetuated by their mothers, and by the whole family, who speak of it constantly. My patient Otto was typical.

The fetishist is trapped between his fear of castration and his fear of his own aggressivity, and deep narcissistic regression is the only solution open to him. That solution results in the fetishistic formation because the awakening of his sensorium converges with an anal erotism that is sustained and confirmed by a seductive mother who colludes with the future fetishist in that respect. The work of Joyce McDougall (1972) and other authors teaches us that the future pervert is greatly influenced by his seduction at the hands of his mother, but the real point is that this is an anal sexual seduction and, moreover, a form of seduction which paves the way for the narcissization of aggressivity, or at least for an attempt to narcissize it.

We find here a certain convergence between the mechanism of *sublimation* on the one hand, and the fetishist's 'creation' on the other. The fetishist uses the anal object to create – in a prepsychotic mode – something resembling a living being (just as God uses clay to create living beings, clay being a euphemism for excrement). Having created a void around himself, he will

13 In my view, the anal stage is preceded by a sort of *proto-anality*. Its existence is discernible throughout postnatal life, and even before postnatal life begins. There is every reason to believe that prenatal life, which supplies the matrix for narcissism (it is also the source of the drives), also contains the basic or primal elements of the future anal dimension. The foetus floats in amniotic fluid, a liquid which is rich in organic material; we know that the mother's *smell* is of vital importance to the infant from the very beginning. And we also know the conclusions ethologists have drawn from this basic datum.

repopulate it, but he does so with a single creature that means everything to him. Being the bearer of both his anality and his triumphal narcissism, the fetish provides a focus for the polarization of the fetishist's entire instinctual and narcissistic problematic, and will in a sense solve all the problems that previously affected the economic organization of his agencies. His creation allows him to live in a world of his own, and to perform miracles. In a sense the fetishist is deified in his own lifetime.

At this point, we obviously have to ask what becomes of his aggressivity – and this is his real problem. He is caught up in a narcissistic delusion, but whilst his anality is covered up and hidden by his ecstasy, it has not been suppressed, and he continues to be affected by anal tension. Although the tonality of his narcissistic ecstasy may borrow an energy specific to the anal nucleus, he is still trapped within its basic dialectic. The fetishist's aggressivity constantly makes its presence felt, if only at the level of his ambivalence towards the fetish itself: we know that primitive men can turn against their fetishes, and I myself have seen a devout Catholic throw a statue of the Virgin out of the window because she refused to help him win the lottery. This action was accompanied by obscene curses. The fetishist may also expend an enormous amount of aggressivity in order to attack those who do not revere the object of his adoration, which explains why it has been said that the bloodiest wars are always wars of religion.

But despite all these attempts, the fetishist is still faced with a basic conflict which takes the form of a dilemma: either he retains a certain lucidity, and is constantly obliged to perform miracles in order to convince himself of the absolute value of his fetish (of his narcissism); or he becomes trapped in delusions in his attempts to defend himself against his own aggressivity, and that is tantamount to allowing himself to be completely overwhelmed by the anal-sadistic component (because it functions in a magical mode, his ego loses most of its attributes). Initially the narcissistic current is like a burst of boundless exhilaration, and the subject obviously cannot sustain this level of intensity for very long; the initial impact of love at first sight brings with it the promise of disenchantment, because the subject will inevitably experience a narcissistic disappointment.

The same conflict can also be seen in the negative solution (precipitated by the displacement of the energetic charge, which plays an essential role in the maintenance of an energetic equilibrium). Berlanga's film *Grandeur nature* provides, in my view, an image which conforms to the clinical reality.

Michel – which is also the forename of the star, Michel Piccoli – has ordered a plastic doll from a factory in Japan, and has real sexual relations with it. Perfect happiness. Michel is in love with his fetish-doll, and he opts for that solution; he leaves his wife and his flat, abandons his clients (he is a dentist) and gives up all his professional activities. Nothing in his behaviour corresponds to the usual aim of the fetishist, who tries, on the contrary, to achieve 'normalization' by using the fetishistic mechanism; this suggests that the mechanism is working badly and that the subject is living with the threat of breakdown.

Michel's mother immediately enters into his fetishistic game. She finds her son's choice perfectly normal, and even 'borrows' his doll and dresses it up in clothes from her own wardrobe. This complicity is in fact no more than a continuation of an earlier seduction. As for maternal aggressivity, the director makes that an attribute of Michel's wife, who has no hesitation about dragging him before the courts. We then see Michel's lawyer, accompanied by his wife, visiting him at his request. Michel greets them in his underpants and ignores the lawyer's wife, and this homosexual exhibitionism can only be understood as an attempted seduction of the father figure Michel needs to protect him. But he cannot protect himself against his own anal-homosexual drive. The mechanism breaks down, and so does the narcissistic fiction.

We see here a process I have described in connection with the 'Suicide of the melancholic' (Grunberger, 1966): the narcissistic self turns against the ego, withdraws its narcissistic charge, and analizes the ego. The 'de-narcissization' of the ego is represented by the 'Christmas party' sequence. Michel invites his concierge and a whole procession of hideously vulgar individuals. This makes him physically sick, but nothing can prevent his house (ego) from being invaded by the process of faecalization. The monstrous and abject creatures who constantly harass and persecute him are his own introjects, which – once they have been set free – become dispersed and, once their narcissistic cathexis has been withdrawn, become the terrible, grimacing figures we see in nightmares, both processes having the same origins. The idol itself (the doll) is carried in a debauched procession. At first she is almost a reliquary (another allusion to the fetish), but she suddenly becomes a disgusting prostitute, and is defiled by swarms of men. Michel throws himself into the river, where he finds what remains of the filthy, deflated doll being carried along by the current like any other piece or rubbish. The anal object has been stripped of its triumphal narcissism, and analized anew.

I have already spoken of Sacher-Masoch's fetishes and of his novella about a 'Brown Venus'. The hero of the story falls in love with his Amazon queen, but after their marriage the queen becomes depressed; in an attempt to cure her, her husband offers her anything she wants, even his life. She accepts his offer, has him roasted, eats him, and is cured of her depression. Here we are at the heart of a deep conflict with the mother, a conflict marked by fantasies of being devoured; there is nothing surprising about that: on the contrary, it is thrown into a certain relief if we recall that the discoverer of masochism went mad and killed one of his precious pedigree cats, even though he passionately loved it (a short while afterwards, he attempted to strangle his wife). The night after he killed his beloved cat, Sacher-Masoch woke up screaming: 'I am being eaten alive – the cats, the cats – they are chasing me' (see Clengh, 1957). We know that in his novel *Venus in Furs* (1886) he compares women dressed in furs to the big cats, and it will be recalled that Konrad dreamed of cats crawling out of women's corpses to persecute him.

We have seen that the fetishist's conflict is primarily a deep conflict with the mother, and that it is presided over by primal maternal imagos; one imago promises a narcissistic and magical omnipotence; the other is an image of the anal-sadistic mother on to whom he projects his own anality and sadism. Both imagos appear in the fetish-object, which represents the transition from identification to projection. (The historical oedipal mother has been ousted by the narcissistic-magical regime, just as the Oedipus itself is ousted by anal erotism and its derivatives.)

The fetishist seems in fact always to have suffered from the lack of a father. Either his father is absent, or he is sadistic. This seems to have applied to Sacher-Masoch, whose father was the chief of police. All these cases are characterized by the absence of a father capable of protecting the child from primitive maternal imagos. As Joyce McDougall stresses, perversions are defences, though the extent to which they are organized may vary, not only against the Oedipus but also against psychosis. The distinguishing feature of the fetishist is his attempt to project – in a localized way – a major conflict bound up with anality by means of a narcissistic projection which puts an end to the conflict. He therefore uses his fetish to create a conflict-free zone, an *inverted phobic object*. The return of the repressed is signalled by aggression, often directed against the fetish, and may result in psychosis (Sacher-Masoch kills the adored cat-fetish which has become his persecutor). In their dreams, fetishists sometimes see the gradual transformation of the fetish into an object of terror.

At a certain level, the fetish also contains the father's anal phallus, and the fetishist attempts to narcissize that too. The fetish thus becomes a condensation of highly ambivalent anal objects which are *simultaneously* erected into idols. We also know that the fetish is a good luck charm, which has to be touched or carried around if the subject is to be surrounded by its beneficent fluid. But it can sometimes have precisely the opposite effect, and some commonly used good luck charms also have the reputation of being unlucky, the number '13' being one example. Within their own regressive dimension, fetishes are rather like primal words: they have antithetical meanings (Freud, 1910b). To a certain extent, and in certain conditions, anality can imply potential narcissization, but the converse is also true: owning a piece of the hangman's rope may bring luck, but in the theatrical world narcissism forbids any mention of that same object. Whilst the sight of the fetish may be lucky, idols are often malevolent deities and reliquaries are always surrounded by grimacing figures from a chamber of horrors which express the subject's primal aggressivity: the primal *anal object* becoming the *phallic* (*narcissistic*) *image*. It also contains all the stages the subject lived through during his transition from one to the other, and tells the story of a metamorphosis which was lived in a prepsychotic mode as an apotheosis.

Chapter Twelve

A study of
the Oedipus

I The Oedipus and narcissism

I HAVE ATTEMPTED, in a series of works dating back to 1956 (Grunberger, 1956), to show that the Oedipus can easily be used to cover up a narcissistic wound. The young child inevitably suffers a narcissistic wound when it realizes that it is not capable of fulfilling its wishes concerning the adult object. The child would rather be forbidden to do something than to have to admit to its impotence, and in a sense it invents the oedipal obstacle so as to defend its honour: 'I am not impotent; I have come up against an external obstacle.'

I am now convinced that we can go further and take the view that as well as being the source of this secondary gain, narcissism can, in a very general sense, be found at the very basis of the oedipal conflict: that the individual 'invents' the Oedipus, and that the Oedipus stems directly from his psychosexual development. I will describe this psychosexual development later, and put forward a hypothesis which has, I believe, the further advantage of explaining the complex's twofold nature: oedipal wishes and their prohibition stem from the same source – that is, from the child. (In Freud's day it was possible to speak of a real threat of castration, but in general that threat no longer exists, and when an analysand tells me in the course of a session that 'Incest is forbidden', I occasionally ask, 'Forbidden by whom?' No one actually tells children that incest is forbidden – indeed, in certain milieus the tendency appears to be to tell them the exact opposite.)

This paper was written in 1983.

For the moment I will deal only with certain aspects of the relationship between the Oedipus and narcissism, but I will anticipate my later remarks by putting forward one of this essay's theses: in my view, the Oedipus essentially means that human instinctuality (which is my translation of the German *Triebhaftigkeit*) is channelled towards the potential completion of a narcissistic project which may be regarded as the natural and spontaneous culmination of the maturation process.

I recently analysed a young priest who, whilst he had not abandoned his priestly vocation, had begun to think about certain problems and to adopt revolutionary, not to say heretical, positions with regard to the Church. He went into analysis because he was having difficulties at the level of social contacts, and in order to put some order – as he put it – into his sexuality. He very quickly brought up some openly oedipal material, illustrated by sexual dreams which could not have been more explicit. But when he told me that he had just made love with one of his cousins to prove to himself that he was capable of doing so, I asked him why (why he thought he might not be able to), and then asked him what he was afraid of. He had no answer. I tried to get him to say that he was afraid of *being a child* and of being impotent, but it did no good. When, in order to make things easier, I told him – in rather unorthodox fashion, it must be said – that 'in theory all adults are supposed to be able to make love', he failed to grasp the line I was trying to throw him. It became obvious that the repression was concerned less with his oedipal wishes than with the narcissistic wound that had been caused by his inadequacy, and that he was masking it by protesting about the tyranny of the Church in forbidding sexuality. It should be noted that in French, as in other languages, the word *pouvoir* has a double meaning: 'to have the right' and 'to have the capacity'; this explains how inadequacy can be projected on to a prohibition (emanating from the superego).

The basic narcissistic wound from which the child suffers (and in my view, the function of oedipal prohibitions is to make reparation for it) is its very condition – in other words, its inadequacy and the fact that it is small. It may try to heal this wound in its fantasies, which are reflected in fairy tales about clever little Tom Thumb outwitting the stupid, clumsy giant (the adult) and, in a different register, in the story of how David was cunning enough to defeat the powerful Goliath. What seems on the face of things to be an oedipal victory is primarily a transcendence of a narcissistic wound that has been inflicted because the child is inadequate, young and small.

The ideologies of our time commonly offer a different solution by celebrating children or, rather, *infantilism*. Adults are made to feel that they have been narcissistically wounded because they do not conform to a model that has been turned into an ideal. This is in fact further defence against the narcissistic wound inflicted by the fact of being a child. In this connection, we should stress the importance of the spontaneous maturation of the child; the process must not be hurried, otherwise the child will be traumatized and its development will be blocked. Parents who want to help their children by treating them as 'pals' are simply reminding them of their humiliating condition, in the same way that workers find it difficult to tolerate the paternalism of their bosses.

A young woman in analysis once told me that as a child (she had several brothers and sisters) she enjoyed letting her brothers caress her stomach, as it gave her (and them; the pleasure was mutual) an extremely pleasurable feeling which spread throughout her whole body, and made them collapse into helpless laughter. Her father, an extremely liberal man, did nothing to forbid these games, and in fact encouraged them. One day, he heard the specific tonality of these manifestations, and said: 'I know that noise; you're playing...' That immediately put an end to the excitement, which turned to a general unease. This same father took his daughter's sexual education in hand in the belief that he was in the vanguard of progress. The result was that the girl developed a particularly prohibitive and sadistic superego as a defence against what she saw as a permanent exercise in seduction which was particularly wounding to her narcissism in that it never led to any satisfaction. When she reached puberty – and there was nothing abnormal about the way she developed – she was frigid, but that was not all; her ovaries would not function, and she suffered from total amenorrhoea together with a total and apparently organic involution of the internal genital organs. The gynaecologists she consulted found the enigma insoluble.[1]

It is above all the fact that they have such small sexual organs that embarrasses children, and we know how common it is to encounter the 'small penis complex' in analysing men (see Chasseguet-Smirgel, 1976; 1985, pp. 35–43). We also know how easily children can displace the Oedipus on to their grandfathers. In regressive situations such as dreams (not to mention mankind's collective dreams, which take the form of mythologies) the Oedipus can also be displaced on to *animals* representing the power and strength of adults. One of the reasons that the primal scene is so traumatic is that the protagonists have such instinctual power, and children give disproportionate emphasis to its sadistic character. Children can easily fantasize that power by projecting their own instinctual power, but at the same time they find themselves unable to discharge it.

The following clinical fragments illustrate the dialectical use of the Oedipus that I have outlined.

The first case is that of Laura, a young artist. This patient had once before

---

1 I am of course adopting a specific view in a somewhat arbitrary manner here, but that does not mean that I am overlooking the classic view of oedipal guilt.

been sent to me by one of my teachers for a classical analysis. I in fact failed to appreciate either the exceptional severity of the nucleus of her depression or the extreme fragility of her ego. Initially, she achieved a narcissistic-oral elational transference; but the narcissistic projection began to include elements of an early instinctual transference. Its libidinal charge was beyond her ability to integrate for the moment, particularly in that the elational transference-projection masked an almost total absence of narcissistic self-cathexis. When the libidinal charge reached a certain threshold, she reacted by mobilizing a regressive pseudo-oedipal conflict. Due to an unexpected incident, it was lived in a catastrophic mode.

I have mentioned earlier that as she was leaving after a session, this patient glimpsed the fleeting appearance of the figure of my wife in the hallway. She suddenly regressed and began to live the oedipal situation in an acutely immediate mode, but refused to recognize this transferential aspect. I asked her to sit down – this was obviously a psychotic regression – and we continued to sit face to face for several months before we could return to the normal analytic setting but the developing fluid of psychotic regression also allowed us to understand what had happened.

As we have seen, Laura initially achieved what seemed to be a positive paternal transference, and it was possible to analyse it at a certain level; but that transference masked a second transference which was taking place at a different level. The incident brought her face to face with her narcissistic inadequacy; until then she had been able to repress it, but not completely. She therefore projected her narcissism on to me (this always happens in analysis, but the process is usually partial) and the narcissistic haemorrhage resulted in a corresponding withdrawal of cathexis from the ego, which had been put in danger. She therefore resorted to a massive reactivation of her oedipal conflict, but she did so in what one might have called a hallucinatory mode, were it not that there was an element of reality about it. As she said, and kept saying, 'I did see that woman; she does exist. It's not transference; it's a fact.' And she described the process she had lived in a psychotic mode: 'When I saw you in all your glory [thanks to a huge narcissistic projection], and then me, an insignificant, pathetic little girl dressed in clothes that didn't fit me, you were my father's marvellous phallus, and I was a little girl's childish and inadequate genitals.' She gave this description much later, after a lengthy process of maturational development; when she had told me about it, she had a sexual dream in which her father penetrated her. But she was lying in the position she had been in when a girlfriend taught her to masturbate. The dream represented both a narcissistic fusion and oedipal coitus. Then she said: 'When I got up and washed in the morning, I saw my genitals as a valuable, precious, living organ for the very first time.'

The other case I would like to describe in this context is that of a man in his forties. He originally came from Central Europe, and his father had emigrated when he was born. He was therefore brought up by a governess (his mother was usually away on business too), but he retained the image of a father who was very narcissistically satisfying, who was idealized because he was absent. At the same time, the image did have a real content, as his father had lived in the tropics and had indeed enjoyed a picturesque and dazzling career. Deeply involved in local and then international politics, he became a famous leader, and the house was full of photographs in which the child could admire him surrounded by his faithful native servants or leading a troop of elephants.

At the age of three-and-a-half the child was put on a ship and sent to join a father he had never seen. The ship called at various ports, and he was taken around by the crew and by various passengers who, as the voyage went on, became increasingly fond of the little boy, who was extremely narcissistic and extremely attractive. They all knew his history. As the ship approached the quay it became possible to make out the imposing figure of his father. The helmsman let the boy take the wheel, and told him he was steering the ship. The boy experienced a feeling of intense joy.

Before analysing this episode, I should complete my account by stressing that until this moment in the analysis, the highly narcissistic transference had always failed to overcome the insistent demands of the drives, which systematically gave rise to resistances. But when the patient came to relate the episode I have just described, I intervened and asked him to try to remember if he had believed the helmsman, and if he had really thought that he was steering the ship. He immediately replied: 'Yes, at first I did believe it. But when I saw my father, who was powerfully built, just as I had imagined him, and realized that he was about to throw his arms around me, I no longer believed it, *presumably because I didn't need to once my father was there.*'

In the first case, the patient resorted to a psychotic mode of regression to the oedipal conflict, and then emerged from it when she was able to use the image of her girlfriend, a double of herself, to 'narcissize' her drives. (As a child, this patient had had an imaginary playmate – another version of the girlfriend in question.) In the second case, the patient let go of his narcissistic omnipotence when he could project it on to his father, partly by identifying with him.

Whilst father figures in general become a focus for narcissistic projection, a father who is unable to assume that task is a major obstacle to the child's development. The result may, for instance, be a rejection of the father, though this must not be confused with a derivative of the oedipal conflict.

II The complex

In my view it is essential to return to the notion of maturation, particularly in that a superficial and extra-analytic conception of that notion is invading our discipline as the result of ideological pressures which, as I have already pointed out, are intended to eradicate the narcissistic wound caused by being small and inadequate by stressing facts which put child and adult, or at least adolescent and adult, on the same level. As a result, maturation tends to be confused with a purely physiological or purely intellectual process, or even with the acquisition of a certain body of knowledge. The growing time-lag between physiological maturation on the one hand and the structuring of the ego on the other is in fact one factor in psychosexual disturbance.

The degree of maturity that has to be attained in both life and analysis is an oedipal maturity because, as we know, it is bound up with the Oedipus and simply cannot be confused with a purely physiological or intellectual maturity.

Analysis is not a matter of intellectual preparation or training. If it were, it would be impossible to understand why training analyses are becoming longer and longer at a time when the younger generation of analysts possesses an undeniable intellectual sophistication and enjoys conditions which are far superior to those experienced by earlier generations. Psychoanalysis is now faced with a crucial problem. The contempt that is displayed for the deep, intimate and visceral aspect of the analytic process is the modern equivalent to the medieval cleric's loathing of anything to do with corporeality. This may be a source of great satisfaction for the analyst's narcissism, but the analysand needs to go through the process of maturation, and to *live* that dimension in the transference. This applies to both therapeutic and training analyses.

My own view is that anality plays a key role in the process of maturation that leads to the integration of the Oedipus. Anality adds a third dimension to the drives. Anality seems to be particularly difficult to accept – and it is usually projected – yet it is anality that gives the drives their connotations of animality, substantiality and materiality, and without those connotations the integration of the drives is purely illusory. A refusal to analyse anality means that the analysis will have no lasting effects and transforms it into a purely intellectual game. Theories which give language primacy over the unconscious represent a move in that direction, but other theories have similar effects.

After these all too brief comments, we can now attempt to outline the process whereby the Oedipus is constituted by looking at the clinical data. As I have stressed elsewhere in my descriptions of the characteristics of prenatal life, the constitution of the Oedipus begins before birth. In order to avoid unnecessary repetition, let me simply say that I refer to the primal life of the drives, to the instinctual combination which will later give rise to sexuality and aggressivity (sexuality is prefigured by the accelerated process of the proliferation of cells; aggressivity by the parasitic cannibalistic relationship between the foetus and its host-mother). Given that the mother automatically supplies the child with everything it needs, the child lives this conflict-free state in an elational mode as a coenesthesis which provides a matrix for the feelings of unlimited happiness and boundless omnipotence it will later experience in the form of a narcissistic component.

This elational state becomes the focus for a gradual but inevitable trauma, and when the child is born it is faced with the need to reorganize its libidinal economy (the transition is made easier by the care-taker who helps it to move from one state to the other; see Ferenczi, 1913a) – with the need, that is, to abandon its narcissistic, parasitic tranquillity and begin to use its sensorium and its respiratory, digestive and motor functions (orality and anality). All this forces it to make a total change of regime. But the primordial element in this dynamic upheaval is the constancy of the child's aim. It constantly tries to recover the narcissistic completeness it has lost. Its new condition will force it to adopt the 'instinctual solution', but it will never really make any final choice, and will often hesitate; unlike the Jews who nostalgically remembered their pots of meat as they wandered through the desert, the child will never stop regretting the happy state which once allowed it to satisfy its narcissism automatically, in absolute terms, and at no cost to itself.

When the child is born, its instincts are, then, mobilized and activated by the new state in which it finds itself, but it is unable to discharge them; the child is therefore a focus for tensions it cannot repress because they are beyond the capabilities of its ego. Its ego is, so to speak, nonexistent and it cannot develop without the very conflict the child wishes to avoid. At this stage, the child (whose ego is preceded by a confused narcissism struggling against instinctual tension) experiences any excitation which exacerbates the conflict as 'bad' and everything else (anything pleasurable) as part of its narcissistic self. It is this narcissistic self which must be preserved at all costs, and it is at this point that the Oedipus intervenes to produce the effects I described earlier.

The role of the Oedipus is to channel primitive drives which are all the more threatening in that they have been unleashed prematurely because, as I have indicated elsewhere, the child is born prematurely in the sense that it is inadequately equipped (this is the essential factor in humanization) – which was not the case before it was born – and because its drives remain unchanged and retain their animal qualities. This is the real source of the child's primal difficulties, and it is faced with the problem of finding a *modus vivendi* in which the specificity of its condition can be reconciled with the animal character of its drives.

The child's primal aggressivity first finds expression in a series of fantasies (conscious and unconscious) which are mainly concerned with the mother – or, rather, with the breast, the first object (the breast gradually becomes an object as the drive becomes separated from the primal narcissistic tendency and turns to the world of objects). The child's sexuality, on the other hand, gradually becomes organized and fixated on primitive mental formations or images of part-objects. Both aggressivity and sexuality find their way into certain basic primal fantasies relating to the 'container–contained' and 'the primal scene', and the child's fantasy activity will produce corresponding variations on these themes.

This fantasy activity will gradually focus on the child's image of its mother. She is its first object and, depending on what is projected on to the libidinal support she provides, a variety of successive images will emerge; these are archaic, primal images which are at once terrifying (projections of the child's aggressivity) and omnipotent images to which the impotent child has to submit; the child comes into conflict with these imago-figures and at the same time identifies with them, combating them with the omnipotent aggressivity it derives from these magical imaginary identifications. But that very omni-potence will fill it with anxiety, because the child is powerless to discharge it.

Here we have a world of nightmares and fairy tales, of gurus and intellectual masters (representations of the archaic maternal imago). And here we find, of course, the schema which will govern the formation of certain pathological fixations and perversions. The fact that in the course of the formation of these fantasies there appear traces of triangulation and traces of the paternal figure does nothing to alter the essence of this pre-oedipal sexual-aggressive life, which is still narcissistic and magical, and it is only with the Oedipus that the child undergoes the qualitative change that releases it from this dimension. It is all the more important to clarify this notion in that sexual desires and aggressive impulses are present before the child reaches this evolutionary turning point. We also find an engram of a certain triangulation of these desires and impulses. As Diderot puts it (1762, p. 126):

If the little savage was left to his own devices, remained totally imbecilic and combined something of the reason of the child in the cradle with the violent passions of a man of thirty, he would wring his father's neck and sleep with his mother.

But the whole point is that the child does not have the strength or the capacity to do so, and it is that which constitutes its basic narcissistic wound. It is at this point that the child encounters the reality of its inadequacy, and therefore reality in general. It finally recognizes reality for what it is, but it also learns to make use of reality by organizing its Oedipus in terms of the formula I have already used: 'I am not inadequate, but I am faced with an obstacle.' 'I am biding my time, and for the moment I will identify with my rival.' 'I am displacing my primal aggressivity on to my rival, etc.'

The child's ego begins the work of adapting to reality (though the continued existence – come what may – of the antagonistic narcissistic solution is still an obstacle). The work of adapting to reality and the process of maturation are one and the same, but the various roles played by the latency period have yet to be determined. The Oedipus will give the process a new orientation and will, above all, make reparation for the initial narcissistic wound. The essential component in this process is the channelling of the libido towards the mother and therefore towards women in general, and an increasingly differentiated organization of the aggressivity which appears to be directed towards the father and, at a secondary level, male members of the phratry (displaced Oedipus). Displacement on to the father may be inverted, at least on a superficial level (sibling rivalry). We know that one of the essential forms of the defence against the Oedipus (a long-term process which demands great effort in the face of an increasing number of obstacles; the whole of modern civilization militates against the integration of aggressivity) is of course the mirror projection of narcissistic regression on to the phratry, and that this takes place under the protection of a magical-narcissistic Primal Mother figure such as an ideology, a religion, an intellectual master or an idol.

The Oedipus is therefore both a wish and a prohibition; and we will now examine its dual character in connection with incest. It is an artificial device, but it is an essential and indispensable device, an evolutionary turning point. It is both an obstacle and a support (Talleyrand said that barriers are also supports). It ends – and the Oedipus complex does come to an end, albeit a very relative end – at the moment when the 'device' allows the subject to channel its libido and aggressivity by integrating them into its ego to such an extent that they can be used, given the right economic conditions, whilst still retaining a certain degree of dynamic tension, for reasons which will be examined below. When man reaches this point, the device has served its purpose and there is no further need for it – at least, not in its differentiated form. In that sense the Oedipus too is an achievement, and it may in a sense merge with the achievement of the narcissistic project that originates in prenatal life; it is at least possible, given the right conditions, to ensure that the subject's 'life project' will lead eventually to its spontaneous achievement.

The conception I am outlining gives primacy to the drives and I therefore invert the terms of Freud's (1924b, p. 176) reference to 'the sexual excitement belonging to the complex'. In my view, it is the complex which results from the sexual and aggressive tension. There are no oedipal drives, merely sexual and aggressive drives.

III Lineage and incest

We have seen that oedipal wishes can be understood as both an expression and a natural survival of prenatal narcissistic bliss. These desires first appear as a neonatal form of fusion with the mother and are gradually enriched with instinctual elements, and it may be assumed that their particular charm is attributable to this combination of factors, especially at the beginning of the process, which is relatively conflict-free. But whilst this combination is the source of a particular kind of libidinal outpouring, the anal-sadistic component means that it also gives rise to certain specific difficulties. The integration of that component is in itself problematic, and the difficulties it creates have little to do with parental 'prohibitions' which, as we have seen, merely mask a basic difficulty relating to the intrinsic *anal* conflict and to the narcissistic wound inflicted by the child's inadequacy.

I had intended to devote some space to a specific discussion of how the subject's fear of its own anality and inability to use it in any adequate way intervenes in the oedipal dialectic, but I will restrict myself to giving a number of quotations from Deleuze and Guattari's enormous *Anti-Oedipus* (Deleuze and Guattari, 1972). The quotations in fact obviate the need to make a complete analysis of this work, as they are an adequate expression of the authors' hatred of the Oedipus and rejection of the whole complex. Thus, when the authors speak of the Oedipus as a 'dirty little family secret', their choice of terminology is in itself a clear indication of the anal character they are attributing to the Oedipus (the expression is modelled on such phrases as 'dirty Jew', 'dirty nigger', etc.). We will look later at the importance of this crudely negative attitude towards the Oedipus, but we can conclude even now that there is something peculiar about it if we recall that the Oedipus is one of psychoanalysis's primary insights: that its existence is not simply known but widely accepted, and has even become banal, thanks to current popularizations of Freud. And that is not all. Not only do we have to differentiate levels of acceptance and integration of this complex, we also have to assess its importance (the 'nuclear complex' of the neuroses) and determine its role in relation to other elements in psychoanalytic doctrine.

Psychoanalysis lives or dies by the Oedipus, because no matter which of the many oedipal solutions we adopt, both psychosexual development and analysis necessarily take place within an oedipal framework because of the channelling of the drives described above. Even if the attempt to channel the drives ends in failure, the subject will be negatively structured by that very failure. This is why it is the Oedipus that comes under attack and, as we shall see, the challenge to the Oedipus has far-reaching implications. Given that the subject's goal is narcissistic, two possibilities are open to him. Either he inserts himself into the natural evolutionary process and attempts to realize his project through his instinctual life (a maturational development involving the Oedipus, the anal-sadistic component and reality), or he begins to look for a purely narcissistic solution by avoiding the Oedipus, by remaining within the imaginary rather than confronting the real, and, in a word, by circumventing the maturational process and living a marginal exist .ice as though neither the father nor reality existed.

We are talking here about basic attitudes towards life, one based upon the Oedipus, and the other upon its denial; about two visions of humanity which occasionally clash (usually within psychoanalysis) and which, to anticipate later arguments, we might describe as being, respectively, patri-oedipal and matri-narcissistic. Those who take the latter view form phratries, narcissistically identify with each other in a play of mirror reflections, and cluster around archaic mother figures which protect them by warding off, fighting and disavowing the father and his entire world.[2]

As I have already said, the child is inserted into the oedipal situation and we have to analyse that situation in detail. In order to do so, we can make use of the notion of lineage. That will give us a better understanding of the essence of incest, both as wish and as 'prohibition' (in a purely psychoanalytic sense; I am not proposing that we venture into social anthropology).

The notion of lineage is banal, and we all know how important it is to man at the level of both his instinctual life and his narcissism. Here we come dangerously close to certain philosophico-biological conceptions which once acquired a certain influence and led Freud and others to speculate about Weissman's germ-plasm theory, and about instincts dedicated solely to the preservation of the species (Freud, 1920). Those speculations finally result in the Eros–Thanatos theory, which I would prefer not to discuss here. We know that there are certain categories of individuals who dedicate their lives to their family name and are willing to die for it. The perpetuation of the family line concerns both the future (Jews refer to the other world as the world to come) and the past, because these individuals are trying both to ensure that they will have a future life and to preserve something they have inherited from their ancestors.

Abraham, the founder of Judaism, proved his loyalty and submission to his God by agreeing to sacrifice his only son Isaac. Abraham became a father late in life, and he was willing to sacrifice his entire line of descent. God rewarded him for this supreme sacrifice by promising him that he would have numerous offspring ('I will multiply thy seed as the stars of heaven, and as the sand which is upon the sea shore' [Genesis 22: 17]). This allows us to conclude that lineage represents something that affects the individual's whole life, that it corresponds to the ideal of narcissistic fulfilment which I situated at the focal point of the individual's project. That project is central and essential to his life.

Religions have of course taken note of and ritualized man's primitive tendency to perpetuate and safeguard his family line, and having no descendants, and particularly no male descendants, is not only a curse but

2 They are indeed archaic mother figures, and not 'genital' figures. It is as though the only choice were between the father and the primal mother, and matters are likely to remain that way.

often a veritable crime. We will return to this point. The curse can be lifted by having recourse to customs which are broadly analogous to the Mosaic custom of levirate. In certain societies, a father who has no male descendants may remedy his deficiency by becoming the nominal father of any male child that might be born to his daughter if she marries a close relative chosen by him (note how close this is to father–daughter incest). The proxy is chosen on the basis of a strict order of succession, and is usually one of the father's brothers. Levirate itself concerns married men who die and leave no children; a childless widow must marry her late husband's brother, who is thus responsible for 're-establishing his brother's house – in other words, his integrity – by becoming a link in the chain of the generations.[3]

The Oedipus is closely bound up with the issue of lineage. I have deliberately omitted matrilineal societies from this discussion; matrilineal societies still exist in some primitive communities, but it can be demonstrated that the apparently matrilineal society of, say, the Trobriand Islands is really a disguised patriarchy. Our own society is patriarchal, and the paternal imago is narcissistically projected on to a God who creates ethics, aesthetics, the ideal of justice and, above all, a scientific method based on causality and logic, and it is no accident that Sophocles has the Sphinx ask Oedipus a riddle about lineage, about the sequence of the three ages (which correspond, in my view, both to the three successive individuals needed to found and continue a family line and to the process of maturation). Oedipus's own ancestry raises the same question: his grandfather Labdakos shares the same characteristic (lameness) and his name has the same meaning (lame); as we know, the word 'oedipus' itself means 'swollen-footed'.

What, then, is a line of descent? We have already seen that it is made up of a continuous sequence of *male* individuals; the founder of the line is therefore the father. It is the father who gives his daughter in marriage to his son-in-law,

---

3 When seen in this light, Mosaic law provides a veritable prototype for oedipal legislation in that it extends its specific provisions to cover the animal kingdom and even the vegetable kingdom: 'Thou shalt not let thy cattle gender with a diverse kind; thou shalt not sow thy field with mingled seed; neither shall a garment mingled of linen and woollen come upon thee' (Leviticus 19:19). It goes without saying that homosexuals (18:22; 20:13), and especially transvestites, are subject to particularly harsh condemnation. These provisions, which are now over three thousand years old, might be criticized on the grounds that they are illiberal or even grotesque. But it seems to me that they are an expression – taken to absurd lengths by the primary process – of the essence of the oedipal world and of the world of lineage. They appear all the more shocking and irrational to us in that we have lost all sense of what they once meant because we live in a much more – and increasingly – matri-narcissistic world.

If we accept that the line founded by the father provides a certain society with an existential basis, we can begin to understand why any perversion that institutes a sexuality which excludes the father, at least in his role of progenitor, can be seen to be sacrilegious, just as adultery – and hybridization in general – can tarnish the purity of the line.

who thus perpetuates his gender. The fact that the line of descent is perpetuated by a sequence of fathers therefore allows us to understand (if not to condone) the morals of those who take a different view of adultery depending on whether it is committed by a man or a woman. In a sense, when Jesus prevents the adulterous woman from being stoned – and he does so in a very poetic and highly moral way – he undermines the law that preserves the purity of the line and can therefore be seen as one of the champions of the matri-narcissistic world (I need scarcely add that I am not in favour of stoning women who commit adultery!). And in Catholicism, the matri-narcissistic world finds its supreme expression in the union between Virgin and child.

It should also be noted that the interpretative technique of Freudian psychoanalysis constantly tries to reinsert the subject into a line of descent – and it is this which so annoys the anti-oedipal party – by saying 'X as such does not matter; X in fact represents your father (or mother).' Because it reduces a multiplicity of images and presentations to parental figures, psychoanalysis is indeed essentially oedipal. Similarly, the *causality* which it establishes between various phenomena (psychic determinism) also relates to the idea of lineage: one thing generates another. Attempts to introduce other disciplines or ideologies into psychoanalysis, or to subordinate psychoanalysis to them, can therefore be seen as so many attempts at hybridization, as attempts to break the line of descent. We can now turn to the dialectic between the oedipal system (lineage) and the matri-narcissistic system which – to allude to Sophocles' drama – might also be called the Sphinx's system. The genius of Sophocles obviously grasped the very essence of this dialectic intuitively. The various twists of the plot might be regarded as a sequence of positive and negative phases:

> Laius refuses to have a son (to be a father) and forms a homosexual couple with Chryssipos; he breaks the line, whereas
> Oedipus is looking for his parents; he would like to be their son, and enters a line of descent. Then,
> having founded a family, he has two daughters and two sons, but his sons kill one another. He therefore breaks the line;
> his daughters could found the line anew by marrying, but they commit suicide, and the line is therefore destroyed.

We can now elaborate a concept of incest on the basis of these remarks on lineage.

Incest represents a search for narcissistic fulfilment by returning directly to the mother's womb (incestuous coitus).[4] In terms of lineage, incest is, so to speak, an attempt to 'go back up the line', to pervert the line of descent. The term incest applies not only to the individual, but to his lineage. Incest breaks or cuts the line. If the line of descent is to be perpetuated, it must be constantly crossed or cut by the introduction of a mother from the outside (exogamy) and the return to the mother leads it into an impasse because coitus with the mother means the death and obliteration of the father. In so far as the prohibition of incest takes a socialized form which gives rise to rites and taboos, we can conclude that it has much more to do with the breaking of the line than with the prohibition of an individual sin.

IV Oedipus and the Sphinx

The story of Oedipus can be reduced to two essential 'contents' which are both contrasted and complementary: the episode with the Sphinx (Sophocles' 'cruel singer') and the drama of incest (the exact order of events is of little importance in the unconscious dimension). And what is the Sphinx? A sort of omnipotent and terrifying Phallic Mother. She is related to demi-goddesses like Medusa and Selene, the moon goddess of Thebes, and is therefore a creature of darkness; she bears a number of phallic emblems, and her realm lies in the most undifferentiated and most archaic depths of pregenitality. Her obscurity reflects the way the child projects on to an archaic mother; it does not understand her, but it knows that it depends on her and that in order to survive it must accept her and identify symbiotically with her. Her obscure words suddenly acquire a narcissistic value which places her beyond the real and which, in a purely imaginary and illusory way, make her exist on a higher plane.

A 'new' psychoanalysis has recently come into being. It has its own liturgy, and its value stems from its obscurity, from its sibylline, esoteric language. One is reminded of the Sphinx in her den, drawing the young people of Thebes to her in order to destroy them with her lessons in confusion, with her rhetoric, and with a false and hollow eloquence which is as deceptive as she is; but she will collapse into nothingness at the first formulation of logic and with the first reference to reality, or to the 'Oedipus'. By calling things by their real names, Oedipus destroys the power of evil spells: clarity is mystery's enemy, which is why an analyst who gives the interpretation 'It's only . . .' is an Oedipus killing a Sphinx.

The oedipal approach is primarily an epistemological approach, and wordplay is designed to conceal that fact. *Oedipus* derives from the root *oida*,

---

4 There are different degrees of incest; the term should really be restricted to incest between mother and son – incest between brother and sister is mainly narcissistic. If mother and son actually commit incest, the result is a sort of psychic death. I have in fact heard a mother's account of her incestuous relations with her twenty-year-old son. The immediate outcome was regression and schizophrenia.

meaning 'to know', 'to understand'. This is why oedipal knowledge obtained by the oedipal method, and with the support of the parallel maturational process, sets man free, releases him from his infantile dependency, and makes him both a father and a son. That is to say, he is his own father; he does not fulfil his oedipal wishes, but he does rise above his infantile servitude.[5]

Psychosexual maturation therefore involves a transition through the Oedipus, which is itself structured by the successive integration of instinctual phases, and that process takes place in a specific and almost visceral dimension.

Whilst the Oedipus, which is a crossroads and a turning point in the maturational process, comes about through the successive integration of developmental phases in which anality plays a primordial role, the negation of this essential dimension of analysis gives rise to the much-sought-after illusion of a pure narcissistic solution which is conflict-free, immediate, total and absolute. The narcissistic solution depends on a tactic which I sometimes refer to as the fantasy of the apocalypse (and I would point out that this word means 'revelation'). The automatic resurgence of this fantasy is the resurgence of the world of prenatal regression, of a primal state of bliss. It is as though the existence of reality and of one of its principal components – anality – were unconscious obstacles to the final and triumphal advent of that state.

The analysis of anality in its various phases and modes of emergence must be pursued and supported by a form of theorization which does not do away with it or suppress it completely. But we are now witnessing the rise of a spiritualizing and aestheticizing discourse which is vague, superficial and impossible to grasp. It conjures away the existence of clinical reality, drives, conflict, affects – or, in a phrase, the existence of the real. I refer to the discourse of the anti-Oedipus. The Oedipus – and any psychoanalysis corresponding to that name – therefore becomes Public Enemy Number One because the collective superego of our time has resolved to destroy it. The fashionable discourse is that of the Sphinx, who sang the praises of darkness and confusion, as opposed to life and existence (I am speaking of the life of the drives and of the senses) – of essential difference between objects, structures, ideas, and individual histories. The discourse that is now in fashion is based on projection and disavowal, and it blames society (the outside world) for the conflict. Even within psychoanalysis itself, man is striving to lay down the burden of his conflicts and his primal narcissistic wound.

So, Oedipus never did defeat the Sphinx, and she constantly rises out of her

---

5 We find the same double inversion at a symbolic level. Rimbaud, for example, took his inspiration from the writers he had been imitating for years: François Coppée, Baudelaire...and in his turn he became a model, a father for future generations of poets.

ashes. My explanation for the difficulties we encounter in analysis – and they mean that the analysis is not simply interminable, but constantly has to be begun anew – is that we are all to some extent tempted to allow ourselves to be drawn into the obscure and fascinating entrails of the Sphinx, and I put that temptation down to our narcissistic nostalgia. Ideologies reactivate that nostalgia. It is therefore vital to ensure that psychoanalysis itself does not take on the bewitching features of the destructive Sphinx.

Chapter Thirteen

Narcissism: genesis and pathology

IN THANKING my hosts for their invitation to speak to you about my theory of narcissism, I feel that I should begin by listing the elements that are to be found in Freud's work, and particularly in 'On narcissism: an introduction' (Freud, 1914). Freud does indeed introduce narcissism, but he does so within a framework based on a theory of the drives which prevents him from constructing a coherent theory of narcissism. For Freud (1914, pp. 73–4) narcissism – which was originally identified as a perversion by Havelock Ellis – is 'the libidinal complement to the egoism of the instinct for self-preservation [*Selbsterhaltungstrieb*]'. He also states that 'it might claim a place in the regular course of human sexual development'. Now Freud makes a distinction between sexuality – and he refers to sexual energy as libido – and the instinct for self-preservation. In that connection, he speaks of 'interests' [*Interesse*]. It is possible to dispel this ambiguity by referring to Freud's idea that the origins of narcissism are very early, or that the two instincts in question can be combined. As to the character of this phase (of development), he extends the notion of 'phase' in two ways, given that he regards narcissism both as an archaic or primal state and as something which is perpetuated throughout human evolution (1916–17, p. 416):

It is probable that this narcissism is a universal and original state of things [*allgemeine und ursprüngliche Zustand*] from which object-love is only later

This paper was presented as a lecture at the Institute of Psychology, University of Bologna, 13 April 1985.

developed, without the narcissism necessarily disappearing on that account.

Freud also notes (1914, p. 77) that 'a unity comparable to the ego cannot exist in the individual from the start; the ego has to be developed', whereas the autoerotic instincts 'are there from the very first [uranfänglich]'. In other words, 'there must be something added to autoerotism – a new psychic action – in order to bring about narcissism.' Even so, it has been established that the origins of narcissism are very early, and that it may even originate in prenatal intrauterine life, as Freud invokes – amongst other factors – the state of sleep in this connection (1916–17, p. 417):

> The picture of the blissful isolation of intrauterine life which a sleeper conjures up once more before us every night is in this way completed on its psychic side as well. In a sleeper the primal state of distribution of the libido is restored – total narcissism [der volle Narzissmus], in which libido and ego-interest, still united and indistinguishable, dwell in the self-sufficing ego.

As Freud (1916–17, pp. 413–14) likens sexuality (and therefore the autoerotism from which narcissism originates) to 'a germ-plasm endowed with virtual immortality', narcissism now implies the notion of eternity; that is also part of my own definition of narcissism, but certainly not in Freud's sense of the supposed permanency of the drive. My own definition will be found above in my essay on Don Quixote [p. 129]. That definition is based on the psychic transcendence of the matrix activity of prenatal coenesthesis, and it necessarily extends beyond a definition based upon a perversion, a libidinal phase, the examination of the psychoses (narcissistic neoroses), the state of being in love, organic illnesses and sleep, as interpreted within the theory of the drives.[1]

As I have said [p. 14–15, p. 91], psychoanalysis is a theory of the drives [Trieblehre], and this point has often been made in attempts to criticize Freud, usually in connection with sexuality ('pansexualism'). Yet whilst the importance of the sexual factor cannot be denied (and I have attempted to show in detail that the role of sexuality in Freud's work can be a source of resistance to psychoanalysis), the attempt to extend its influence to infinity in fact restricts its validity. The same point can be made with respect to

---

[1] It is in this connection that Freud (1914, p. 77) describes the difference between 'a speculative theory and a science erected on empirical interpretation'. He adds: '... these ideas are not the foundation of science, upon which everything rests: that foundation is investigation alone. They are not the bottom but the top of the structure, and they can be replaced and discarded without damaging it.' He then discusses developments in physics, and expresses the hope (p. 78) that 'our provisional ideas in psychology will presumably one day be based on an organic substructure.'

narcissism, which was – for this very reason – a relatively late discovery and one which never really developed into a complete theory.

The same could be said of love, and I would remind you that whilst Freud does analyse the state of 'being in love', he never speaks of love in the true sense. As for friendship and tenderness, it is certainly not enough to regard the former merely as a sublimated derivative of homosexuality, or the latter as being restricted to the dimension of affection. In fact, we find in both love and narcissism an element – and it is probably their most characteristic element – or a factor which cannot be confused with sexuality but must, on the contrary, be contrasted with it. We will come back to this point, but for the moment let me quote Freud himself (1916–17, p. 76; emphasis added): ' ... or in connection with the higher aspirations, which we are occasionally in the habit of *contrasting* with "sensuality" under the name of "love"'.

According to Freud, the conflict is one between object-libido and ego-libido, and as one is employed, the other becomes depleted. This is Freud's description of the duel:

> The highest phase of development of which object-libido is capable is seen in the state of being in love, when the subject seems to give up his own personality in favour of an object-cathexis; while we have the opposite condition in the paranoiac's phantasy (or self-perception) of 'the end of the world'.

Observation of lovers gives the lie to this description, as we find that exalted happiness and an overevaluation of the object imply the overevaluation of the subject too. The worm falls in love with a star which shines and radiates a happiness, which is in fact the narcissistic elation that has been projected on to it, but the worm – who happens to be a poet – also benefits from it. Both love and narcissistic elation (which have a common core) transcend the drives, probably because of the presence of the element I call *pure narcissism*, which is devoid of any instinctual element.

This pure narcissism exists in a dialectical relationship with the drive factor, and it is the key to a number of pathological phenomena, but it also provides a key to the understanding of certain forms of relationship and forms of mass behaviour, to say nothing of its mental and intellectual expressions. Pure narcissism does not merge with the drive component, and may come into conflict with the instinct for self-preservation. I have described this conflict in connection with the 'Suicide of the melancholic' (Grunberger, 1966) and it provides an explanation for certain pseudo-accidental deaths, the course of certain illnesses, the sudden death of infants and a whole range of self-destructive behaviour. Freud rightly felt that some mysterious noninstinctual factor was at work here, and his intuition finally led him to discover the 'death drive'. It is not in fact a drive but a nostalgic longing for a purely narcissistic intrauterine life, in which the foetus's host – the mother – takes complete responsibility for its instinctual life, whilst the foetus itself lives like a happy parasite, is sheltered from conflict, and is its own sovereign master.

Self-sufficiency and inaccessibility are typical characteristics of prenatal life, but Freud's examples of narcissistic existence include children, women, large beasts of prey, and criminals:

> The charm of a child lies to a great extent in his narcissism, his self-contentment and inaccessibility, just as does the charm of certain animals which seem not to concern themselves about us, such as cats and the large beasts of prey. Indeed, even great criminals... (1914, p. 98)

Freud's short list is heteroclite and strangely inconsistent, particularly if we think of the economy of the drives. According to Freud, women are castrated, the child is a miniature man, and the instinctual force of the criminal is directed into aggressivity. Women, children, animals and criminals maintain a libidinal position which we once adopted and which we abandoned long ago, and Freud explains their charm in terms of their narcissistic cathexis. It is, however, easier to explain Freud's list if we adopt a different viewpoint and take the criminal as our starting point, as I do in a note appended to my study of Don Quixote [see note 2, p. 126]. As Freud himself puts it (1914, p. 89): 'It is as if we envied them for maintaining a blissful state of mind – an unassailable libidinal position which we ourselves have since abandoned.' In 'Libidinal types', Freud (1931, pp. 217–18) makes a distinction between 'the narcissistic type', 'the erotic-obsessional', the 'erotic-narcissistic' and the 'narcissistic-obsessional'. We can now add to this horizontal classification by giving a vertical or chronological description of the evolution of the individual, as seen in the light of narcissism.

II

The role of narcissism in the psychosexual evolution of the individual can take on very varied forms, but in order to simplify matters we can make a distinction between two basic modes of evolution. In the first, the oedipal (instinctual) current evolves parallel to the narcissistic current; this is a double process of narcissizing ('egotizing') the drives (through the integration of conflict) and of integrating narcissism into instinctual maturation, and eventually into the ego. This evolution results in a relative synthesis. This narcissism obviously has nothing in common with the initial 'pure narcissism', and it is ego-syntotic. We will not dwell upon the so-called 'normal' mode of maturation here, but will go on to look at another way in which narcissism can function in relation to the drives. Here, the synthesis of drives and narcissism does not occur in the normal way, and may not occur at all, and this raises the question of prematuration, much as it might displease certain analysts.

We may begin with the newborn child which comes into the world. It does so with a memory of prenatal elation, perfect bliss, absolute sovereignty and omnipotence. It has no memory of this in the psychological sense, but it has therefore 'recorded' it all the more indelibly and will constantly demand to return to it. It does so all the more insistently in that it really did once experience that state, and interpreted a coenesthetic state corresponding to a physiological reality on the basis of that experience. The child therefore comes into conflict with itself, so to speak, as its demands are physiologically based, whereas its whole life is now bound up with its new postnatal instinctual position. But it is dominated by its wish to preserve its pure narcissism; it is therefore caught up from the outset in a contradiction which cannot be reduced. The narcissist strives to cling to the 'existential solution', and to retreat from both instinctual life and the oedipal maturation which organizes reality.

We know that in the early stages of a child's life those around it – especially its mother – try to re-create the conditions of prenatal life, and as its mother takes full responsibility for it, the child can avoid primal conflict so long as it can avoid frustration by remaining in a parasitic state. Thanks to its mother, it can remain safe from conflict and can sustain its narcissistic illusion of completeness. At this point, the mother is not yet an object but an intimate environment assuring the infant that its narcissism will survive. She thus confirms the child's narcissism. Mother and child form what I call a *monad* [as described above in chapter 1]. The monad is constituted by narcissism, which is reflected on to the future maternal object and is conveyed by *reflections* and by the *gaze*. The child is both unaware of its environment and part of it (compare Winnicott's [1967] notion of the mother as environment).

Freud writes (1921, p. 101) of the extreme sensitiveness and violent aggressivity displayed by certain men in the crowd, and sees it as an expression of their immature narcissism. Having cited Schopenhauer's simile of the porcupines who crowded close together to protect themselves from the cold, but were forced to separate again because they soon felt the effects of one another's quills, he goes on to describe the aversion to people who are different. And this brings us back to the narcissist, who can cathect his image only if he sees it in a mirror, and who decathects or 'analizes' others:

> In the undisguised antipathies and aversions which people feel towards strangers with whom they have to do we may recognize the expression of self-love – of narcissism. This self-love works for the preservation of the individual, and behaves as though the occurrence of any divergence from his own particular lines of development involved a criticism of them, and a

demand for their alteration. We do not know why such sensitiveness should have been directed to just these details of differentiation; but it is unmistakable that in this whole connection men give evidence of a readiness for hatred, an aggressiveness, the source of which is unknown, and to which one is tempted to ascribe an elementary character.

In his paper on libidinal types, Freud (1931, p. 218; emphasis added) describes the narcissistic type as follows:

> The third type, justly called the *narcissistic* type, is mainly to be described in negative terms. *There is no tension between ego and superego* (indeed, on the strength of this type one would scarcely have arrived at the hypothesis of a superego), and there is no preponderance of erotic needs. The subject's main interest is directed towards self-preservation: he is independent and not open to intimidation. His ego has a *large amount of aggressiveness* at its disposal, which also manifests itself in readiness for activity. In his erotic life *loving is preferred to being loved*. People belonging to this type impress others as being 'personalities'; they are especially suited to act as a support for others, to take on the role of leaders and to give a fresh stimulus to cultural development or to *damage the established state of affairs*.

The monad assures the child that something of its prenatal bliss will live on, and at the same time supports it in its attempts to adapt to a postnatal way of life – to the instinctual conflict that results in the Oedipus. But if it is to do that, the conditions must be right, and this is not always the case. If the conditions are not right, the child will cling to women because they support a primal maternal imago; the mother in question is an asexual component of the monad (a narcissistic ideal) which is later transformed into a sexual object. The child cannot, however, become an oedipal conqueror. It remains under the mother's influence in so far as she is the monad in a narcissistic (oral-anal) sense, and will adopt a pseudo-oedipal position as a defence against the Oedipus (by refusing to engage with it). Its frustration will result in a certain aggressivity, and the child will project its difficulties not on to the father himself but on to the very possibility of oedipal evolution, on to the principle of paternity, on to causality and the real, and on to pragmatism and the pragmatic aspects of things in general. Rather than fighting the father in order to be like him (in either a positive or a negative sense), to overcome him and then to become a father in its turn, the child will constantly rail against the 'system', behave as a marginal, and express contempt for the world of the father. The narcissist will not fight his historic father, but will ignore him or ridicule him; he will behave in a similar way towards the oedipal world and the principle of paternity.

Adolescence is a period in which sexual maturation sets the senses alight and there is a sudden surge of narcissism which finds its expression in a heightened self-esteem which, in so far as it represents coenesthesis, becomes conscious. It is a sudden revelation. The young narcissist suddenly experiences the feeling of being different from others (but not from all his contemporaries, because some of them are like him in that they are going through the same process) and especially from his family. He feels superior to them (an interpretation of his sudden feeling of narcissistic hypertrophy, supported by sexuality). But the ego-nucleus on which this evolution centres is fragile (because of the oedipal deficit), and that gives him a feeling of insecurity; he reacts to that deficit by panicking, and that transforms his elation into weakness and a narcissistic wound. In his confusion, he will look for support to anyone who is like him and will happily become involved in mystical and ideological movements, in utopias which foster the illusion that he is conforming to a narcissistic ideal which can stand in for the ego; at the same time, it is quite possible that he will abreact his frustrated aggressivity.

If we now return to Freud's description, we find that the primary characteristic of this structure is indeed the absence of tension between ego and superego: the superego is the classically typical formation of this period of life, but no superego can be constituted if the ego is inadequate. If that is the case, we can at best speak of an archaic maternal superego [as described in chapter 9]. The narcissistic adolescent is contemptuous of the superego and all its derivatives, but he does not simply abandon it. He either inverts it or ridicules it in an attempt to outbid it.

The weakness of the ego provides an adequate explanation of the overwhelming need to be loved, but the subject's narcissism may reject love and may, like Deleuze and Guattari (1972), speak of the 'abject wish to be loved' because he cannot tolerate his dependency upon the object: that constitutes a narcissistic wound, as does any surrender to an instinctual urge. He has to be 'cool'. We are only too familiar with the large amount of aggressivity that can be provoked by the impossibility of integrating narcissism. It may take an explosive form. This is a way of avoiding the Oedipus; the systematic transgression and rejection of every manifestation of the paternal order is based on a primitive maternal ideal and its aesthetico-cultural derivatives stem from a type of mental activity (speech and writing) which appears to be brilliant but which, in the absence of the oedipal component, is grounded in certain disturbances of the thought processes. Freud is not mistaken when he speaks of those who are capable of giving 'a fresh stimulus to cultural development' and of those who can 'damage the existing state of things'.

This phase in evolution is, however, unavoidable, as the problems which arise here must arise; the point being that we should not dwell on them for too long.

The apparent nonexistence of this phase is equally worrying, as it indicates that the subject's defences are too great and too stubborn. Both the absence of any narcissistic *élan* and the predominance of the vegetative life of the drives can make it impossible to achieve an authentic synthesis of narcissism and the instinctual factor under optimal conditions.

Adolescents despise adults who conform too much because they have adapted too well to the instinctual solution. 'Being an adult' may mean achieving a certain psychological maturity, but that in itself means that we have not given up a prenatal narcissistic completeness, which still has a role to play. As he evolves, man relies upon the initial *élan* which leaves its mark on all his attempts to realize specific projects and transcends his material existence. To a certain extent, it outlives the purely pragmatic use he makes of it, and it is only in pathological cases that, because of frustration, it results in an outburst of primitive aggressivity that overwhelms the individual. Man's choices are not limited to being either an incendiary like Herostratus or a human louse.

Bibliography

(The place of publication is London unless otherwise indicated.)

Abraham, K. (1924) 'A short study of the development of the libido, viewed in the light of mental disorder', in *Selected Papers of Karl Abraham*, Hogarth, 1949, pp. 418–502.

Andreas-Salomé, Lou (1921) 'The dual orientation of narcissism', Stanley A. Leavey, trans., *Psychoanal. Q.* 31:1–30.

――― (1958) *The Freud Journal*, Stanley A. Leavey, trans. Quartet, 1987.

Anzieu, D. (1971) 'L'Illusion groupale', *Nouvelle Revue de psychanalyse* 3: 73–93.

Aron, R. (1955) *The Opium of the Intellectuals*, Terence Kilmartin, trans. Secker & Warburg, 1957.

Bachofen, J. J. (1861) *Myth, Religion and Mother Right. Selected Writings of J. A. Bachofen*. Princeton, NJ: Princeton University Press, 1967.

Balint, M. (1932) 'Character analysis and new beginning', in Balint, *Primary Love and Psycho-Analytic Technique*. Tavistock, 1965, pp. 151–64.

Balter, L. (1969) 'The mother as source of power: a psychoanalytic study of three Greek myths', *Psychoanal. Q.* 38:217–74.

Baudelaire, C. (1887) *Intimate Journals*, Christopher Isherwood, trans. Panther, 1969.

Beá, J. and Hernández, V. (1984) 'Don Quixote: Cervantes and Freud', *Int. J. Psycho-Anal.* 65:141–53.

Boss, M. (1953) *Sinn und Gehalt der sexuellen Perversionen*. Bern/Stuttgart: Hueber.

Bromberg, N. (1971) 'Hitler's character and its development', *Am. Imago*

28:289–303.

Bromberg, N. and Small, V. V. (1973) *Hitler's Psychopathology*. New York: International Universities Press.

Brosses, C. de (1760) *Culte des dieux fétiches ou, parallèle de l'ancienne religion de l'Égypte avec la religion actuelle de la Nigritie*. Paris.

Byron, W. (1988) *Cervantes: A Biography*. New York: Paragon.

Cahn, R. (1983) 'Le Procès du cadre, ou la passion de Ferenczi', *Revue française de psychanalyse* 47:1107–33.

Camus, A. (1951) *L'Homme révolté*. Paris: Idées, 1970.

Castres, H. (1976) *La Terre sans mal*. Paris: Seuil.

Cervantes, M. de (1604–14) *The Adventures of Don Quixote*. J. M. Cohen, trans. Harmondsworth: Penguin, 1950.

Chasseguet-Smirgel, J., ed. (1974) *Les Chemins de l'Anti-Oedipe*. Toulouse: Privat.

——— (1976) 'Freud and female sexuality. The consideration of some blind spots in the exploration of the "Dark Continent"', *Int. J. Psycho-Anal.* 57:275–86.

——— (1984) *Creativity and Perversion*. Free Association.

——— (1984) 'The archaic matrix of the Oedipus complex', in Chasseguet-Smirgel, *Sexuality and Mind: The Role of the Father and the Mother in the Psyche*. New York: International Universities Press, 1986, pp. 74–91.

——— (1985) *The Ego Ideal: A Psychoanalytic Essay on the Malady of the Ideal*, Paul Barrows, trans. Free Association.

Clengh, J. (1957) *The Marquis and the Chevalier*. New York: Duell, Sloan & Pierce.

Clérambault, G. G. de (1908) 'Passion érotique des étoffes chez la femme', *Arch. d'anthrop. crim.* 23:439–70.

Cocteau, J. (1934) *La Machine infernale*. Paris: Grasset.

Crémant, R. (1979) *Les Matinées structuralistes*. Paris: Laffont.

Deleuze, G. and Guattari, F. (1972) *Anti-Oedipus*, Robert Hurley, Mark Seem and Helen R. Lane, trans. New York: Viking, 1977.

Deutsch, H. (1937) 'Don Quixote and don quixotism', in Deutsch, *Neuroses and Character Types*. New York: International Universities Press, 1965, pp. 218–25.

Diderot, D. (1762) *Le Neveu de Rameau*. Paris: Livre de poche, 1966.

Dostoevsky, F. (1869) *The Idiot*, David Magarshack, trans. Harmondsworth: Penguin, 1955.

——— (1871) *The Devils*, David Magarshack, trans. Harmondsworth: Penguin, 1971.

——— (1880) *The Brothers Karamazov*, David Magarshack, trans. Harmondsworth: Penguin, 1958.

Erikson, E. H. (1956) 'The problem of ego identity', in Erikson *Identity and*

Life Cycle. New York: *Psychological Issues, Monograph 1*, 1959:101-64.

Evans-Pritchard, E. E. (1956) *Nuer Religion.* Oxford: Clarendon.

Fain, M. (1971) 'Préludes à la vie fantasmatique', *Revue française de psychanalyse* 30:871-82.

Faurisson, R. (1961) *A-t-on lu Rimbaud?.* Paris: Pauvert.

—— (1978) 'Le Problème des chambres à gaz', *Défense de l'occident*, June.

Federn, P. (1919) 'Zur Psychologie der Revolution: Die vaterlose Gesell-schaft', *Der österreichische Volkswirt* 11:571-4, 595-8.

—— (1953) *Ego Psychology and the Neuroses.* Imago.

Ferenczi, S. (1909) 'Introjection and transference', in Ferenczi (1952), pp. 35-93.

—— (1911a) 'On obscene words', in Ferenczi (1952), pp. 132-54.

—— (1911b) 'On the organization of the psychoanalytic movement', in Ferenczi (1955), pp. 299-307.

—— (1912a) 'On the definition of introjection', in Ferenczi (1955), pp. 316-18.

—— (1912b) 'On transitory symptom-constructions during the analysis', in Ferenczi (1952), pp. 193-213.

—— (1912c) 'The symbolic representation of the pleasure and reality principles in the Oedipus myth', in Ferenczi (1952), pp. 253-70.

—— (1913a) 'Stages in the development of the sense of reality', in Ferenczi (1952), pp. 217-40.

—— (1913b) 'A little Chanticleer', in Ferenczi (1952), pp. 240-53.

—— (1913c) 'On the ontogenesis of symbols', in Ferenczi (1952), pp. 336-40.

—— (1913d) 'Taming of a wild horse', in Ferenczi (1955), pp. 336-40.

—— (1914) 'On the ontogenesis of an interest in money', in Ferenczi (1952), pp. 319-33.

—— (1924) *Thalassa: A Theory of Genitality.* New York: Norton, 1968.

—— (1925) 'Pyschoanalysis of sexual habits', in Ferenczi (1950), pp. 259-97.

—— (1929) 'The principle of relaxation and neocatharsis', in Ferenczi (1955), pp. 108-35.

—— (1931) 'Child analysis in the analysis of adults', in Ferenczi (1955), pp. 126-42.

—— (1933) 'Confusion of tongues between adults and the child', in Ferenczi (1955), pp. 156-67.

—— (1950) *Further Contributions to Psychoanalysis.* Hogarth.

—— (1952) *First Contributions to Psychoanalysis.* Hogarth.

—— (1955) *Final Contributions to the Problems and Methods of Psycho-Analysis.* Hogarth.

—— (1970) *Oeuvres complètes, Psychanalyse II, 1913-19.* Paris: Payot.

—— (1985) *Journal clinique.* Paris: Payot.

Fernandez, D. (1982) *Dans la main de l'ange*. Paris: Grasset.

Fornari, F. (1964) *Psicanalisi dela guerra atomica*. Milan: Feltrinelli.

Freud, A. (1936) *The Ego and the Mechanisms of Defence*. New York: International Universities Press.

Freud, S. (1894) 'The neuro-psychoses of defence', in James Strachey, ed. *The Standard Edition of the Complete Psychological Works of Sigmund Freud*, 24 vols. Hogarth, 1953–73, vol. 3, pp. 45–62.

—— (1900) *The Interpretation of Dreams. S.E.* 4–5.

—— (1905a) *Jokes and their Relation to the Unconscious. S.E.* 8.

—— (1905b) *Three Essays on the Theory of Sexuality. S.E.* 7, pp. 125–245.

—— (1907) *Delusions and Dreams in Jensen's 'Gradiva'. S.E.* 9, pp. 1–95.

—— (1908) 'The sexual theories of children'. *S.E.* 9, pp. 205–76.

—— (1909a) 'Analysis of a phobia in a five-year-old boy'. *S.E.* 10, pp. 1–145.

—— (1909b) 'Notes upon a case of obsessional neurosis'. *S.E.* 10, pp. 151–249.

—— (1910a) *Leonardo da Vinci and a Memory of his Childhood. S.E.* 11, pp. 57–137.

—— (1910b) '"The antithetical meaning of primal words"'. *S.E.* 11, pp. 155–61.

—— (1913) *Totem and Taboo. S.E.* 13, pp. 1–161.

—— (1914) 'On narcissism: an introduction'. *S.E.* 14, pp. 73–102.

—— (1916–17) *Introductory Lectures on Psychoanalysis. S.E.* 15–16.

—— (1918) 'From the history of an infantile neurosis'. *S.E.* 17, pp. 1–122.

—— (1920) *Beyond the Pleasure Principle. S.E.* 18, pp. 1–64.

—— (1921) *Group Psychology and the Analysis of the Ego. S.E.* 18, pp. 65–143.

—— (1923a) *The Ego and the Id. S.E.* 19, pp. 3–61.

—— (1923b) 'The infantile sexual organization'. *S.E.* 19, pp. 139–45.

—— (1924a) 'The economic factor of masochism'. *S.E.* 19, pp. 155–70.

—— (1924b) 'The dissolution of the Oedipus complex'. *S.E.* 19, pp. 171–9.

—— (1924c) 'The loss of reality in neurosis and psychosis'. *S.E.* 19, pp. 181–7.

—— (1925a) 'Negation'. *S.E.* 19, pp. 233–9.

—— (1925b) 'A note upon the "mystic writing pad"'. *S.E.* 19, pp. 227–32.

—— (1925c) 'Some psychical consequences of the anatomical distinction between the sexes'. *S.E.* 19, pp. 241–58.

—— (1926) 'Inhibitions, symptoms and anxiety'. *S.E.* 20, pp. 75–125.

—— (1927) 'Fetishism'. *S.E.* 21, pp. 147–57.

—— (1929) *Civilization and its Discontents. S.E.* 21, pp. 57–145.

—— (1931) 'Libidinal types'. *S.E.* 21, pp. 215–20.

—— (1933) *New Introductory Lectures on Psychoanalysis, S.E.* 22.

—— (1938) *An Outline of Psychoanalysis. S.E.* 23, pp. 139–207.

—— (1939) *Moses and Monotheism. S.E.* 23, pp. 1–137.

_____ (1940 [1938]) 'Splitting of the ego in the process of defence'. *S.E.* 23, pp. 271–8.

_____ (1961) *Letters of Sigmund Freud 1873–1939*. Hogarth.

_____ (1985) *The Complete Letters of Sigmund Freud to Wilhelm Fliess, 1887–1904*. Jeffrey Moussaief Masson, ed. and trans. Cambridge, MA: Belknap.

Gagnebin, M. (1984) 'L'Irreprésentable ou les silences de l'œuvre', *Écriture*, January.

Garma, A. (1956) 'The meaning and genesis of fetishism', *Int. J. Psycho-Anal.* 37: 414–15.

Garnier, C. and Fralon, J. (1951) *Le Fétichisme en Afrique noire*. Paris: Payot.

Genet, J. (1949) *Journal d'un voleur*. Paris: Gallimard.

Gennep, A. van (1909) *Les Rites de passage*. Paris: Nourry.

Ghiotto, R. (1967) *Scacco all regina*. Milan: Rizzoli.

Girard, R. (1978) *Des Choses cachées depuis la fondation du monde*. Paris: Livre de poche, 1986.

Glover, E. (1930) 'Grades of ego differentiation', in Glover, *On the Early Development of Mind*. Imago, 1956, pp. 112–22.

Goethe, J. W. von (1809) *Elective Affinities*, R. J. Hollingdale, trans. Harmondsworth: Penguin, 1971.

Goncharov, I. (1858) *Oblomov*, David Magarshack, trans. Harmondsworth: Penguin, 1954.

Green, A. (1976) 'Un Autre, neutre', *Nouvelle Revue de psychanalyse* 13: 37–80.

Greenacre, P. (1941) 'The predisposition to anxiety', in Greenacre, *Trauma, Growth and Personality*. Hogarth, 1953, pp. 25–37.

Grunberger, B. (1956) 'The analytic situation and the dynamics of the healing process', in Grunberger (1979a), pp. 38–59.

_____ (1959) 'A study of anal object-relations', in Grunberger (1979a), pp. 143–65.

_____ (1964) 'On the phallic image', in Grunberger (1979a), pp. 202–18.

_____ (1966) 'The suicide of the melancholic', in Grunberger (1979a), pp. 241–80.

_____ (1967) 'The child's treasure horde and the avoidance of the Oedipus complex', in Grunberger (1979a), pp. 281–302.

_____ (1971) *Le Narcissisme. Essais de psychanalyse*. Paris: Payot.

_____ (1979a) *Narcissism, Psychoanalytic Essays*. New York: Int. Univ. Press.

_____ (1979b) 'From the "active technique" to the "confusion of tongues": on Ferenczi's deviation', in S. Lebovici and D. Widlöcher, eds. *Psychoanalysis in France*. New York: International Universities Press.

_____ (1983) 'Narcisse et Anubis, ou la double imago primitive', *Revue française de psychanalyse* 47:921–38.

Hermann, I. (1945) *Az Atizemitus Lélekana*. Budapest: Bibliotheca.

Howe, S. (1989) 'Living with a Nazi past', *New Statesman and Society*, 17 February, pp. 30–3.

James, M. (1962) 'Infantile narcissistic trauma: observations on Winnicott's work in infant care and child development', *Int. J. Psycho-Anal*. 43: 69–79.

Jones, E. (1954) *The Life and Work of Sigmund Freud*. 3 vols. Hogarth.

Kafka, F. (1919) 'A country doctor', in *In the Penal Settlement: Tales and Short Prose Works*. Secker & Warburg, 1949, pp. 132–40.

Katan, M. (1965) 'Fetishism, splitting of the ego, and denial', *Int. J. Psycho-Anal*. 45: 237–45.

Kessel, J. (1961) *France-Soir* 13–21 April.

Khan, M. M. R. (1965, 1979) 'Fetish as negation of the self: clinical notes on foreskin fetishism in a male homosexual', in Khan, *Alienation in Perversions*. Hogarth, 1975, pp. 139–77.

Klein, M. (1933) 'The early development of conscience in the child', in *Contributions to Psycho-Analysis, 1921–1945*. Hogarth, 1948, pp. 267–77.

—— (1952) 'The origins of transference', in *Envy and Gratitude, and Other Works, 1946–1963*. Hogarth, 1975, pp. 48–57.

Kohut, H. (1972) 'Thoughts on narcissism and narcissistic rage', in P. H. Orstein, ed. *The Search for the Self: Selected Writings of Heinz Kohut: 1950–1978*. New York: International Universities Press, vol. 2, pp. 615–58.

Krafft-Ebing, R. von (1892) *Psychopathia sexualis*, C. G. Chaddock, trans. London/Philadelphia: F. A. Davies.

Lacan, J. (1953) 'The function and field of speech and language in psychoanalysis', in *Écrits: A Selection*, Alan Sheridan, trans. Tavistock, 1977, pp. 30–114.

—— (1967) 'Proposition du 9 octobre 1967 sur le psychanalyste de l'École', *Scilicet* 1, 1968:14–30.

—— (1973) *The Four Fundamental Concepts of Psycho-Analysis*, Alan Sheridan, trans. Hogarth, 1977.

Laplanche, J. and Pontalis, J.-B. (1967) *The Language of Psychoanalysis*, Donald Nicholson Smith, trans. Hogarth, 1973.

Letarte, P. (1983) 'Le dessous d'un fétiche "porte = mère"', *Revue française de psychanalyse* 47:364–75.

Lichtenberg, G. C. (1844) 'Nachrichten und Bemerkungen des Verfassers über sich selbst', in *Vermischte Schriften, 1844-7*. Göttingen.

Loewenstein, R. M. (1952) *Psychanalyse de l'anti-sémitisme*. Paris: PUF.

Malcolm, J. (1984) *In the Freud Archives*. Cape.

Masson, J. M. (1984) *The Assault on Truth: Freud's Suppression of the Seduction Theory*. New York: Farrar, Straus & Giroux.

McDougall, J. (1972) 'Primal scene and sexual perversion', *Int. J. Psycho-Anal*. 53:371–84.

Mendel, G. (1986) *La Revolte contre le père: une introduction à la socio-psychanalyse*. Paris: Payot.

Meyer, B. C. (1964) 'Psychoanalytic studies on Joseph Conrad: fetishism', *J. Amer. Psychoanal. Assn.*

Mitscherlich, A. (1967) *Society without the Father: A Contribution to Social Psychology*, Eric Nosbacher, trans. Tavistock, 1969.

Money-Kyrle, R. E. (1951) *Psychoanalysis and Politics: A Contribution to the Psychology of Politics and Morals*. Duckworth.

Moser, T. (1974) *Years of Apprenticeship on the Couch: Fragments of my Psychoanalysis*. Anselm Hollo, trans. New York: Urizen, 1977.

Nacht, S. (1948) 'Du moi et son rôle dans la thérapeutique psychanalytique', *Revue française de psychanalyse* 12:27–53.

Olivieri, D. (1965) *Dictionary of Etymology*. Milan: Ceschina.

Ovid, *The Metamorphoses*, Mary M. Innes, trans. Harmondsworth: Penguin, 1955.

Parkin, A. (1964) 'On fetishism', *Int. J. Psycho-Anal.* 44:352–61.

Pasche, F. (1969) *À partir de Freud*. Paris: Payot.

Payne, S. (1939) 'Some observations on the ego-development of the fetishist', *Int. J. Psycho-Anal.* 20:161–70.

Pichette, J. P. (1980) *Guide raisonné des jurons*. Montreal: Les Quinze Editeurs.

Pierrard, P. (1984) *L'Église et les ouvriers en France*. Paris: Hachette.

Poliakov, L. (1951) *Bréviaire de la haine*. Paris: Calmann-Lévy.

Pontalis, J.-B. (1970) 'Seeing in-between', in *Frontiers in Psychoanalysis: Between the Dream and Psychic Pain*, Catherine Cullin and Phillip Cullin, trans. Hogarth, 1981, pp. 68–76.

Proust, M. (1919) *A L'Ombre des jeunes filles en fleur*. Paris: Livre de poche, 1966.

Rauschning, H. (1939) *Hitler Speaks*. Thornton Butterworth.

Renard, J. (1896) *La Maitresse* in *Œuvres II*. Paris: Bibliothèque de la Pléiade, 1971, pp. 8–50.

Revel, J.-F. (1978) *The Totalitarian Temptation*, David Hapgood, trans. Harmondsworth: Penguin.

Rimbaud, A. (1883) 'Le Bateau ivre', in *Poésies complètes*. Paris: Livre de poche, 1966.

Roazen, P. (1969) *Brother Animal. The Story of Freud and Tausk*. New York: Knopf.

Roheim, G. (1934) *The Riddle of the Sphinx: Or, Human Origins*. Hogarth.

Rousseau, J.-J. (1782) *Les Confessions*. Paris: Garnier-Flammarion, 1968.

Sacher-Masoch, L. von (1886) *Venus in Furs*. Sphere, 1969.

Sade, D.-A.-F. de (1785) *Les 120 Journées de Sodome, ou l'école de libertinage*, in Sade, *Œuvres complètes*. Paris: Au Cercle du livre précieux, vol 13, 1967.

_____ (1796) *Juliette, ou les prospérotés du vice*, in Sade, *Œuvres complètes*,

Paris: Au Cercle du livre précieux, vol 5, 1966.

Sadger, I. (1921) Die Lehre von den Geschlechtesverwirrungen. Leipzig Vienna: Deuticke.

Sartre, J.-P. (1944) *Huis clos, suivi de Les Mouches*. Paris: Folio, 1974.

—— (1946), *Réflexions sur la question juive*. Paris: Idées, 1969.

—— (1952) *Saint Genet: Comédien et martyr*. Paris: Gallimard.

Schatzmann, M. (1973) *Soul Murder: Persecution in the Family*. Allen Lane.

Schubert, E. H. von (1808) *Ansichten von der Nachtseite der Naturwissenschaft*. Darmstadt: Wissenschaftliche Buchgesellschaft, 1967.

Simmel, E. (1946) *Anti-Semitism: A Social Disease*. New York: International Universities Press.

Spitz, R. (1953) *No and Yes: On the Genesis of Human Communication*. New York: International Universities Press.

Stéphane, A. (1969) *L'Univers contestataire, ou les nouveaux chrétiens. Etude psychanalytique*. Paris: Payot.

Sterba, R. (1982) *Reminiscences of a Viennese Psychoanalyst*. Detroit, MI: Wayne State.

Stewart, H. (1961) 'Jocasta's crime', *Int. J. Psycho-Anal.* 43: 424–30.

Stewart, S. (1972) 'Quelques aspects théoriques du fétichisme', in *La Sexualité perverse*, pp. 159–92. Paris: Payot.

Sterren, H. A. van der (1948) *Oedipe, une étude psychanalytique d'après les tragédies de Sophocle*. Paris: PUF, 1976.

Stoller, R. J. (1968) *Sex and Gender. On the Development of Masculinity and Femininity*. Hogarth.

Vidal-Naquet, P. (1980) 'Un Eichmann de papier', *Esprit*, September, 8–52.

Villiers de l'Isle-Adam, A. de (1890) 'Axël', in Villiers de l'Isle-Adam, *Oeuvres complètes*, Paris: Bibliothèque de la Pléiade, 1986, vol 2, pp. 532–680.

Wilde, O. (1891) *The Picture of Dorian Gray*. Harmondsworth: Penguin, 1949.

Winnicott, D. W. (1956) 'Primary maternal preoccupation', in *Collected Papers: Through Paediatrics to Psychoanalysis*. Hogarth, 1958.

—— (1967) 'Mirror-role of mother and family in child development', in *Playing and Reality*. Harmondsworth: Pelican, 1974, pp. 130–8.

Yonnel, P. (1983) 'Rock, pop, punk', *Le Débat* 25, May.

Index

This first edition of
New Essays in Narcissism
was finished in August 1989.

It was typeset in 10/13 Bodoni
on an AM Compset 560 by Photosetting, Yeovil
and printed on a Timson T32
on to 80g/m² vol. 18 Book Wove.

This book was commissioned by Robert M. Young,
edited by Ann Scott and Selina O'Grady,
copy-edited by Gillian Beaumont,
indexed by Peva Keane,
designed by Wendy Millichap
and produced by Miranda Chaytor
and Martin Klopstock for
Free Association Books.